Fair
Isn't Always
Equal

Fair Isn't Always Equal

Assessing & Grading in the Differentiated Classroom

Rick Wormeli

Stenhouse Publishers
Portland, Maine

National Middle School Association
Westerville, Ohio

Stenhouse Publishers
www.stenhouse.com

National Middle School Association
www.nmsa.org

Credits
Page 19, Figure 3.1: From cartoonist W. E. Hill, 1915, as adapted from an 1888 postcard advertising the Anchor Buggy Company.

Library of Congress Cataloging-in-Publication Data
Wormeli, Rick.
    Fair isn't always equal : assessing and grading in the differentiated classroom / Rick Wormeli.
       p. cm.
       Includes bibliographical references and index.
       ISBN 1-57110-424-0
       1. Grading and marking (Students)—United States. 2. Educational tests and measurements—United States. 3. Students—Rating of—United States. I. Title.
LB3060.37.W67 2006
371.26'4—dc22   2005057975

Cover and interior design by Martha Drury
Cover and interior photographs by the author

Manufactured in the United States of America on acid-free paper
11 10 09 08 07 9 8 7 6

For my parents, Paul and Nancy Wormeli,
who teach me every day to:
change what is unjust,
serve others to find purpose,
and be brave just five minutes longer.

Grading is one of the most bizarre aspects of teaching. No two teachers grade alike, and everyone thinks their way is best. I've been doing this for thirty-seven years, and I'm still not happy with the way I grade. Does a grade truly reflect what a student has learned, or how hard they tried, or what they're capable of doing?

—Charlie Lindgren, Secondary Teacher

Checking is diagnostic, teacher is an advocate. Grading is evaluative, teacher is a judge.

—Dr. Thomas R. Guskey, University of Kentucky

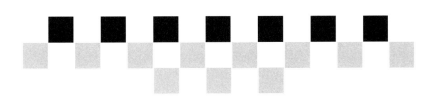

Contents

Preface

This is a compilation of my own thinking as an educator, as well as a distillation of ideas from colleagues working in today's secondary classrooms, and the ideas presented by those who have written extensively about grading, assessment, and differentiated instruction. While declarations of preferred grading and assessment practices in differentiated classes are made throughout the book, I make no claims about being the wisest of the bunch in what I offer.

This book, then, is a beginning. It is meant to do four things: 1) be a catalyst for serious reflection on current grading and assessment practices in differentiated classes—'no becalmed waters here; 2) affirm effective grading and assessment practices we're already employing; 3) provide language and references for substantive conversations with colleagues and the public; and 4) feed a hunger growing larger every day for coherent and effective grading practices in a high-stakes, accountability-focused world.

While I hope the ideas are useful, I know not every idea will mesh with every reader's teaching philosophy. That's fine; cognitive dissonance and discourse elevate all of us. Don't throw the book out the window, however, because one idea on one page gives you heartburn. Give the concepts some thought, try some of them with your students, then shape and share your own thinking regarding grading and assessment in differentiated classes with others. We look forward to hearing your wisdom. It will serve us well.

Rick Wormeli
March 2006

Acknowledgments

I am indebted to the following individuals for their unflinching candor and compelling insights into differentiation, grading, and assessment:

Bobby Biddle, Moosa Shah, Sue Howell, Tom Pollack, Susan Clark, Aaron Kalman, Kathy Bowdring, Marsha Ratzel, Bill Ivey, Chris Toy, Keith Mack, Anne Jolly, John Norton, Cossondra George, Brenda Dyck, Susie Luatua, Bruce Campbell, Michael Shackleford, Linda Allen, Robert Marzano, Carol Tomlinson, Catherine Taylor, Susan Nolen, Douglas Reeves, W. James Popham, Kelly Gallagher, Tom Guskey, Jane Bailey, Susan Brookhart, Ken O'Connor, Alfie Kohn, Susan Winebrenner, Rick Stiggins, Judith Arter, Jan Chappuis, Stephen Chappuis, Sheryn Northey, Grant Wiggins, Jay McTighe, Debra Pickering, Lynda Rice, Jim Grant, Jerry Newberry, Brenda Quanstrom, Ellen Berg, Jennifer Beahrs, Paul Bogush, Charlie Lindgren, Marg Soderberg, Deb Bova, Marie Bahlert, Paula Schmierer, Susan Bischoff, Lisa Pierce, Eileen Bendixen, Melba Smithwick, Rick Spreigner, Carolyn Beitzel, and Laurie Wasserman.

In addition, I am extremely grateful for the wise counsel of my editors at Stenhouse Publishers, Philippa Stratton, Bill Varner, and Jay Kilburn. Be assured, the reader's experience is dramatically improved over the original draft for their clear-headed, cut-the-extra-words, make-it-meaningful-to-the-reader approach.

As always, my greatest thanks go to my wife, Kelly, and my children, Ryan and Lynn, who good-naturedly accept the appendage attached to my hip bone—my laptop. I thank them, too, for reminding me of the more important parts of life: sports, hiking, music, games, wave-runners, laughing, love, good pizza, and diving deeply into imagination.

CHAPTER 1

The Differentiated Instruction Mind-set: Rationale and Definition

ecall your days as a student in middle and high school. Did your teachers differentiate for you? Think carefully.

If you consider it long enough, clear examples of differentiated practice from your childhood will flood into your mind's eye. If your teacher ever rephrased a question; extended a deadline; provided a few extra examples in order to help you understand something; stood next to you to keep your attention focused on the lesson; regrouped the class according to student interest, readiness, or the way students best learned; gave you a choice among assignments based on something she knew about you; or let you redo a test or project if at first you didn't succeed, she differentiated instruction. They may not have called it "differentiated" back then, but our teachers differentiated instruction.

In the first fifteen minutes of a successful, secondary school math class in today's world, we see the following easy evidence of differentiated practice.

Students have homework laid out on their desks for teacher checking. Some students have done alternative problems based on yesterday's level of mastery prior to receiving the homework.

Some students have preferential seating because of attention problems.

The teacher moves physically closer to some students, using proximity to him or her to keep them focused.

Desks are clustered, or if in rows, movable, for flexible grouping later in the lesson.

Students are discussing difficult problems from last night's homework in small groups because the teacher recognizes that small-group work best meets the needs of some students in the class. Later she does whole-class and independent work to meet other students' needs.

If the day's lesson isn't one about basic calculations or graphing, but about advanced and abstract concepts instead, the teacher allows the use of TI-83 calculators to keep the momentum of the lesson and prevent students from getting bogged down by tenacious calculations and simple arithmetic errors. She wants to keep students focused on the new concept of the day for now.

The teacher offers one student a second example of a math concept when the one given to the class doesn't clarify the concept for him.

Students who are struggling with an assignment while a teacher is working with four students in the back of the room are working through a list of "What to do when I'm stuck and the teacher is not available" ideas previously taught to them.

The teacher has two students who serve as "graduate assistants" whom she knows have mastered the concepts and she has identified to the class as good resources if they have questions.

The teacher provides a few moments for students to think reflectively regarding a prompt before he guides their thinking. Those students who need intrapersonal contact appreciate the time to think, and many others would benefit from learning how to think reflectively.

These are all examples of teaching in a fair and developmentally appropriate manner—that is, differentiating instruction.

The exciting thing for today's teacher is that we've learned more about how the brain learns and about differentiated practices in the last twenty years than in all of civilization put together. For good reason, the 1990s were known as the Decade of the Brain, and that is expected to continue into the 2000s and beyond. There are two problems, however.

First, what we know about the brain is still being tested, and that means most of our assertions about it should be preceded by the words "seems to be" or "as of our understanding today." Cognitive theory and neuroscience are very dynamic fields and what we quote as fact this year may be proven otherwise next year. It's difficult to keep track with so much on an educator's plate, so we are indebted to those who make sense of the research and share it with us—folks like David Sousa, Pat Wolfe, Robert Sylwester, Spencer Rogers, Marilee Sprenger, Howard Gardner, William Bender, Thomas Armstrong, Robert Marzano, Debra Pickering, Art Costa, Marian Diamond, Eric Jensen, the Caines, among others.

The second and far more daunting problem, however, is how to get our modern classroom to reflect what has been distilled from the research. Of course, we don't want to drop everything we find effective in teaching for the sake of an interesting conjecture by a cognitive theorist; the leap from observing the behavior of neurotransmitters in our synapses to how we should write information on the board is too great—we're not there yet. There's enough positive correlation to warrant further experimentation and discussion, however.

We have salient patterns that suggest what would be successful in a classroom, and teachers are finding them useful. Teachers are on the frontlines of these applications, and it's time they use what has stood the test of time so far. Our fear is that teachers from the 1950s, 1960s, 1970s, or 1980s could transfer through time, end up in our classrooms, and be completely at home. The more hopeful result is that they would be fish out of water: They'd ask us why we're doing what we're doing, and upon hearing our explanation, they'd lament, "Wow, I wish I had known that back in '69. I could have really helped Rudy in my fourth period class."

When first learning about differentiated practices, many of us focus primarily on differentiation principles and structures such as scaffolding, tiering, respectful tasks, flexible grouping, learner profiles, readiness, and anchor lessons. At the same time, however, we are wise to explore cognitive science as well, realizing that our strategic application of cognitive principles is actually one of the best ways to differentiate effectively. For example, in order to provide scaffolding for students who need it, we sometimes structure struggling students' interactions with text, labs, field trips, and DVDs by providing them with graphic organizers in advance of those learning experiences. This not only primes their minds for what to identify as salient in the experience, but it also structures information for meaningful management and retrieval later. Sometimes, then, we don't spend energy identifying tasks for high-, medium-, and/or low-functioning groups so much as we consider whether we've taught in a way the brain best processes.

Professional development and creating a culture of teachers focused on cognitive theory and differentiated instruction are great fodder for other books. For purposes of *this* one, we will assume readers have a basic understanding of both topics and that they embrace the principles therein. The bibliography contains suggestions for further reading. To ensure a common frame of reference, however, let's review the basic logic behind differentiated practices.

Definition. *Differentiated instruction* is doing what's fair for students. It's a collection of best practices strategically employed to maximize students' learning at every turn, including giving them the tools to handle anything that is undifferentiated. It requires us to do different things for different students some, or a lot, of the time in order for them to learn when the general classroom approach does not meet students' needs. It is not individualized instruction, though that may happen from time to time as warranted. It's whatever works to advance the students. It's highly effective teaching.

If we accept this premise, then every aspect of our teaching, including our grading and assessment practices, should be fair to students; and it should maximize the students' learning. Anything that does not provide for such is suspect.

Let's push our acceptance of differentiated practices a little further. What would happen if we differentiated for a particular student every single time he needed it, kindergarten through twelfth grade? (Notice the clarification that differentiation is done as needed—not all the time.) What kind of students would graduate from our high schools?

Some of us claim students from such experiences would be highly competent, independent thinkers. These students would be tolerant of others, and they would be creative and willing to take risks. Such students would be well-prepared for the world beyond high school.

What is it about differentiated practice that yields those results? Competence and diverse approaches to learning lead the way. Students for whom teachers have differentiated instruction learn well; they're competent. They understand themselves as learners, and because of that, they are better equipped to advocate for themselves. They see classmates as being at different points on the same journey, and differences from their own point on the journey are not seen as weak—just different. They are not threatened by difference; it's seen as strength. These students consider themselves beginners at some things, experts in others, and this variance is natural.

Looking at these traits, you'd think differentiated practice leads to an almost utopian, model citizen. Could there be a downside with too much differentiation? For example, could students become dependent on others to differentiate for them in the real world? After all, since age five, the adults in their educational lives have always made it easier for them to learn and succeed.

There's the rub: Differentiated instruction does *not* mean we make learning easier for students. Instead, it provides the appropriate challenge that enables students to thrive. Because we know our students so well, we know what buttons to push. We teach in a responsive manner: If students are becoming too dependent, we do whatever it takes to create personal autonomy within them. When we teach in the way a student's mind best processes information and skills, he or she finds the lessons compelling. What gets easier is classroom management; appropriately challenged students are cooperative.

Some educators and parents still see differentiated instruction and assessment as a crutch. In truth, they are correct—but not in the negative sense they intend. In their minds, a *crutch* refers to something leaned on too much. Students limp around, never really growing autonomous, always dependent because things are made easier for them when the teacher differentiates.

Nothing could be farther from the truth. In the last few decades, we've witnessed amazing heroes of our time—Canada's Terry Fox and Rick Hansen, the United States's Christopher Reeve, to name just a few—who've achieved greatness through the use of prosthetic legs, crutches, and wheelchairs. These objects (and their analogous applications to the classroom) allow individuals to rise, be held accountable, and soar. We wouldn't dream of limiting them by removing their support devices. Because of the differentiated approaches, they become full individuals, identified first for who they are inside, and labeled only much farther down the road with an almost incidental comment that they happen to be in a wheelchair or have a fake leg. This is what can happen when we differentiate instruction and assessment for students who struggle.

When we differentiate, we give students the tools to handle whatever comes their way—differentiated or not. This is why differentiated instruction and standardized testing are not oxymoronic: Students will do well on standardized, undifferentiated tests only if they have learned the material in the class, and differentiated practices are the ways we maximize students' learning at every turn. Standardized tests can only sample learning, making observations about mastery inferential at best. They are meant to look at trends and patterns for a school, not exclusive evidence about an individual student's or teacher's performance. State and provincial policy makers want us to focus on our true goals: to teach students how to interpret graphs, obtain insight from historical events, understand the scientific processes of living organisms, incorporate healthy diet and exercise into everyday life, and create the jarring beauty of music written with just the right dynamics. Anything we do to enable students to become their own advocates in this cause is worthy, and differentiated practices do just that.

What if students experience differentiated practices in middle or high school, yet the next grade levels (high school and college, respectively) do not differentiate? Won't they be expecting it, and when they don't get it from their teachers, be disabled?

No. They will do well in the next grade levels, differentiated or not, if they know the material of the earlier grade levels and they know themselves as learners. Differentiated approaches provide both of these in abundance when done well.

Here's a clarifying example used by many educators: Two students are seated at the back of the classroom. One of them is nearsighted and cannot see anything clearly that is more than a few feet away. He wears thick glasses to see long distances. The teacher asks both of them to read, record, and learn the information written in small print on the front board, on the opposite side of the room. In order to be equal, however, the teacher removes the nearsighted child's glasses and asks both students to get started. The child needing glasses squints but can't read anything on the board.

Did the teacher make it harder or easier for the nearsighted child? Most educators claim the teacher made it harder. On the contrary, however, the teacher made it much easier. We learn from cognitive scientists that the brain is a survival organ—it's out for its own self-preservation. With the removal of the glasses, the student has an excuse: he can cop out, escape. When we give him his glasses, which are analogous to scaffolding (providing support) and differentiating, he is compelled to read the board and consider its content. He thrives. We didn't make it easier by providing him with his glasses, we made it more demanding. *Undifferentiated* classes are the easy ones because the "my approach or nothing" teacher conveys to students that they can coast or drop out if the lesson is not working for them. In differentiated classes, teachers know them so well that they know how to get students engaged with their learning, and they use it. These classes are challenging. Students are held accountable and they achieve more.

Is providing support and differentiation fair for both children? To answer this question, let's look at the results of the next day's test on the board's material: If we remove the glasses, will both children have fair opportunities for success? No. If we don't provide the glasses to the student who needs them, the grade he earns on the test is not accurate. The grade does not indicate his true mastery of the topic; he didn't have the tools to learn well. So now, not only did the child not learn, but also any grade we give him is distorted and cannot be used to document progress, provide feedback, or inform instructional decisions. In short, by not differentiating, we defeated the whole purpose of schools and grading.

As we do when providing students with their glasses, we provide fair support like this in many ways: We allow the use of graph paper or turning lined paper sideways for some students so that their numbers will line up in columns as they complete math problems; we allow some students to use "focus frames" (Forsten, Grant, and Hollas 2002) with interlocking L's to direct their eyes while reading; we allow some students to hear their history textbooks on compact disc rather than having to read them silently. In all these ways, students learn the material, and any assessments given to them will accurately render their mastery, assuming there are no issues with the assessment formats and test protocols themselves.

What is fair isn't always equal, and our goal as teachers is to be fair and developmentally appropriate, not one-size-fits-all equal. If we give a graphic organizer to four students who are struggling with text but not to their classmates who do not need it, we are still being fair. The same test will be given to all students at the end of the unit, and the grades are legitimately earned. While some tests are about procedures and processes, most tests are about essential understandings—knowledge, concepts, and skills—not how students came to know the information.

Would we announce the availability of that graphic organizer to the rest of the class and allow other students to use it if they wanted to? Sure. Will we require some students to use it even if at first they are not interested? That depends. If we want students to appreciate the great success achieved via the graphic organizer, we might let them work without it and subsequently do poorly on the assessment, but then offer them another chance to succeed using the scaffolding (the organizer) and record the new, improved grade. In some cases, however, differentiated approaches are non-negotiable. If a student declines, he or she is committing insubordination by defying the teacher. We handle it as a discipline issue. This doesn't happen often, however, because students find differentiating teachers are out for their success. That encouragement is powerful motivation.

Let's examine the real world as well. Is the real world differentiated? Absolutely. Imagine a garage mechanic charged with fixing the timing in a car's engine, but it's a car he's never serviced or studied before. In such a circumstance, he consults the manufacturer's manual or even with the manufacturer directly. He can ask for guidance from a senior mechanic, and he can even extend the deadline by telling the customer that, though he promised it would be ready by 5:00 P.M., the car won't be ready until the next day at 10:00 A.M. In the real world, we gravitate toward careers with tasks for which we have some proclivity. We don't spend an entire day working in our weak areas.

On the surface, the military seems fairly rigid, no-nonsense, with little accounting for individual learning styles. Yet it's a perfect example of differentiated practices. When young recruits are learning how to take apart and put back together an assault rifle in the field, for example, some need nine times of disassembly and reassembly; others need only four times before they get it done without thinking. Some recruits look at the manual, while others concentrate on their trainer's words. Some require their trainers to physically move their fingers to find the safety release mechanisms, while others don't. Some need to practice on less complex firearms in clear daylight, while others are ready for learning how to assemble more complex assault rifles in total darkness. Each of these approaches demonstrates differentiated practice.

How about surgery? Absolutely. We hope our surgeon differentiates. If she opens our bodies for surgery and finds something unexpected, for our sakes she better be able to adapt and go a different direction, perhaps with a different procedure, piece of equipment, or length of time to complete the task. Yes, the real world is differentiated.

What if we never differentiated instruction for students who needed it, kindergarten through twelfth grade? What kind of students would graduate from our high schools?

It's a trick question. In all likelihood, they wouldn't graduate. If differentiated instruction advances a student's learning, lack of differentiated instruction puts competence in jeopardy and passing graduation assessments in question. It's a little absurd to think that a one-size-fits-all approach by every teacher a child has kindergarten through twelfth grade is the best way for that child to learn day after day, week after week, month after month, year after year—and how can that be true of all children at the same time?

Nobody cares what we teach—not our principals, our superintendents, or our legislative bodies. No one. In fact, what we teach is irrelevant. It's what our students learn after their time with us that matters. What students learn is the greatest testimony for us as teachers, as schools, and as communities. Let's rally our assessment and grading energy around that fact.

Differentiation provides focus. It is a compelling, highly effective approach that is equal parts technical dexterity and professional can-do attitude. That commitment to all students and their learning extends to grading and assessment, and *this point is key:* We commit to students and to sound grading practices. Unsuccessful teachers deny their own involvement in their students' success or lack thereof. Secondary school educator, Ellen Berg comments:

> *In my experience, there are teachers who put 100 percent of the responsibility on the kids, teachers who share the responsibility, and teachers who take 100 percent of the responsibility. Teachers in that middle category seem to be the most successful at my school.*
>
> *The thing is, if I took a look at my end grades and saw a huge percentage of F's, I'd be disturbed. I'd look for causes (missing work, low scores, etc.) and figure out what types of strategies to try with those students. I am the teacher, and so it is up to me to teach the kids I have, be they unprepared, irresponsible, etc. . . . I'm not saying that's easy, but if what we're doing isn't getting us the desired results, doing the same thing over and over and expecting something different is not only nonproductive, it creates stress and unhappiness in our lives.*

Most teachers who dive into differentiation's mind-set and practices feel liberated, not burdened. They breathe a little easier because they experience students' learning as a direct result of their decisions, and those students are learning at a level otherwise not achievable through non-differentiated practices. The cement overshoes of cynicism and settling for less are cast off, replaced by hope and by students achieving every day. We rediscover ourselves as teachers and as students when we differentiate. Yeah, it has that much of an impact.

When it comes to difficult grading decisions, having a differentiated mind-set illuminates correct paths readily. We sort through competing priorities and choose the most effective response. In fact, if we are hesitant or confused about our differentiated rationale, grading becomes tortuous and we doubt our enterprise. If we are struggling to accept the rationale for differentiated approaches, the material presented in the remaining pages of this book will be difficult to swallow. If we've accepted differentiated approaches as the great positive they are, regardless of our skill development with them, the remainder of this book will be like a visit with a good friend, one who affirms our efforts yet also pushes us to explore new territories in pursuit of our cause—student growth. That's pretty good for something that's been around since the Ancient Greeks and earlier. Not even close to being a passing fad, differentiated instruction is good teaching, and it's here to stay. Let's hope we're wise enough to use it.

It's just as true today as when Dr. Haim Ginott (1993) said it decades ago:

I have come to the frightening conclusion that I am the decisive element in the classroom. It is my personal approach that creates the climate. It is my daily mood that makes the weather. As a teacher, I possess tremendous power to make a child's life miserable or joyous. I can be a tool of torture or an instrument of inspiration. I can humiliate or humor, hurt or heal. In all situations it is my response that decides whether or not a crisis will be escalated or de-escalated, and a child humanized or de-humanized. I am part of a team of educators creating a safe, caring and positive learning environment for students and teaching them in a manner that ensures success because all individuals are capable of learning.

With this mind-set, let's explore assessment and grading in the differentiated classroom.

CHAPTER 2

Mastery

In a study of ninth-grade science classrooms, . . . Nolen (2003) found that when students perceived their classrooms as ability-based meritocracies, their performance on a district-wide, curriculum-based test was compromised. Students in other classes who saw teachers and peers to be focused on mastery and independent thinking performed significantly better on the district test.

—Nolen and Taylor 2005, p. 186

Original prompt: $(2x + 4)(x - 3) = ?$
Student's response: $2x^2 + 4x - 6x - 12 = 2x^2 - 2x - 12$

Was the student's response correct? Yes.

What can we conclude about the student's mastery of this topic? Not much with just one problem. Possibilities, however, include: She knows how to multiply binomials and combine like terms in a polynomial, as well as how to multiply and add positive and negative integers.

Are these the concepts and skills we were trying to teach? Yes.

Can we conclude that she has mastered this concept? Not necessarily. We have to see clear and consistent evidence of these skills in her work, not just one or two examples.

Original prompt: Circle one *simile* in the following paragraph.

Life was a Ferris wheel to Betina, always circling, coming around again, and always leaving a small lump of something in the pit of her stomach as she descended from the uppermost view where she could look out across the world. It was always sad for her to come down the far side of something exciting in life, the ground rising to meet her like the unwanted rush of the tide she's helpless to turn away.

Student response: He circles, "like the unwanted rush of the tide."

Did this student demonstrate mastery of similes? Sort of. He circled the "like" portion of a correct example, but he did not circle both of the items being compared: the "ground rising to meet her" and the "unwanted rush of the tide she's helpless to turn away." What can we conclude about his understanding? He seems to know the difference between a simile and a metaphor because he did not circle the metaphor in the first sentence, but he circled only part of the simile in the last sentence. This could be a guess on the student's part, too. And is mastery indicated by circling samples in text? Isn't it more?

Definitions

In both of these examples, are we making an inference that may not be valid? Are we using our best "guess" about the students' level of understanding? Yes. Grades are momentary inferences at best, and for both students, we have only one example in one particular situation to examine.

So what is mastery? Ben Franklin aptly wrote, "Tim was so learned, that he could name a horse in nine languages; so ignorant, that he bought a cow to ride on" (*Poor Richard's Almanac* 1750). Mastery is more than knowing information, of course, but it can even go beyond manipulating and applying that information successfully in other situations. Ask members of your faculty to define mastery for their subjects and their responses will vary.

At a future gathering of faculty or just your department, ask teachers to finish the statements, "Mastery is . . . ," "Understanding is like . . . ," and "My students are literate in my subject area when they . . . ," and see what everyone assumes the endings to be. If the school promotes itself as one in which teachers focus on true mastery, then it's wise to have a commonly accepted definition of what that means. Breaking it down into public-friendly soundbites helps everyone—teachers, students, administration, parents, policy makers—grasp the idea and be on the same page.

Howard Gardner says that understanding ". . . involves the appropriate application of concepts and principles to questions or problems posed" (1991). Jean Piaget claimed that, "Real comprehension of a notion or a theory

. . . implies the reinvention of this theory by the student. . . . True understanding manifests itself by spontaneous applications" (McTighe and Wiggins 2001, p. 53). A particular favorite definition of mine is adapted from the Center for Media Literacy in New Mexico: "If we are literate in our subject, we can: *access* (understand and find meaning in), *analyze, evaluate,* and *create* the subject or medium."

Can our students not only understand math but also break it down into its component pieces (analyze), critique (evaluate) it against criteria, and can they create math? Can they create grammar? Can they create technology, science, social studies, geography, art, drama, and physical well-being? You bet. Our students can be math literate, science literate, grammar literate, geography literate, art literate, physical education literate—*literate* (masterful) in every subject.

In their book, *Understanding by Design,* Jay McTighe and Grant Wiggins list six facets of true understanding:

- Explanation
- Interpretation
- Application
- Perspective
- Empathy
- Self-knowledge

They explain that students really understand a topic when they can demonstrate proficiency with each of the following aspects within the subject: They can explain it, interpret it for others or other situations, apply it, acknowledge and explore alternative perspectives on the topic, experience empathy for the topic (or appreciate the experience of others who do), and accurately identify and reflect on their own self-knowledge regarding the topic (McTighe and Wiggins 2001).

For purposes of our discussions here, let's pull these ideas together within the context of a teacher dealing with his or her lesson plans and gradebook every day. Here's a working definition of mastery:

Students have mastered content when they demonstrate a thorough understanding as evidenced by doing something substantive with the content beyond merely echoing it. Anyone can repeat information; it's the masterful student who can break content into its component pieces, explain it and alternative perspectives regarding it cogently to others, and use it purposefully in new situations.

Given this definition, let's look at the examples and non-examples of mastery in Figure 2.1.

Figure 2.1 Examples and Non-Examples of Mastery

Mastery	Not Mastery
The student can hear or read about a situation that requires repeated addition and identifies it as a multiplication opportunity, then uses multiplication accurately to shorten the solution process.	The student can repeat the multiplication tables through the 12's. (This is more about *automaticity*— how automatic a student is when reciting the information or solutions. Automacity often comes with mastery but sometimes it is just recitation, not understanding.)
A student accounts for potentially contaminating variables in a lab by taking extra steps to prevent anything from affecting an agar culture with bacterial growth she's preparing, and if accidental contamination occurs, she adjusts the experiment's protocols when she repeats the experiment so that the sources of the contamination are no longer a factor.	A student prepares an agar culture for bacterial growth by following a specific procedure given to her by her teacher. She calls the experiment a failure when unknown factors or substances contaminate the culture after several weeks of observation.
The student uses a variety of basketball passes during a game, depending on the most advantageous strategy at each moment in the game.	The student uses primarily the bounce pass in the basketball game regardless of its potential effectiveness because that's all he knows how to do.
The student can point to any word in the sentence and explain its role, and explain how the word may change its role, depending on where it's placed in the sentence.	The student can match each of the following parts of speech to its definition accurately: noun, pronoun, verb, adverb, adjective, preposition, conjunction, gerund, and interjection.

Acceptable Evidence of Mastery

What are we willing to accept as evidence of mastery? According to Nolen and Taylor, ". . . there are two ways to obtain sufficient evidence of mastery: 1) multiple assignments, and 2) tracking the progress of a few important works over time" (2005, p. 289).

To explore what we mean by acceptable evidence further, let's look at an example from geography class. If we're teaching latitude and longitude, which of the following tasks would best demonstrate our students' mastery of these concepts?

1. On the sphere provided, draw a latitude/longitude coordinate grid. Label all major components.
2. Given the listed latitude/longitude coordinates, identify the countries. Then, identify the latitude and longitude of the world capitals and bodies of water that are listed.

3. Write an essay about how the latitude/longitude system came to be.
4. In an audio-visual presentation, explain how our system of latitude and longitude would need to be adjusted if Earth was in the shape of a peanut (narrow middle, wider edges).
5. Create a collage or mural that represents the importance of latitude and longitude in the modern world.

What are the pros and cons of each assessment? What content and skills does each one require students to demonstrate? Do some limit what we'll find out about a student's understanding of latitude and longitude? Do some get us away from the unit's objectives?

We can't answer too many of these questions unless we know the specific *objectives*—the essential and enduring knowledge and skills of the lesson, the prime foundations for differentiated lesson design. If we're trying to evaluate the appropriateness of an assessment, therefore, we must always examine how it illuminates or obfuscates those essential understandings and questions. For example, if we want students to be able to use latitude and longitude in a practical manner, item 2 is the best choice. If we want them to look at the big picture of latitude and longitude, we'd ask them to complete tasks 1, 3, and 5. If we want them to extrapolate a bit, items 4 and 5 look good. The point is that we have to be clear in our objectives before we can differentiate instruction and properly assess our students' attainment of those objectives. Obtuse objectives make for deadly differentiation.

Take a moment and brainstorm a list of options that all teachers have for enabling students to demonstrate what they know and are able to do. These can include, but are not limited to, the following: tests, quizzes, portfolios, checklists, learning contracts, models, demonstrations, exhibitions, performances, essays and other writings, videos, CDs, Web sites, animations, art projects, panel discussions, rubrics, Socratic seminars, drawings, mindmaps, displays, discussions, and portrayals. These are tools or products that can convey students' mastery, but they don't demonstrate mastery themselves. We wouldn't want to declare students masterful because they can produce the medium. There has to be substantive content and skill demonstration via the product. Successful teachers consider and communicate the criteria expected for mastery in each one. This means we're back to the focus on what's essential and enduring in the lesson.

It may be helpful to examine naïve versus sophisticated understandings—given a specific topic, what would indicate a simplistic, undeveloped response, and what would indicate a complex, fully aware response?

To do this, let's examine an education standard or benchmark you have to teach this year. If you don't have one readily available, consider the following sample from Virginia:

The student will compare the United States Constitution system in 1789 with forms of democracy that developed in ancient Greece and Rome, in England, and in the American colonies and states in the 18th century.
—Virginia, Grade 12, United States and Virginia Government (as of 2006)

After reading a standard or benchmark, do we have enough information about what students should know and be able to do? Usually we don't. In such cases, we have to spend time "unpacking" the standard into its benchmarks and component pieces: What specific skills and content will be necessary to teach students in order for them to demonstrate mastery of the standard, and what specific information and skill sets will we accept as evidence of mastery?

For example, when we teach students to make inferences about an author's meaning, we can't just ask them to infer the author's meaning from the given text. There's more to it. Some of the skills readers use when inferring include:

- Recognize and use context clues
- Identify an author's purpose and intended audience for writing
- Activate their own prior knowledge on the subject and consider how what they're reading fits with what they know
- Make predictions that are more than wild guesses—they're based on sound reasoning
- Use background information to make sense of new material

To demonstrate sophisticated mastery, we'd like students to make an inference and elaborate on how they arrived at their conclusion in writing, orally, or some other way. We don't accept unexplained, one-line responses like, "He was speaking about man's mortality in that passage." For many math problems, students can arrive at the correct answer for that one problem, but whether they've developed the thinking process for strategic employment of the new math formula in varied situations remains a mystery.

Sometimes, then, we ask students to write out their explanations for how they solved the problem. Written responses reveal misconceptions in ways oral retelling cannot. In oral retelling, students can use voice inflections and body language to smooth over rough areas of thinking, making it easier for us to assume they understand the concepts. You can't get away with that in writing. Through writing we see levels of mastery, high and low, not otherwise detectable.

The complex nature of mastery as more than recitation is true in every subject. Consider spelling, for instance. Just because a student memorizes and spells a list of ten words correctly on Friday's quiz doesn't mean he or she has mastered spelling and that the spelling grade should be an A on the report card. How about assessing skill in identifying misspelled words in general text, or in applying knowledge of spelling rules to figure out the spelling of a previously unknown word? How about assessing use of appropriate resources to proofread writing work for spelling errors before submitting the final version? Many of us are not the greatest spellers, but we become masterful because we take steps to correct our mistakes. Teachers cannot draw any conclusions—that is, we cannot determine a grade for a student—with one write-the-word-the-teacher-says spelling quiz. Maybe given the whole year's worth of quizzes we can see a pattern of success and make an inference, but a declaration of sophisticated mastery? No. Sophisticated mastery is more than this.

In the Grade 12 Government Standard of Learning from Virginia mentioned before, what would a simplistic demonstration of mastery be? The student might mention one or two ways our 1789 constitutional system was similar to indirect democracy and a republic, then he might mention a connection to the Magna Charta and one other milestone in England's democratic evolution during the seventeenth and eighteenth centuries.

A sophisticated response would trace the roots and eventual evolution of democratic thinking that laid foundations for the 1789 Constitution, including influences from some of the following:

- Direct and indirect democracy—advantages and disadvantages of each
- Rise of republics, senator citizens (patricians), and the common folks (plebeians)
- Democratic development during Rome's Pax Romana—200 years of peace and government development
- The Code Napoleon, declaring all men equal before the law
- Adam Smith's *Wealth of Nations,* which explained capitalism and the free market system
- The rise and impact of imperialism for countries promoting democracy
- Alexis de Tocqueville's *Democracy in America*
- Thomas Hobbes's *Leviathan,* which described a social contract in which everyone consents to obey the law as the justification for government
- John Locke's claim that individuals have natural rights, including life, liberty, and property
- Jean-Jacques Rousseau's idea that there is a general will that pursues a common good, promoting liberty, equality, and fraternity
- Thomas Paine's *Common Sense,* which many say was the fodder for the American Revolution, as American colonies were struggling with unfair taxation and parliamentary representation

We see that the sophisticated responses rely on concepts beyond the first token moments in democracy or the one-line subtitles in basal textbooks. The student connects the dots among a variety of democratic influences using primary and secondary sources, offering specific and plentiful evidence to back up claims made. We could even ask him or her to consider how history might have evolved differently if one or more of these factors never existed. Such mental dexterity with the topic is a good indicator that the lessons will last beyond next week's test. The student mastered the standard.

Determining What's Important to Master

How do first-year teachers or teachers new to the subject area figure out what's important in a unit of study? The text material is massive and not all of it is salient. What if we emphasize information and concepts that are not the same as our colleagues; or what if what we teach isn't even on the state or provincial exam, or worse, it's on the exam but we didn't think it was important enough to teach?

We have many resources from which to choose to get up to speed on how to unpack the specific standards we have to teach. Let's make good use of them. It would be unprofessional not to pursue those sources but, instead, to just hope we have it right. Such helpful resources include:

- Mentor or colleague teachers
- Subject-specific listservs
- Professional organizations
- Curriculum guides
- Posted benchmarks
- Standards of learning
- Programs of study
- Textbook scope and sequence
- Other teachers' tests and assessments
- Professional listservs
- Personal reflection after studying the field yourself (easier to do after we've been teaching a few years, of course)

Interestingly, veteran teachers need to do this as well as new teachers. We all have to be vigilant against complacency or subject myopia (tunnel vision in which all we see is what we know, and we do not open our minds to other perspectives or ways of thinking). In addition, what is deemed important in society and in our expertise areas can change. We all have to keep up with those changes. Annually is not too often to examine benchmarks, standards, and what we consider essential. The point is to always be open to the conversation.

Grade subjectivity and students' varied states of readiness and learning styles make strict adherence to equal grading for all disquieting. It's even more so when we consider the varied interpretations of mastery, how it's manifest by our students, and how it gets translated into grades on report cards. Annual focus on defining mastery for each of the topics we teach is a good use of time and resources. We have to be clear as to what is evidence of mastery versus evidence of almost-mastery mixed with a lot of hard work. Julie Greenberg, a math teacher at Montgomery Blair High in Maryland, says, "My guiding principle in teaching is that telling the truth about mastery is the best thing I can do for now. We're way too new at this process of finally trying to evaluate mastery to stop in our tracks and encourage grading that blurs effort and mastery" (Mathews 2005, p. A10).

In an effort to streamline and safeguard definitions of mastery and to be assured that every child has the same foundations and standards across the district, some districts provide scripts for teachers to follow: "On day one of week five, all students in this grade level in this subject will be on page 71. To start this lesson, say the following: . . ."

This type of pacing guide for teachers is great for those learning to teach the units for the first time, but even guides are subject to multiple interpretations by teachers and principals: Are the guides suggestions from which we can veer as necessary to respond to the needs of our students, or are they declarations that cannot be violated, packaged in user-friendly "guide" language?

Clear communication regarding pacing guides requires attention, but we also need to recognize that regardless of how scripted or "teacher-proof" a year's curriculum becomes, we all emphasize some aspects over others. Given restrictions on time and resources as well as very diverse groups of students each year, we're always deciding what to prune and what to keep, when to just introduce versus when to push for mastery, and what constitutes mastery —all of these can vary from teacher to teacher.

Curriculum is subject to a teacher's interpretation, and this is not necessarily a bad thing. Instead of spending so much energy trying to defy such realities, let's embrace them. We can use each other's wisdom and experience to shape what we teach, and we can structure our days and priorities in order to create time to share those ideas. Regular conversation via e-mail or face-to-face interactions will go a long way toward keeping us focused on high standards for all children across our districts.

Isolation may be one of the great hurdles to mastery learning. Without focused conversations about mastery, lesson plans become a series of shots in the dark. While presenting them, we hope we do no harm. The clarity required by differentiated instruction and assessment defeats such vague and ill-spun pedagogy, for they force us to begin with the end in mind. Once we have that clear picture, we're ready to assess students and begin our lessons.

CHAPTER 3

Principles of Successful Assessment in the Differentiated Classroom

A university professor screened a group of undergraduates to make sure they had never seen this graphic before. Once the larger group was selected, he divided it in half, and invited the first half to come into a room and look at the graphic. The other half waited outside.

He displayed the graphic for the first group. It was the same graphic you see here, except he had used shading and thicker lines to emphasize the *older* woman. In fact, it was difficult to see the younger woman. He asked this first group to memorize the picture for seven minutes.

When the time was up, he asked the group to wait outside, and he invited the second group into the room. Before they entered, however, he quickly switched the picture with one that emphasized the *younger* woman. The second group sat down and observed this new picture for seven minutes, just like the first group did with their version of the picture. After the time period, they left the room and waited outside.

When the room was empty again, the professor removed the second picture, and replaced it with the one above that emphasizes both the younger and older women equally. He invited both groups back into the room and asked them to describe for each other what they saw.

The first group started describing the older woman, and the second group described the younger woman. Both groups said they couldn't understand how the other group couldn't see what was plainly in front of their eyes. Both sides argued for their perceived "truth." In just seven minutes, they had been conditioned to see only the one perspective.

Extrapolate to our classrooms: Our students come to us "biased" on how to see the world of math, language arts, history, physical education, sexuality, grammar, literature, science, technology, foreign language, and other topics for five to eighteen years via school and living their lives. It can get murky. Many adults, for example, still think it's warmer in the summer and colder in the winter in the northern hemisphere because the Earth is closer and farther from the heat source, the sun. This is not correct, of course. It's the 23.5 degrees tilt of the Earth off its vertical axis that causes direct and indirect rays to heat and cool the atmosphere, causing seasons. Because throughout their lives students have had occasion to be closer and farther from heat sources, however, students think it's the same cause for seasonal changes.

Into this fray of arguing fallacies walks the teacher. He or she has to understand each student's "truth," and convince students that their perceptions are incorrect or incomplete, and that the "truth" the teacher has is the one they should adopt. This is a difficult task when one teaches thirty or more students, or even twenty.

We can't teach in a vacuum. What are the three most important things in real estate? The most common reply is, "Location, location, location." It's the same thing in differentiated instruction: location, location, location of the student's mind. We cannot teach blind to our students. All differentiated instruction is based on informal and formal, 24–7, assessment.

Introduction

In a differentiated classroom, assessment guides practice. Instructional decisions are based not only on what we know about curriculum, but also on what we know about the specific students we serve. We have to be diligent, however. Dividing students into flexible groups, for example, might be creative or break up boring lesson routine, but it only becomes true differentiated instruction when we assign students to different groups based on something we know about those students. The Latin root of *assessment* is "assidēre," meaning "to sit beside." This means that assessment is a coaching, nurturing tool. Its emphasis is not so much on documenting deficiencies as it is on shaping our instructional decisions. Some teachers would use assessment simply to see how a child doesn't measure up. Assessment expert Douglas Reeves reminds us that, "Too often, educational tests, grades, and report cards are treated by teachers as autopsies when they should be viewed as physicals" (O'Connor 2002, p. 112).

Begin with the End in Mind

Just as we discussed in Section I, great differentiated assessment is never kept in the dark; it always begins with clearly understood, developmentally appropriate mastery. We do everything we can do to avoid being

> Students can hit any target they can see and which stands still for them.
>
> —Rick Stiggins, educator and assessment expert

cryptic with our lesson's objectives. It's similar to the real world: We don't pull our car with faulty brakes into a mechanic's shop and tell the mechanic, "There's something wrong with this car. If you can figure out what it is and fix it, I'll pay you." In the real world, we always know what the outcome is supposed to be.

It may be a bit radical, but go ahead and give students the end-of-unit test on the first day of teaching the unit. That's right, the actual piece of paper on which they will record their answers. Clarify each question with students. Now when you teach the unit and mention an answer to one of the test questions, students will perk up and listen, elevating the information to importance. This is a great thing! You're not making it easier for students. You're teaching so that they learn the material, which is your goal. On the day of the test, the students show you their still-blank copies before the test begins, and wow, they're ready to show their mastery by completing it.

This works best, of course, if you use constructed response items in which students generate their own information in response to prompts. If a student shouts to classmates during our unit lecture, "Hey, that's the answer to number 12. Everyone write that down," be proud; it's exactly what should happen.

If we're using forced-choice formats (matching, true/false, multiple choice), then we rearrange the items so students can't memorize an answer pattern. In math classes, we reserve the right to change the numerical values in the problems, but we'll have the same number of problems that deal with cosine, sine, secant, cosecants, tangents, and cotangents.

Students achieve more when they have a clear picture of the expectations. We teach a novel in our English classes, for instance, by first identifying for or with students the intended outcomes of the unit:

Class, today we start our study of Remarque's All Quiet on the Western Front. *In this unit, we will concentrate on three areas: Theme—What are the themes of a novel? How does an author communicate the theme, and how does a reader determine the theme? Authenticity—How does an author create historical fiction authentic to the time period, and what impact does that have on the reader's experience? Literary Devices—What are some of the common devices employed by writers, and what is their impact on the reader's experience?*

Students are likely to do the homework assignment if they have a clear picture of the finished product. If the assignment is fuzzy, they won't; it takes too much effort to distill coherence. "I'll put it off another day," they reason. Examples of fuzzy assignments include: "Respond to the novel's style," "Consider economic alternatives," "Vary your response according to the artwork's theme," "Practice the vocabulary terms," or "Study for the test."

Very few things are as frustrating to a student as working long hours on a project over several weeks' time only to find out she wasn't doing it correctly. As teachers, how would we feel if we found out that what we were studying was incorrect, and that we have to go back and undo what we've learned? In both scenarios everyone's frustrated; the teacher ends up answering to the student's parents, the administration, and his or her own spouse or significant other who resents the hurt that's been caused and all the time he or she spends fixing the problem.

Nothing in the post-school world is kept a secret, so we shouldn't play games with students, coyly declaring that we maintain the right to choose anything we want from the chapter text when they ask what's on the test. "You'll just have to read every word," we say, "and study every concept really well in order to get an A. I'll know whether or not you read every word."

This isn't teaching. It's not important that the students read every word, yet now you've made it so. The important thing is that they learned the material. We haven't done our job if a child ever asks, "Will this be on the test?"

EEK a.k.a. KUD

Great assessments in a differentiated classroom focus on essential and enduring knowledge (EEK), concepts, and skills. Some folks label it as: *Know, Understand, Able to Do* (KUD). *Know* refers to what students have retained from the learning: "A prepositional phrase consists of a preposition, modifiers, and the object of the preposition." *Understand* refers to concepts/relationships/connections students understand as a result of the unit: "Energy is transferred from the sun to higher-order animals via photosynthesis in the plant (producer) and the first-order consumers that eat those plants. These animals are then consumed by higher-order animals. When those animals die, the energy is transferred to the soil and subsequent plants via scavengers and decomposers. It's cyclical in nature." *Do* refers to specific skills students can demonstrate: "When determining a percentage discount for a market item, students first change the percentage into a decimal by dividing by one hundred, then multiply the decimal and the item price. This new amount is subtracted from the list price to determine the new, discounted cost of the item."

Essential understandings are often placed in the context of essential questions you want students to pursue. Essential questions are larger questions that transcend subjects, are usually interesting to ponder, and have more than one answer, such as "How can an ordinary individual have an extraordinary impact on the world?" As understandings or questions, they are often broken down into component pieces for our lessons.

For example, what if the essential question in our unit on Reconstruction was, "How does a country rebuild itself after civil war?" We'd have to ask questions about state versus federal government rights, the economic state of the country, the extent of resources left in the country, the role of the military and industry, the effects of grassroots organizations established to help, and the influence of the international scene at the time, among others. In each of these topics, there would be subsets of information as well. While there are usually one to five essential questions for a unit of study, there can be many subsets of information. Beyond the material that's essential and enduring, it's often wise to include information for enrichment purposes: "What's nice to know?"

For units we're teaching for the first time, this one section of the unit plan can take weeks as we unpack the standards, confer with colleagues, and come to know the material ourselves. In *Test Better, Teach Better,* Dr. James Popham says one way to prioritize standards and objectives is to lay them all out in front of you and categorize them as: essential, highly desirable, desirable.

Essential would be those items you consider vital to current growth and future success. *Highly desirable* refers to those items that are very important to students, but not absolutely necessary. *Desirable* standards are items that would be great to know but aren't as important or necessary as the others. He adds, "There's a whopping difference between content standards that are simply sought and content standards that are truly taught" (Popham 2003, p. 36).

Remember, we all prune. No matter how scripted the curriculum, we all elevate some instructional objectives to great importance over others and we all place some objectives on the instructional back burner. We're human, and humans are messy. Over the years, there's

You are asked to teach "Agriculture Revolution" to your secondary students. How do you figure out what is essential in the unit? Here's a think-aloud that might help clarify the process.

Look over your new categories and ask, "What will I accept as proof students have mastered this?" For example: *Agriculture Revolution* means what? To get a better fix on it, we read further in the standards. We see standards 6.1 and 6.2. What does "Explain the emergence of agriculture, irrigation, and domestication of animals" really mean? I don't know, so I need to read the text, talk to colleagues, and do whatever it takes to fully understand all the little pieces I'll be teaching—concepts, terms, patterns, skills, and connections that I want students to learn. It's only when I've looked at the pieces and big picture that I might be able to create those categories.

One of the best ways to encapsulate all these ideas is to focus on essential questions. A few that come to mind are: What is a culture? What factors affect a culture's development and how do they do so? How does geography affect a culture's growth? How do economics affect a culture's growth? What enabled technological advances to occur in Mesopotamia? How did the development of technology affect a culture's growth? Why is the Fertile Crescent known as the birthplace of civilization? Wouldn't it be cool to have your own ziggurat? (Okay, this last one wasn't completely serious.) With the essential questions, you can now organize your lessons.

And you might ask, "What do I write at the top of the gradebook columns, however?" Perhaps each of your standards or essential questions . . . You can, of course, have categories for tests, quizzes, projects, writings, homework, classwork, etc., but those wouldn't be tied to your objectives or standards, which means they wouldn't help your differentiated instruction cause.

wisdom, but in the moment, there may not appear to be. No amount of standardization mandates will change this fact, though to be honest, that doesn't toll the death bell of education as some would have us believe. The truly effective differentiating teacher takes every opportunity with colleagues and alone to reflect on what is essential in the curriculum versus desirable or highly desirable. Insights gained from reflection and from others' insights that don't exactly align with his or hers actually moves the teacher forward. In all of it, the teacher is responsive to the students before him or her, not just to the mandated curriculum.

Determining what is essential in a unit takes time. We might begin the effort weeks ahead. If it's the first time we've ever differentiated the unit, we can ask colleagues to share their tests so that we can see what they consider salient. We look for advice about the important concepts and questions via a professional listserv or file folder on our school's intranet. We look to how our subject's professional organization has "unpacked" national standards with benchmarks and look-fors. And, after teaching a unit, we can go back and revisit what we consider to be essential and enduring and make a note of any revisions in our thinking in a "tickler" file we'll use next time we teach the unit.

For those who are teaching a unit for the first time, here are some great places to get guidance on what is essential and enduring:

- Standards of learning (Unpack them—What specific skills and content within this standard will be necessary to teach students in order for them to demonstrate mastery of the standard?)
- Programs of study
- Curriculum guides
- Pacing guides
- Tests from other teachers
- Professional journals
- Mentor or colleague teachers
- Textbook scope and sequence
- Textbook end-of-chapter reviews and tests
- Subject-specific listservs
- Professional organizations
- Quiet reflection

As we pre-assess, plan for, and teach students, we'll find some of them have more success than others. This is normal, of course, but we wonder nevertheless: "What in our lessons should we adjust so that all students can succeed?" We look at our teaching methods, resources, accommodations, and even assessments. Along the way, we often revisit our essential understandings and all the objectives inherent within them.

It's important to hold tight to those objectives. The milestones are there for a reason, and they are not meant to be dismissed easily. We can rearrange objectives, benchmarks, and standards in efforts to make curriculum understood and meaningful, but they are the compass heading we should maintain. When we have to adjust essential and enduring content and skills, it's always done with solid record-keeping of what was and was not achieved, with the clear intent of returning to those essentials later in the unit or via another route. So, while we might alter or remove an essential learning here and there for struggling students, we find ways to remind ourselves of that temporary detour and get students back on the right road, complete with missing mileage. For advanced students, we make sure they have all the essentials necessary for the next portion of the trip, but we don't require the mileage—that is, doing the same work as everyone else— if it's not needed.

Determining Students' Readiness

After identifying essential understandings and the objectives within them, we identify specific tasks we can employ to determine our students' levels of readiness regarding the topics. These are diagnostic pre-assessments. Our analysis of student responses to such pre-assessments will shape our lessons and units of study. The influence is so great, in fact, we often do not plan the first learning experience or activity of a unit until the pre-assessments are completed and analyzed.

If we plan in this sequence, we are not thinking, "I have to teach inertia. What activities can I do in this unit?" Instead, and more effectively, we're thinking, "These are the things students must learn and here's where they are already. What experiences do I need to provide in order for them to master this material?" The former focuses on accountability: "Here are the experiences, now let me see whether you can jump through this hoop I've set for you." The latter focuses on students' mastery: "How can I help you have the most success with this material?"

Where do the pre-assessments come from? If possible, they should come from the summative assessment—the unit test or culminating project. Summative assessments reflect all we deem important to know, so let's start with them as we initially identify students' backgrounds in the material we have to teach. Pull specific skills and concepts from your summative assessments and use them as the pre-assessments. This way you can examine before-and-after levels of readiness with greater validity and authority.

Avoid anything too large and complex for a pre-assessment; keep it as short and to the point as possible. If the unit project, for example, is for students to design a lunar or underwater colony incorporating three-dimensional solids in the shapes of the buildings (e.g., cube, sphere, rectangular pyramid, rectangular prism, pentagonal pyramid, pentagonal prism, cone, cylinder), for the unit pre-test ask students to simply identify each shape and its corresponding number of faces, edges, and vertices. Then have them draw the two-dimensional design for folding paper together to create the three-dimensional shape for the pre-assessment. In other math units, ask students to solve three math problems of the type you are teaching in the unit ahead that reflect different aspects of the concept you're to teach.

As a pre-assessment in science, ask students to identify the scientific method within a given lab procedure, and if something was amiss, to describe it for you and how they would change the experiment to correct the concern. If the student is supposed to compose a brilliant persuasive essay at the end of the unit, assign the pre-unit assessment prompt: "Using your most persuasive techniques, write an essay in which you persuade me to your way of thinking regarding an issue encountered in everyday living. Use whatever resources and writing process you think are necessary to be successful, except for any specific advice from classmates, family, or others." See where they are regarding the topic right here and now, cold turkey. You're going for baseline data.

As you create the pre-assessment, consider:

- What are the essential and enduring skills and content you're trying to assess?
- How does this assessment allow students to demonstrate mastery?
- Is every component of that objective accounted for in the assessment?
- Can students respond another way and still satisfy the requirements of the assessment task? Would this alternative way reveal a student's mastery more truthfully?
- Is this assessment more a test of process or content? Is that what you're after?

How do we know an assessment assesses what we want it to? Several ways: We do the task ourselves, then we circle the portions of our responses that elicit the essential and enduring knowledge and skills listed at the top of our unit. We read each component of the essential and enduring knowledge and skills, then check off on the assessment where demonstration of that knowledge and skill is required. We ask someone else to compare the lesson's essential and enduring knowledge and skills to the assessment to make sure they're in sync. The point is to take the time once in a while and make the correlations.

Designing the Assessments

Assessments are based on the essential understandings/questions. There are three types of assessments we need to design: pre-, formative, and summative. While there is a suggested sequence to design these, we recognize how fluid this process is. In the course of designing a summative assessment, for example, we may realize we need to change the essential understandings slightly or we might think of a great learning experience that would be more effective than what we've been planning to do. As we design those essential understandings and learning experiences, on the other hand, we might think of a better way to assess students. Be open to the back-and-forth nature of unit planning.

Although we've just listed the three types of assessments in the order in which students will experience them, they are usually designed in a different order. As mentioned before, we start with where we're going—summative assessments. Design this one first, and make sure everything in the unit's objectives or understandings is accounted for in the summative assessment, and that it doesn't assess anything beyond the unit's goals. Keeping focused means we literally write out or type the culminating project or unit test before we design our first lesson with the material.

Once summative assessments are identified, we can determine our pre-assessments. They are smaller pieces and versions of the summative assessments. If the summative assessment is a complex project, of course, we cull the basics from the project and ask students to do sample tasks that reveal their readiness levels regarding mastery.

Finally, we identify frequent and plentiful formative assessments that will guide our instruction. Again, if formative assessment ideas suggest themselves while planning other portions of the unit, write them down right away.

To clarify, let's be clear on the purpose of each type of assessment.

Pre-assessments. These assessments are used to indicate students' readiness for content and skill development, and to guide instructional decisions.

Formative Assessments. These assessments are en route checkpoints, done frequently. They provide ongoing and helpful feedback, informing instruction and reflecting subsets of the essential and enduring knowledge. See the next section for more information on formative assessments.

Summative Assessments. These assessments are given to students at the end of the learning. They match objectives and experiences, and their formats are negotiable if the product is not the literal standard and would prevent students from revealing what they know about a topic. They reflect most, if not all, of the essential and enduring knowledge.

The Wisdom of Formative Assessment

Assessment is never kept exclusively for the end of a unit. On the contrary, students achieve more with frequent formative assessment throughout the unit.

> *After reviewing 7,827 studies on learning and instruction, researcher John Hattie . . . reported that providing students with specific information about their standing in terms of particular objectives increased their achievement by 37 percentile points. To dramatize the implications of this research, assume that two students of equal ability are in the same class learning the same content. Also assume that they take a test on the content before beginning instruction and that both receive a score that puts their knowledge of the content at the 50th percentile. Four weeks go by and the students receive exactly the same instruction, the same assignments, and so on. However, one student receives systematic feedback in terms of specific learning goals; the other does not. After four weeks, the two students take another test. Everything else being equal, the student who received the systematic feedback obtained a score that was 34 percentile points higher than the score of the student who had not received feedback. It was his dramatic finding that led Hattie to remark: "The most powerful single innovation that enhances achievement is feedback." (Marzano et al. 2001, p. 23)*

Many teachers make the mistake of spending considerable energy designing a culminating project or test, but its end-of-unit nature limits impact on student learning. Students can't use the feedback they gain from such assessments to grow. A better use of energy, then, is for teachers to spend considerable time and effort designing and using *formative* assessments offered en route to summative achievements. These frequent checkpoints are where students learn the most. They allow teachers to change course mid-journey, and they keep students and their parents informed—positives all around.

This really is significant. If we rally our resources, creativity, and focus around students' summative experiences, we miss critical opportunities to positively affect learning. When designing a lesson or unit, the wise teacher spends time inserting ideas for formative assessments, making sure they are frequent and substantive, then finds time and inclination throughout the unit to consider those assessments and make instructional changes accordingly. It's not too much, then, for a principal or colleague to pass a teacher in the hallway or stop by his or her classroom and ask, "What's one thing you changed in the last two weeks in your instruction because of something you observed while assessing students?" Or put more directly: "What did you learn about a student today and what did you do with that knowledge?"

Figure 3.1 Topics with Sample Formative Assessments

Topic	Formative Assessments
Verb Conjugation	Conjugate five regular verbs.
	Conjugate five irregular verbs.
	Conjugate a verb in Spanish, then do its parallel in English
	Answer: Why do we conjugate verbs?
	Answer: What advice would you give a student learning to conjugate verbs?
	Examine the following ten verb conjugations and identify which ones are done incorrectly.
Balancing Chemical Equations	Define reactants and products, and identify them in the equations provided.
	Critique how Jason calculated the number of moles of each reactant.
	Balance these sample, unbalanced equations.
	Answer: What do we mean by balancing equations?
	Explain to your lab partner how knowledge of stoichiometric coefficients helps us balance equations.
	Prepare a mini-poster that explains the differences among combination, decomposition, and displacement reactions.

Formative assessment can take many formats. See Figure 3.1 for examples of topics and their sample formative assessments.

Take Action as a Result of What We Learn

Besides their critical role in diagnosing students' needs and informing teachers' decisions, assessments result in action. Many teachers do a myriad of assessments, including multiple intelligence surveys, learning style inventories, standardized state or provincial exams, interest surveys, Myers-Briggs Personality Type profiles, Bernice McCarthy's 4MAT learning styles system, and unit pre-assessments. Chapter 1, "Getting to Know Your Students," of Sheryn Spencer Northey's wonderful book, *Handbook on Differentiated Instruction for Middle and High Schools,* is one of the best sources available for these instruments.

Unfortunately, some teachers (and earlier in my career me included) do all these assessments, yet still go ahead and do what they were going to do anyway. They do not know how to differentiate nor do they have a large enough repertoire of strategies from which to choose. Instead of spending all that time coming to know their students via those assessments, they would better serve students if they just went ahead and taught without assessing. Of course it wouldn't be very good teaching, but it would be a better use of time. Pre-testing students without taking action with the results isn't assessment.

Assessment forces action in many ways. If we get test scores back that indicate boys at our school don't do as well on standardized reading tests, for example, we figure out why and take multiple actions to raise boys' reading proficiency on standardized tests as well as proficiency in normal reading for learning and enjoyment. We teach them standardized test-taking savvy, and we provide extended practice with test-similar materials and questions. We point out positive reading habits by males in their lives, teach them how to make sense of text, and provide ample and varied background experiences so they can understand text scenarios and attach new learning to what's already in long-term memory. We provide many opportunities to build and sustain advanced vocabulary, and we cultivate their belief that reading is transformative (Tatum 2005): It is the key to unlocking doors in life. All of this action is based on our assessments, and it's targeted at those boys who need it. Assessment informs practice, and we take action.

Varied and "Over Time" Assessment

Imagine your supervisor comes to your classroom to observe your success with that new teaching technique. Your salary and final evaluation are tied to the evaluation. Up to this particular day, everything has been going well—the students were learning and you were succeeding with the technique. You're quite good at it, in fact. On this one day, however, the students are a mess, everything goes down the tubes, and you're rushing through things because you have something for which the students must be prepared the next day. Add to that, the air conditioning has conked out, the room is stifling, it's after lunch, and the front office has interrupted your class three times with p.a. announcements requesting students to come pick up band instruments and other items left by their parents. The lesson bombs and your evaluation rating is much less than desirable.

As an adult professional, you would resent the rating given you for that observation. It represents one snapshot out of multiple days of success. You'd appeal the evaluation as not indicative of your true expertise, and you'd request another chance to prove your expertise, or at least another means by which to demonstrate it. It's a frustrating situation for mature, stable adults; to your students, it's the end of the world.

Educational Testing Service and other standardized test makers are the first to inform educators that their tests are never meant as the sole diagnostic tool for an individual student. They are meant to indicate trends and patterns for a school or district, and to be included as one of many sources of information about a student. Yes, they may provide an initial indicator of achievement or aptitude regarding a student, but they should always be used in conjunction with other assessment tools in order to make important decisions regarding an individual child. This applies to evaluating teachers of that individual student as well.

In order for assessment to be valid, it must be varied and done over time. A student might know the material today, but to determine whether he or she has learned it, assess the student on the same material a while later. This is not always possible, of course, but we can incorporate earlier content and skills in new units of study. For example, if we taught students how to write expository paragraphs two weeks ago, we should ask them to write expository paragraphs on our current studies of taiga, tundra, temperate, rain forest, marine, and desert biomes today. We can assess easily whether they still retain an understanding of expository paragraph structure and technique.

We can also allow students to redo work for full credit—a concept explained in Chapter 9. The point here is that students aren't "on" 100 percent of the time. No one is. There are so many justifiable reasons students may be distracted on the day of the assessment—growling stomach from lack of food, thirst, emotional angst because of parents/friends/identity/tests/college/politics/birthday/sex/blogs/parties/sports/projects/homework/self-esteem/acne/holiday/report cards/money/hurricane/terrorism/disease/future—that it's more than reasonable to allow students every opportunity to show their best side, not just one opportunity. It's civil, and it's merciful. We are teaching adults-in-the-making, not adults.

Before readers get too hung up on their interpretation that such extensions and multiple attempts would never be allowed in the real world, they are encouraged to reexamine two premises: First, for most grade levels and in all subjects, it's developmentally inappropriate to hold students to adult-level competencies and deadlines. We're preparing students for being who they are right now, and they are just now coming to know the subjects we teach. They are not supposed to have an adult-level proficiency with them. Second, the real world *is* like this. In almost every professional situation, we can set things up for extended deadlines (or finishing projects with enough time left to make multiple attempts to fix our mistakes before the deadline).

When we assess students through more than one format, we see different sides to their understanding, too. Some students' mindmaps of their analyses of Renaissance art rival the most cogent, written versions of their classmates. If we never gave them that additional opportunity to use the mindmap format, we would never have seen their thinking. Accepting the power of varied assessments over time makes us wonder what student gifts go undeclared over the years due to our singular focus on single-shot assessments.

Can we always offer multiple assessments over time? No, but we can do it a majority of the time. And we can allow students to approach us and ask whether they can negotiate how to demonstrate mastery. Again, we want an accurate portrayal of a student's mastery, not something clouded by a useless format or a distorted snapshot that doesn't represent true proficiency.

The best phrase to apply here is "clear and consistent evidence." What can we do to have clear and consistent evidence of our students' development? This means we grade on a pattern of achievement, not all achievement. Anything that is a serious anomaly in the student's performance record, especially if it's a particularly low score in a parade of wonderful scores, is examined closely to determine its relevance. If it's a fluke, we don't let one low score influence the accurate, overall grade represented by the more consistent performance pattern.

Authentic Assessment

Authenticity refers to two aspects of assessment. First, the assessment is close to how students will apply their learning in real-world applications. For instance, there is no business or company that asks students to write five-paragraph essays. In fact, most companies say that we do a disservice to our students and their future employees when we teach the five-paragraph essay as the Holy Grail of writing. Employers expect employees to be able to discern the proper number of paragraphs for a successful document, splitting and combining paragraphs as warranted by content, audience, and the writer's purpose. So rather than assess students on a topic by asking for a five-paragraph essay, we need to ask for a properly done essay, regardless of its length. This is more authentic to how students will use their learning in the real world.

Students shouldn't feel the need to ask, "When will we ever use this?" or "Why are we doing this?" Remember, though, that real-world applications are secondary. Holding students accountable for adult-level proficiency as would happen in their lives beyond school is often inappropriate. Sometimes the only meaningful rationale for studying and assessing certain topics is the rhetoric and reasoning skills, such as the following, that study of the topic provides. Not many of us graph parabolas in our daily routine as adults, for example; however learning how to do so teaches us many skills and concepts applicable throughout our lives.

- Accounting for variables
- Getting enough data (points) to plot the curve (at least three ordered pairs) so that we can be sure of our answer
- Following logic to its conclusion
- Explaining our thinking symbolically to others
- Being thorough
- Persevering

- Extrapolating to predict outcomes
- Checking the reasonableness of conclusions
- Remaining organized
- Following protocols
- Weighing the use of alternative strategies

It's worth overtly sharing skills and concepts with them as justification for what we teach, then show students how they're doing in mastering them.

Does every assessment have to be authentic to real life? Of course not. In fact, it's wise for teachers in grades kindergarten through early years of high school to realize that their lessons and assessments are in preparation for living the current year, not just for something occurring years down the road, or even next week. Some teachers get so focused on "preparing these kids for the real world" that they dismiss what they know as developmentally appropriate for the age-group. Subsequent lessons are not as meaningful to students, solid learning is threatened, and students become disillusioned. We have to remember that many of our students are literally at the "How can this [the lesson] prepare me for the rest of this day?" point, let alone the rest of the week or beyond.

The second aspect of authenticity refers to the assessment being authentic to how students are learning. For example, we don't conduct our math lessons focusing on numeric computations, only to then assess students on that content through word problems. We don't teach science students via verification labs (recipe labs in which students obtain a predetermined result) then test them using an inquiry lab (labs in which students design the investigation question and methodology themselves, the result of which is unknown to both students and teacher until the investigation is done).

If assessment is not authentic to how students learned and what they were supposed to learn, then all subsequent grades are questionable. In such cases, grades and scores are not accurate renderings of what students know and are able to do. They do not reflect what was taught. In some cases, the injustice of this is obvious—for example, assessing students on their knowledge of persuasive advertising techniques by asking them to design a commercial from scratch when they have only talked about commercials during the unit but never designed one. It can easily be overlooked in more subtle situations, however. Some teachers design tests to assess content knowledge, but they don't see the other prerequisite skills needed in order to express that mastery.

For example, we can assess students' understanding of a math principle by asking them to respond to a series of word problems, but those word problems also require good reading comprehension skills. In another class, we ask students to prepare a multimedia presentation on a topic so that we can assess their mastery of the topic, but this also requires solid technical skills with the presentation software. Will lack of skill with presenting the information unduly influence the accuracy of the grade earned on the project? Definitely. Will the grade be useful to teachers as a way to document progress, provide feedback, or inform instructional decisions? No.

In sum, while it's critical for assessment to be authentic to how students learn the material, it may or may not be essential for assessment to be authentic for real-world applications.

Be Substantive—Avoid "Fluff"

Some students aren't ready to analyze literary devices in a novel via writing. So while the class works on that, we ask struggling students to color murals depicting scenes from the book.

This brings shame on our profession. Don't do it. Instead, find alternative routes for students at low readiness levels to access those same literary devices.

Here are some examples of "fluff" assignments to be avoided when determining full mastery, followed by their substantive versions—consider what is being learned and what is being assessed in each one.

Fluff Assignment. Make a poster for each math formula on page 70. (Most activities like this are nice activities to do after school hours, but it does not advance the students' understanding of the concepts. If the poster required students to explain concepts and procedures in detail, there may be some learning benefit, however.)

Substantive Assignment. Analyze the relative success of five different students' responses to problems 17 through 22 on page 71.

Fluff Assignment. Make an acrostic poem about chromatography using each of its letters. (This force-fit of ideas doesn't advance students understanding and retention of chromatography lessons.)

Substantive Assignment. Explain how chromatography paper separates colors into their component colors, and identify one use of chromatography in a profession of your choosing.

Fluff Assignment. Define the terms "manifest destiny" and "imperialism," and use them properly in a sentence.

Substantive Assignment. Identify one similarity and one difference between the concepts of "manifest destiny" and "imperialism," then explain to what extent these two concepts are alive and well in the modern world.

Please don't ever hold an ancient Greece festival where all students learn is how to keep togas tied to their shoulders. Always err on the side of substance, not fluff. Students will spot a lightweight approach every time and they will resent it, even those you are supposedly letting off the hook. If students can't analyze literary devices to the level of their classmates, then ask them to focus on one literary device at a time with literature that more vividly than subtly displays the device. Ask them to create the device in their own writing. Really hammer it home, then introduce the next one, but don't let anyone off the hook from learning it. Check out Chapter 5 on tiering lessons for more ideas on how to raise the complexity of assessments for all levels of readiness.

Inclusion classes provide even more opportunities to consider fluff versus substance. Inclusion is done via accommodations that enable students with learning challenges to take on the regular classroom curriculum. We try our best not to dilute anything. Inclusion teacher, Jeanne, has a point when she talks about teachers who tell their special education students all they have to do is attempt the work, regardless of whether they understand it, in order to pass the class:

> *Wow, as a special education teacher . . . yes, I think this is wrong . . . wrong on the way the entire inclusion program is set up. If a child is putting forth effort, and still can't pass, then the program just isn't right!*
>
> *The idea of inclusion . . . is to find a way that a child with special needs can be successful in a general education setting. The first and best way is for the child to master the same material through a system of accommodations and supports. For example, a child who can't read has a peer buddy who reads to him, or a child to whom he dictates his answers. We've had kids where an aide would spend additional time reviewing the material and helping the child study. Perhaps the child with one arm learns to type using only one hand.*

Assessment-Guided, Differentiated Lesson Planning Sequence

Given this emphasis on assessment, here are the twelve basic steps for planning a successfully differentiated lesson:

1. Identify the essential and enduring knowledge (understandings, questions, benchmarks, objectives, skills, standards).
2. Identify your students with unique needs, and what they will need in order to achieve. They may need changes in content, process, product, affect, or learning environment (Tomlinson 2003). This is where you refer to any information you have in your learner profiles that

may influence a student's success with the lessons. For a description of student factors affecting instruction see the next section.

3. Design your formative and summative assessments. Literally write them out, if possible.

4. Design and deliver your pre-assessments based on the summative assessments and essential and enduring knowledge discussed earlier.

5. Adjust assessments or essential understandings and objectives based on your further thinking while designing the assessments.

6. Design the learning experiences for students based on the information gathered from pre-assessments. Don't be afraid to adjust essential understandings or assessments based on further thinking you've done while planning these experiences. See the next page for a further description of this step.

7. Run a mental tape of each step in the lesson sequence to make sure things make sense for your diverse group of students and that the lesson will run smoothly. While doing this, check the lesson(s) against criteria for successful differentiated instruction and revise as necessary. Be sure you can point to evidence in the lesson of your expertise with students of this age, with cognitive theory, and with differentiated practice. If you can't point these out, the lesson may need revision.

8. Review your plan with a colleague. Lesson design is very subjective, and as a result, we miss opportunities others can see through their objective perspective. At least twice a year, exchange lessons with a colleague and critique each other's approach. It's amazing how much we discover when we do this.

9. Obtain and/or create materials needed for the lesson. Be completely provisioned.

10. Conduct the lesson.

11. Evaluate the lesson's success with students. What evidence do you have that the lesson was successful? What worked and what didn't, and why?

12. Record advice for yourself on changes for when you do this lesson in future years. Also include notes in your plan book for any aspects you'll have to change in tomorrow's lesson in light of what happened during today's lesson.

Student Factors Affecting Instruction (Step #2)

This section refers to any factors that affect students' readiness to learn. These include, but are not limited to, giftedness, poverty, learning styles, multiple intelligences, LD, dyslexia, ODD (Oppositional Deficit Disorder), bipolar issues, depression, current events (such as devastating earthquakes, tsunamis, or terrorist attacks in their home countries), fetal alcohol syndrome, substance abuse, physical challenges, emotional challenges, gender, family struggles, personal interests, after-school care, nationality, and ESOL status. While we don't resurvey or assess these factors for every lesson we design, we maintain a running file or log on each student so we can have this information as it is needed.

In my own case, I use a lot of sticky notes during the day and evening, recording observations about students—good, bad, and in-between—that I need to address in my lessons or grading tomorrow or down the road. These get thrown into individual folders I keep on each student in a file cabinet. Yes, some years I've used 160 file folders, one for each student I taught.

I don't have time to take out a student's folder every time he or she does something worth noting for later reference, so the sticky notes work well. By the end of the day, I have a pocketful or a small, messy stack of notes on the corner of my desk. It takes three minutes to toss these notes into their respective student folders before I leave for home. Two or three times during a grading period, I'll sit down with each class's folders and transcribe information from the sticky notes to a running record stapled to one side of the folder. *Important:* If the comment I make about the student on a sticky note is for immediate consideration, that note gets inserted in the next day's lesson plan, not the student's folder where it might sit unheeded for three weeks. In today's high-tech classes, a PDA that allows you to use a stylus to record these notes works well.

Remember to divide and conquer with this information. If another teacher does multiple intelligence surveys, for example, ask that the data get entered into a schoolwide database for all teachers to use. If any teacher gets wind of something going on with a student or his or her family that will affect the student's school performance, establish a system by which that information gets shared with all teachers who have that student.

Learning Experiences (Step #6)

This is your actual lesson plan. The thinking here is, "What experiences do I need to provide these particular students in order for them to achieve 100 percent on every assessment?" This is different from providing a bunch of experiences, then asking students to jump through hoops of assessment to document how they measure up or down.

In a differentiated class, much of this lesson plan is a menu of options in a rough hierarchy (ranking) of challenge—from concrete to abstract, structured to open-ended, single facet to multifaceted—similar to the equalizer ideas from Tomlinson (2003). This is where we tier the learning for student success. The lessons can be compartmentalized as necessary for mini-lessons. Everything focuses on skills and content listed for each essential understanding. Planning for this section is also fluid: Go back and forth between this section and your assessments, adding, deleting, and modifying as appropriate.

Don't forget the myriad of approaches we can offer. We can do the four-block lesson design with some lessons and some students, but on another day, we decide Bernice McCarthy's 4MAT approach is best for the whole class. Constructivism might be the best way to go with the next lesson or with a specific group of students, while others would benefit from direct instruction templates. Some students in the upcoming lesson might respond better via certain of their multiple intelligences, so we provide experiences that invite those proclivities to shine; and others call for a strict adherence to Madeline Hunter's lesson design (Hunter 2004). Some students have no personal background in the topic we're teaching tomorrow, so today's experiences need to build that personal background so they can fully participate in tomorrow's learning.

We also make sure students have adequate opportunity to experience the content in whole-class, small-group, and individual instruction, and we might use an anchor activity on some days. In anchor activities, the whole class is working on one multistep activity for an extended period of time while the teacher pulls out mini-lesson groups for two to twenty minutes at a time to focus on specific skills and content. The class knows what to do when the teacher is working with others and not available for assistance, and the teacher periodically circulates to assess students and answer questions.

Again, while we're putting all these ideas down on paper, we're constantly going back to the assessments and enduring understandings, asking:

- "Does this learning experience enable these particular students to learn this material well?"
- "Whose needs are not being met with these learning experiences?"
- "Is there any portion of these understandings that the lessons don't address?"
- "Is this lesson necessary for all students?"
- "How am I meeting the needs of students who already understand this material or who learn it very quickly and need something else?"
- "How will I know that students have mastered this material?"
- "How have I taken the instructional pulse of the students via formative assessments regarding this material so that I can make the best instructional decisions?"
- "Is this unit going the way I want it to go? If not, how can I get back on track?"

Summary and Further Thinking

Some teachers think that if they ask a student whether he or she understands something and sees a nod, then the student has mastered the topic. This is not assessment, nor does it indicate mastery. Let's be clear, then, on what constitutes good assessment in a differentiated classroom.

- Good assessment advances learning, not just documents it; it's accepted as *integral* to instruction, not *outside* of instruction. We cannot have good instruction that does not assess, just as we cannot have good assessment that does not inform. They are inseparable. In the same planning breath when we design our assessments, we think about how we will use the information in instructional decisions; and as we design our lessons, we plot useful assessments and, most important, formative ones.

- Good assessment determines what's worth being assessed. We assess what's important, not just possible to assess. All assessment rallies around the essential and enduring understandings and skills. This means for every assessment we design, we look back at those essential understandings to make sure they're in line with our goals, and all that we're after is represented.

- Good assessment provides enough information to the teacher to inform instructional practice. We ask ourselves, "Can I gather what I want to know about students from this assessment?"

- Assessment is never saved for the end of a unit. It's ongoing and emphasizes formative over summative feedback. Spend as much time designing formative checkpoints as you do unit tests or culminating projects.

- Good assessment is never kept a secret. It begins with the end in mind. Students never feel the need to ask, "Is this going to be on the test?" because they have a clear picture of what's on the test already. We are never coy with assessments or their format.

- Good assessment focuses on developmentally appropriate, enduring and essential content and skills (a.k.a. KUD—what students *K*now, *U*nderstand, and are able to *D*o). As such, it emphasizes students' readiness levels instead of abilities and is flexibly applied, often resulting in tiering assessments according to readiness.

- Good assessment is authentic to the learning experience—the assessments are similar to what students experience during the lessons, and when appropriate it is authentic to life outside of school. It reflects concepts and skills students will encounter in their later lives as thinkers, doers, and parents.

- Good assessment is a highly valid indicator of what students know and are able to do, not something diluted by inappropriate testing formats, inclusion of effort/behavior/attendance grades, or refusal by a teacher to differentiate when it was warranted. Dr. Popham notes, however, that, "It's not the test itself that can be valid or

Life science teacher Moosa Shah grades every lab students do. He says there's plenty to grade and students have ample opportunity to explore and master the concepts while doing the lab. Laboratory experiences in Shah's class are not just learning experiences; in the end, they're demonstrations of mastery. "Other science teachers I know," Shah says, "only give feedback on labs, or if they grade them, it's a small grade. To really grade students on their mastery, they give tests after the labs that assess students' knowledge gained while doing the labs. That works for them."

Chemistry teacher Kathy Bowdring uses a mixture of grades. "I grade my students on pre-lab work, actual lab work, post-lab discussions, data analysis, and conclusions drawn. I also grade them on their explanations of models of sample sets of data, and they have to show how they've revised their thinking given the evidence presented."

All of these work. Successful assessment assesses what it is supposed to assess. In order to be valid, we only do summative assessments (i.e., graded assessments) when students are ready to demonstrate proficiency, not while they're coming to know the material. Both scenarios adhere to that criterion.

invalid but, rather, the inference that's based on a student's test performance. Is the score-based inference that a teacher has made a valid one?" (2003, p. 43). So, while we try to make our assessment tasks and prompts valid, we have to remember it's the score on the assessment that we're really talking about when we question validity: "Can we conclude what we want to know with this assessment?"

■ Good assessment is reliable. One meaning of this is that the assessment will yield the same accuracy when repeated over time. We can't always know this when designing classroom assessments each week, but it's something to try to factor into their design.

■ Good assessment does not happen on the same day every week because that's test day. It occurs because it's appropriate at this point in the learning to assess mastery, not because it's Friday.

■ Good assessment often engages more than one discipline. Life is rarely compartmentalized. In almost every profession that our students will one day work in, employees do more than one thing at the same time, often in complex and varying situations. We don't do one hour of math, one hour of art, one hour of writing/reading/spelling, one hour of science, and so on. We are dexterous with what we know and can do, integrating readily.

■ Good assessment often calls for the use of different tools and products. We're mindful of the old phrase, "If all we have is a hammer, everything looks like a nail." When we assess, then, we ask students to employ more than one tool, if possible. Art Costa, Bena Kallick, and other *Habits of Mind* educators remind us that it's often better to learn three ways to do one thing than it is to learn one way to do three different things.

■ Good assessment often uses tasks that reveal common misunderstandings so teachers can see whether students have truly learned the material. Examples of this include the math multiple-choice selections in which the given student responses differ only in terms of decimal placement, asking students to correct sentences whose structures reflect local colloquialisms but are grammatically incorrect, or inserting popular misconceptions regarding a topic into class discussions or activities to see whether students catch them. It's also advisable to insert perfectly performed or completed examples to see whether students can recognize them. Finding mistakes where there are none indicates insufficient mastery.

- Good assessment often includes those being assessed in determining its form and criteria, and in analyzing their personal progress. When students determine the evaluative criteria for a product, those criteria move to the front of their working minds. They are referenced while students are working on the assignment/assessment, instead of being disregarded until a quick glance after the project is done.

- Good assessment is often conducted with multiple experiences over time. This increases accuracy. One spelling test does not assess spelling skills—only the spelling of those words on that particular test. Multiple tests over the year will set a pattern from which we can infer ability (Popham 2003).

Educators have undoubtedly questioned the wisdom of so much state standardized testing of students. It seems as if policy makers think more testing equates to more learning, and that time spent practicing all the individual skills required on the standardized test will yield better academic health. Notice, though, that everyone's goal is learning (academic health), not high test grades, but sometimes this gets lost. Teachers themselves can get caught up on this, so it's worth pointing out that in assessment, we can't confuse correlation (if teachers use best practices, students will learn and increase the likelihood of good performance on state tests) with causality (because we have state tests, our students are learning at high levels).

It would be ludicrous to practice the doctor's physical exam as a way of becoming fit and well. The reality is the opposite: If we are physically fit and do healthy things, we will pass the physical. The separate items on the physical are not meant to be taught and crammed for; rather, they serve as indirect measures of our normal healthful living. Multiple-choice answers correlate with more genuine abilities and performance; yet mastery of those test items doesn't cause achievement. (McTighe and Wiggins 2001, p. 132)

Assessment in a differentiated classroom is highly fluid. It's shaped to a high degree by instruction and the students involved. Because assessment in a differentiated classroom is so authentic to the student's learning experience, both teachers and students can take clear action as a result of what assessment reveals. To be so integral to students' success, differentiated assessment is formative, not saved for the end of the unit. This is where differentiating teachers spend the majority of their assessment energy. These teachers are ceaseless assessors, valuing informal, formal, and varied assessments over time instead of one-shot declarations of mastery. Because they want to assess what they think they are assessing, they use more rubrics and standards-based assessments than pure averaging of scores from tests. Differentiating teachers are not coy with assessments, either; they keep everything visible so that students can hit the target. They see assessment as the pivotal instructional tool that it is.

CHAPTER 4

Three Important Types of Assessment

Portfolios

Portfolios are an excellent way to determine accurate grades for students in differentiated classes. With portfolios, teachers can collect and examine work over time. Because of portfolios' longitudinal nature and the big picture they provide of students' development, teachers don't have to make as many inferences about students' mastery based on single samplings (a.k.a. tests and quizzes). As a result, interpretations of students' mastery are more valid, and subsequent decisions we make are more effective.

With portfolios, students get opportunities to reflect on their own progress when they are asked to choose works to include in their portfolios and to explain their rationale for those inclusions. They reflect as well when they are asked to explain how an included work came to be, and what it reveals about their understanding. Students can also use their thinking about their portfolio work to set goals for the next grading period. Portfolios are a wonderful mirror for students to see their own development and take charge of their learning.

Portfolios can be as simple as a folder of collected works for one year or as complex as multi-year, selected and analyzed works from different areas of a student's life. Most appropriately for our discussion on differentiated assessment and grading, portfolios are often showcases in which students and teachers include representative samples of students' achievement regarding standards and learning objectives over time. They can be on hard copy or electronic, and they can contain non-paper artifacts as well. They can be places to store records, attributes, and accomplishments, as well as a place to reveal areas in need of growth. They can be maintained by students, teachers, or both. Though they are stored most days in the classroom, portfolios are sent home for parent review at least once a grading period.

Portfolios are very flexible. Differentiating teachers in every single secondary subject have used them to great success, including those subjects we might not at first think of as portfolio-friendly, such as math, physical education, biology, government, world civilizations, peer mediation, and Latin.

In their book, *Classroom Assessment,* Nolen and Taylor provide one of the best explanations of the different types of portfolios teachers use, and they give specific instructions and examples of how to design and manage them for various subjects. Stiggins et al. provide an equally helpful explanation of portfolios in *Classroom Assessment for Student Learning.* Since definitive explanations of portfolios and their use are beyond the purview of this book, Chapter 10 of Nolen and Taylor (2005) and Chapter 11 of Stiggins et al. (2004) are highly recommended.

Do all teachers who differentiate well use portfolio assessment? No. We can differentiate well without ever maintaining student portfolios. Portfolios promote the ideals of differentiated classes, however; and they provide the mechanics for the kinds of assessment described in this book. Portfolios are common in differentiated classrooms for good reason, even if only in truncated forms, such as when gathering three or four student works over time to make a decision regarding a student's mastery of an essential understanding. They are worth serious consideration by any teacher interested in differentiating instruction.

Rubrics

Rubrics are a popular approach for focusing learning and for assessing and reporting student achievement. Designing rubrics may be more complex than teachers realize, however, but we get better at it with each one we do. Rubrics are so powerful as assessment tools, it's worth getting good at designing them.

Take a moment and design a rubric for a specific task, just to see how it goes. Here are some suggested tasks that might work:

- Ordering a pizza
- Telling a joke
- Giving an oral presentation
- Tying a shoe
- Drawing a circle

Okay, what are the qualities of a well-drawn circle and how do we draw one? How about listing literally what we do when we tie a shoe properly? We can get bogged down in the details quickly. When we examine the steps someone takes in order to create a good rubric for these tasks, we realize that we have to identify several factors: what the task requires, what constitutes proficiency in the task, whether some steps are more important than others, whether our criteria are clear to the performer of the task, and so on.

Great guiding questions as we design sound rubrics for differentiated classes include the following:

- Does the rubric account for everything we want to assess?
- Is a rubric the best way to assess this product?
- Is the rubric tiered for this student group's readiness level?
- Is the rubric clearly written so anyone doing a "cold" reading of it will understand what is expected of the student?
- Can a student understand the content yet score poorly on the rubric? If so, why, and how can we change the rubric to make sure that doesn't happen?
- Can a student understand very little content yet score well on the rubric? If so, how can we change so that it doesn't happen?
- What are the benefits to us as teachers of this topic to create the rubric for our students?
- What are the benefits to students when they create their own rubric and the criteria against which their products will be assessed?
- How do the elements of this rubric support differentiated instruction?
- What steps did we take to make the rubric?
- What should we do differently the next time we use this rubric?
- After completing one, what tips would we give first-time rubric creators?

Rick Stiggins and his coauthors of *Classroom Assessment for Student Learning* use a "Metarubric Summary" to determine the quality of a rubric. They say that teachers need to examine their rubrics in terms of: content (Does it assess the important material and leave out the unimportant material?), clarity (Can the student understand what's being asked of him or her? Is everything clearly defined, including examples and non-examples?), practicality (Is it easy to use by both teachers and students?), and technical quality/fairness (Is it reliable and valid?). Later, they add "sampling" to the mix—"How well does the task represent the breadth and depth of the target being assessed?" (Stiggins et al. 2004, p. 220). Chapter 7 of their book is recommended.

Let's take a look at how a teacher designs a successful rubric for a differentiated class.

How to Design a Rubric

1. Identify the essential and enduring content and skills you will expect students to demonstrate. Be specific.

2. Identify what qualifies as acceptable evidence that students have mastered content and skills. This will usually be your summative assessments and from these, you can create your pre-assessments.

3. Write a descriptor for the highest performance possible. This usually begins with the standard you're trying to address. Be very specific, and be willing to adjust this descriptor as you generate the other levels of performance and as you teach the same unit over multiple years. Remember, there is no such thing as the perfect rubric. We will more than likely adjust rubrics every year they're used.

4. At this point, you'll have to make a decision: holistic or analytic? If you want to assess content and skills within the larger topic being addressed, go with analytic rubrics. They break tasks and concepts down for students so that they are assessed in each area. Analytical rubrics also require you to consider the relative weights (influences) of different elements. For example, in an essay, if "Quality of the Ideas" is more important than "Correct Spelling," then it gets more influence in the final score.

   If you want to keep everything as a whole, go with holistic rubrics. Holistic rubrics take less time to use while grading, but they don't provide as much specific feedback to students. In some cases, though, the difference in feedback is minor, and the work inherent with an analytical rubric doesn't warrant the extra time it takes to design and use, especially at the secondary level where teachers can serve more than 200 students.

   Another way of looking at the difference is this: The more analytic and detailed the rubric, the more subjective the scores can be. The more gradations and shades of gray in a rubric, the more the score is up to the discretion of the teacher and is likely to differ from teacher to teacher, and even from day to day. The more holistic the rubric, the fewer the gradations and shades of gray and thereby, the more objective and reliable the scores can be. Of course, the more detailed the rubric, the more specific feedback we get for both teacher and student. It's very rare to generate a rubric that is highly detailed and analytical while remaining objective and reliable teacher to teacher and over time.

   Here are two examples: In a holistic rubric, we might ask students to write an expository paragraph, and the descriptor for the highest score lists all the required elements and attributes. With the same task in an analytical rubric, however, we create separate rubrics (levels of accomplishment with descriptors) within the larger one for each subset of skills, all outlined in one chart. In this case, the rubric might address: Content, Punctuation and Usage, Supportive Details, Organization, Accuracy, and Use of Relevant Information.

In a chemistry class's holistic rubric, we might ask students to create a drawing and explanation of atoms, and the descriptor for the highest score lists all the features we want them to identify accurately. With the same task using an analytical rubric, however, we create separate rubrics for each subset of features—Anatomical Features: protons, neutrons, electrons and their ceaseless motion, ions, valence; Periodic Chart Identifiers: atomic number, mass number, period; Relationships and Bonds with Other Atoms: isotopes, molecules, shielding, metal/non-metal/metalloid families, bonds (covalent, ionic, and metallic).

Remember how powerful this becomes when students help design the rubric themselves. After working with a few rubrics that you design, make sure to give students the opportunity to design one. Determining what's important in the lesson moves that knowledge to the front of students' minds, where they can access it while they're working. This happens when they have a chance to create the criteria with which their performances will be assessed.

5. Determine your label for each level of the rubric. Consider using three, four, or six levels instead of five for two reasons: 1) They are flexible and easily allow for gradations within each one, and 2) a five-level tiering quickly equates in most students' and parents' minds to letter grades (A, B, C, D, F) and such assumptions come with associative interpretations—the third level down is average or poor, depending on the community, for instance. The following list shows collections of successful rubric descriptor labels. Though most are written in groups of five, which I advise teachers not to use, they are provided in such groupings because that is what educators most commonly find on their district assessments. Look at the list's entries as a sample reservoir of word choices.

- Proficient, capable, adequate, limited, poor
- Sophisticated, mature, good, adequate, naïve
- Exceptional, strong, capable, developing, beginning, emergent
- Exceeds standard, meets standard, making progress, getting started, no attempt
- Exemplary, competent, satisfactory, inadequate, unable to begin effectively, no attempt

Descriptor terms need to be parallel; it's important to keep the part of speech consistent. Use all adjectives or all adverbs, for example, not a mixture of parts of speech. Notice how this sequence on a rubric could be awkward for assessment and confusing to students:

■ Top, adequately, average, poorly, zero

6. Write your descriptors for each level, keeping in mind what you'll accept as evidence of mastery. Once again, be specific, but understand that there is no perfect rubric. Alternative: Focus on the highest performance descriptor, writing it out in detail, and then indicate relative degrees of accomplishment for each of the other levels. For example, scoring 3.5 on a 5.0 rubric would indicate adequate understanding but with significant errors in some places. The places of confusion would be circled for the student in the main descriptor for the 5.0 level.

   In my own teaching experience, this alternative has great merit. When students are given full descriptions for each level of a rubric, many of them steer themselves toward the second or third level's requirements. They reason that there's no need to be "exemplary"—the top level—when they'd be happy with the label "good" or "satisfactory." These students either don't believe themselves capable of achieving the top score's criteria, or they see the requirements as too much work when compared with the lower level's requirements. To lessen the workload, they are willing to settle for the lower-level score.

   Don't let them do this; don't let them lose sight of full mastery. When all that is provided to students is the detailed description of full mastery, they focus on those requirements—it's the only vision they have. All of their efforts rally around those criteria and, as a result, they achieve more of it.

7. "Test drive" the rubric with real student products. See whether it accounts for the variable responses students make, ensuring those who demonstrate mastery get high scores and those who don't demonstrate mastery earn lower scores. Ask yourself: "Does this rubric provide enough feedback to students to help them grow? Does it assess what I want it to assess? Does it help me make instructional decisions regarding students' learning?" If it doesn't do one or more of these things, the rubric may need to be reworked. Check out the rubrics in Figures 4.1, 4.2, and 4.3.

Figure 4.1 Sample Rubric

Generalized Scoring Scales for Evaluation

Level 4

Shows complete knowledge of the subject.

Expresses ideas clearly and succinctly.

Discusses ideas in a highly logical manner.

Addresses all of the questions posed.

Shows complete preparation when responding.

Makes highly detailed responses.

Describes concepts without errors.

Level 3

Shows good knowledge of the subject.

Expresses ideas adequately.

Discusses ideas in a logical manner.

Addresses all of the questions posed.

Shows adequate preparation when responding.

Misses few details when responding.

Demonstrates minor misconceptions when
   responding.

Level 2

Shows some knowledge of the subject.

Expresses ideas with some disorganization.

Shows some illogical thought in discussion.

Addresses most of the questions posed.

Shows some preparation when responding.

Includes some details when responding.

Demonstrates major misconceptions when
   responding.

Level 1

Shows very little knowledge of the subject.

Expresses ideas in a very disorganized manner.

Shows much illogical thought in discussion.

Addresses very few of the questions posed.

Shows little preparation when responding.

Misses most details when responding.

Demonstrates that conceptions are mostly in error.

Grid

Scale: Criteria:				

Scale refers to the numerical or one-word rating, such as 3, 2, 1, 0 or "Proficient, adequate, limited, poor."
Criteria refers to the areas of assessment, such as craftsmanship, accuracy of information, reasoning skills,
preparation, and presentation.

Source: Created by Bruce Campbell, 2004. Used with permission.

Figure 4.2 Persuasive Writing Rubric (Analytic Style)

Name: Date:
Period:

Scale: Criteria:	Writing Structures/Techniques	Persuasive Structures/Techniques	Mechanics/Usage
5 *The Standard of Excellence*	• Well organized, logical/clear • Demonstrates an unusual ability to use language well (strong word choices, good sentence variety, powerful images) • Half or more page (typed), more than one page handwritten • Good use of transitions • Evidence of conference and revisions	• Good opening to get the reader interested • Positively stated proposition • Successfully used at least six of the persuasive techniques identified in class (stronger points at the beginning and end, emotional appeal, testimonies, using facts/research, using logic more than emotion, respected the reader, anticipated arguments and answered them, used enough information to prove points, used vivid examples, repetition, strong conclusion) • Reasons are relevant to the point the writer is making • Expresses unusual insight (meaningful connections or analogies, clever logic and/or resources, mature thinking)	• Used correct spelling • Used correct punctuation • Used correct grammar • Used correct capitalization • There, their, they're used correctly • To, two, too used correctly • Pronouns have clear antecedents
Weight:	2x	3x	1x

(*Note:* Circled items are areas for improvement.)

4 = The student demonstrates *good* understanding and skill. Most of the listed characteristics in the standard of excellence describe the student's work—a few are missing or done improperly.

3 = The student demonstrates a *satisfactory* understanding and skill. Approximately 3/4 of the listed characteristics in the standard of excellence describe the writer's work—1/4 of the characteristics are missing or done improperly.

2 = The writer demonstrates *some* understanding and skill. Only 1/2 of the listed characteristics in the standard of excellence describe the student's work; 1/2 of the characteristics are missing or done improperly.

1 = The writer demonstrates *little or no* understanding or skill. Few of the listed characteristics in the standard of excellence describe the writer's work—more than 1/2 of the characteristics are missing or done improperly.

0 = Not completed or unscorable.

Your Grade:

Writing Structures/Techniques   ——————— x 2 = ———————
Persuasive Structures/Techniques   ——————— x 3 = ———————
Mechanics/Usage   ——————— x 1 = ———————
        Total: _____ ÷ 6 grades = ———————
Additional Comments:

Final Grade: _____

Figure 4.3 Scoring Rubric for the Historical Fiction Book Project (Holistic Style)

5.0 Standard of Excellence:

- All material relating to the novel was accurate
- Demonstrated full understanding of the story and its characters
- Demonstrated attention to quality and craftsmanship in the product
- Product is a realistic portrayal of media used (examples: postcards look like postcards, calendar looks like a real calendar, placemats can function as real placemats)
- All writing is free of errors in punctuation, spelling, capitalization, and grammar
- Had all components listed for the project as described on the other side of this sheet

4.5, 4.0, 3.5, 3.0, 2.5, 2.0, 1.5, 1.0, .5, and 0 are awarded in cases in which students' projects do not fully achieve all criteria described for excellence. Circled items are areas for improvement.

Student:

Date:
Score: Grade:

Additional Comments:

Student Self-Assessment

A student's self-assessment is an important aspect of successful differentiation. It provides invaluable feedback and helps students and their teachers set individual goals. There are many ways for students to self-assess.

One of the best ways is to make the first and last task/prompt/assessment of a unit the same, and ask students to analyze their responses to each one, noting where they have grown. In addition we can use the following strategies:

- Likert scale (Place an X on the continuum: Strongly Disagree, Disagree, Not Sure, Agree, Strongly Agree) and other surveys. Use smiley faces/symbols/cartoons/text, depending on readiness levels.
- Self-checking rubrics
- Self-checking checklists
- Analyzing work against standards
- Videotaping performances and analyzing them
- Fill-in-the-blank or responding to self-reflection prompts (How do I know I don't understand? criteria). This is a list of questions students ask themselves in order to ascertain their level of understanding. Reflective questions include: Can I draw a picture of this? Can I

explain it to someone else? Can I define the important words and concepts in the piece? Can I recall anything about the topic? Can I connect it to something else we're studying or I know?

Cris Tovani's book, *I Read It, but I Don't Get It* (2001) has more ideas on how to help students with this and much more.

- Asking students to review and critique previous work
- Performing in front of a mirror. (Fill one of your classroom bulletin boards with a large, dresser-type mirror. It makes your classroom seem larger, and students can use it in many ways both instructionally and affectively.)
- Reading notations; students can use these to help with their thinking:
  - ✓ I agree with this.
  - X I disagree with this.
  - ?? I don't understand this.
  - !! Wow! (Elicits a strong emotion)
  - CL General *Claim*
  - EV *Evidence* for the Claim (These can be numbered to also indicate their sequence: EV1, EV2, EV3 . . .)

Students can use the notations as they read material assigned to them. These are primarily for nonfiction reading. Author/educators Stephanie Harvey, Laura Robb, and others advocate symbols for fiction reading, too. Reading notations force students to make personal responses to everything they read and to assess their level of understanding regarding the material. The notations act as quick-reference icons for class discussions and other interactions with the material during subsequent days of study.

Journals and learning logs are other great media for students to self-assess. Sample prompts for these structures include:

- I learned that . . .
- I wonder why . . .
- An insight I've gained is . . .
- I've done the following to make sure I understand what is being taught: . . .
- I began to think of . . .
- I liked . . .
- I didn't like . . .
- The part that frustrated me most was . . .
- The most important aspect/element/thing in this subject is . . .
- I noticed a pattern in . . .
- I know I learned something when I . . .
- I can't understand . . .

- I noticed that . . .
- I was surprised . . .
- Before I had this experience, I thought that . . .
- What if . . .
- I was confused by . . .
- It reminds me of . . .
- This is similar to . . .
- I predict . . .
- I changed my thinking about this topic when . . .
- A better way for me to learn this would be . . .
- A problem I had and how I overcame it was . . .
- I'd like to learn more about . . .

Interactive notebooks are popular for self-assessment as well. In such notebooks, students record information and skills they learn, then make personal responses to their learning, followed by teachers' responses to students' explorations. The notebook contains everything that is "testable" from the lessons, including handouts, charts, graphics, discussion questions, essays, and drawings. In addition to teachers' insights into students' thinking, the notebooks provide students themselves with a place to give feedback on their own learning. For great resources on interactive notebooks, consider:

- *Notebook Know-How* by Aimee Buckner (2005)— www.stenhouse.com
- http://interactivenotebook.jot.com/WikiHome
- www.historyalive.com (from the Teachers' Curriculum Institute)
- http://pages.prodigy.net/wtrucillo/interactive_notebook.htm

Readers are directed to *Classroom Assessment for Student Learning* by Stiggins et al. (2004) for a more thorough discussion of student self-assessment. It is a wonderful compendium of philosophy and practicality on self-assessment, as well as on assessment of students' learning in general.

Figure 4.4 Project Evaluation Template

Name: Date:

Project Topic:

Research Question:

Teacher and Peer Assessment: (left score—teacher, right score—peer)

Research:

	Excellent		Satisfactory		Needs Work	
Used at least three sources	3	3	2	2	1	1
Documented sources	3	3	2	2	1	1
Gathered interesting and new information	3	3	2	2	1	1
Identified new topics to pursue	3	3	2	2	1	1
Seemed to prepare well	3	3	2	2	1	1

Presentation:

Was well-prepared and organized	3	3	2	2	1	1
Demonstrated good delivery skills	3	3	2	2	1	1
Used multiple delivery modes	3	3	2	2	1	1
Demonstrated understanding of topic	3	3	2	2	1	1
Answered questions effectively	3	3	2	2	1	1

Teacher and Peer Comments:

Student Self-Assessment:

On the back of this paper or on another sheet of paper, please respond to the following prompts:

1. Explain what you learned about yourself and about working on a project.
2. Explain what you learned about doing a presentation.
3. Explain the most difficult part of this project.
4. Explain the most enjoyable part of this project.
5. If you did this project over, how would you do it differently?

Source: Adapted from an idea by Bruce Campbell. Used with permission.

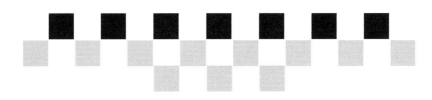

CHAPTER 5

Tiering Assessments

Walk-Through Example

Graphing Linear Inequalities
Graph the solution set of each of the following:
1. $y > 2$ 2. $6x + 3y \leq 2$ 3. $-y < 3x - 7$

Here's how to respond to one of these problems:

2. $6x + 3y \leq 2$
     $3y \leq -6x + 2$
     $y \leq -2x + 2/3$

Plug in values for x to determine corresponding *y* values, then create an *x, y* chart to show ordered pairs for graphing:

x	y
0	2/3
3	−5 1/3

Now, graph the solution.

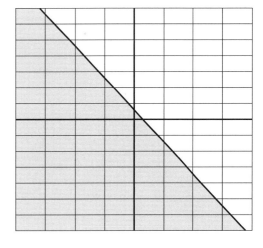

The figure here is how a student who is on grade level might respond. How might we tier these types of math problems for different readiness levels? The following are some suggestions.

For Early Readiness Students

■ Limit the number of variables for which students must account to one in all problems (example: $y > 2$).

■ Limit the inequality symbols to "greater than" or "less than," not "greater than or equal to" or "less than or equal to."

■ Provide an already set up four-quadrant graph on which to graph the inequality.

■ Suggest some values for x such that when solving for y, its value is not a fraction.

For Advanced Readiness Students

■ Require students to generate the four-quadrant graph themselves.

■ Increase the parameters for graphing with equations such as: $-1 \leq y \leq 6$.

■ Ask students what happens on the graph when a variable is given in absolute value, such as: $/y/ > 1$.

■ Ask students to graph two inequalities and shade or color only the solution set (where the shaded areas overlap).

Definitions and Pearls of Wisdom

Some differentiated instruction experts give tiering a broader definition than I use here. They define *tiering* as how teachers adjust assignments and assessments according to students' readiness levels, interests, and learner profiles. The last two, interests and learner profiles, suggest lateral adjustments, however, not the vertical adjustments expressed by the definition of *tier*, such as in terracing or varying levels of something. For purposes of this book, then, *tiering* will be described as similar to what differentiation expert, Dr. Carol Ann Tomlinson, calls "ratcheting" up or down the challenge level. This means we are primarily emphasizing the adjustments we make in assessments according to students' readiness levels, not interests or learner profiles, though these last two are critical elements of successful differentiation and not to be discarded.

There are several pieces of advice that will serve first-time assessment "tiers" well: First, we usually start tiering by expecting every student to demonstrate full proficiency with the standard, not something less. The minimum expectation, then, is the standard or benchmark performance. It's wiser to start here, designing the on-grade-level task, and raise the challenge level, than it is to start lower than the standard and move up to designing the standard performance and beyond. If we start lower or higher than the standard performance, we tend to distort our expectations for the on-grade-level performance, losing sight of the learning outcomes or benchmarks. If we start by designing the tasks for early readiness students first, we sometimes settle for less when designing for the on-grade-level standard performance.

Second, realize that most of the material we teach has subsets of skills and content that we can break down for students and explore at length. It's helpful to literally list every skill or bit of information a student must use in order to meet the needs of the task or assignment successfully. It is in this analysis that we see plenty of opportunities to tier an assignment. For example, in the preceding math problem, just attending to the switching of positive and negative signs as we manipulate the inequality to isolate the variable, *y,* is a skill students must have.

In addition, there won't always be high, medium, and low tiers. Respond to the unique characteristics of the students in front of you instead of imposing a predetermined leveling. There are times when we have four high-achieving groups and only one struggling group, and other times when this is reversed. As they say, we don't always have kids in groups like "Blue birds," "Red birds," and "Buzzards."

Also remember that we don't tier every aspect of every lesson. It's often okay for students to do what everyone else is doing. We might extend the time period for some of them, but there's no need to adjust the level of complexity.

To avoid a potential pitfall with tiering, be *sure* to stay focused on one concept or task. For example, you can choose a topic like teaching the moon's phases, but there are so many factors in teaching this topic that it can become cumbersome, especially as you first learn to tier. In your first attempts, isolate one facet of moon phases, such as the ideas of waxing and waning, and tier that facet alone. When first tiering students' analysis of bias in newspaper articles, design tiered tasks that focus just on one of the following, then add more: fact versus opinion, conjecture, use of persuasive techniques, use of logical fallacies, slant, motivation for writing the piece, analyzing what authors don't include in their pieces, identifying who's paying for the piece to be written.

Increasing Complexity and Challenge

To increase the complexity of an assignment or assessment, consider adding the following attributes gathered from the writings of Tomlinson, Wiggins, and Wormeli. To decrease the complexity of an assignment or assessment, remove one or more of the attributes in this list.

Increasing Assignment or Assessment Complexity
- Manipulate information rather than just echo it
- Extend the concept to other areas

- Integrate more than one subject or skill
- Increase the number of variables that must be considered; that is, incorporate more facets
- Demonstrate higher-level thinking; for example, Bloom's Taxonomy, Williams's Taxonomy
- Use or apply content/skills in situations not yet experienced
- Select from several substantive choices
- Work with advanced resources
- Add an unexpected element to the process or product
- Work independently
- Reframe a topic under a new theme
- Share the background of a concept; that is, how it was developed
- Identify misconceptions within something
- Identify the bias or prejudice in something
- Negotiate the evaluative criteria
- Deal with ambiguity and multiple meanings or steps
- Use more authentic applications to the real world
- Analyze the action or object
- Argue against something taken for granted or commonly accepted
- Synthesize two or more unrelated concepts or objects to create something new
- Critique something against a set of standards
- Work with the ethical side of the subject
- Work in more abstract concepts and models
- Respond to more open-ended situations
- Increase automaticity with the topic
- Identify big-picture patterns or connections
- Defend completed work

Here are some examples for several of the suggested attributes in the preceding list:

- Manipulate information rather than just echo it: "Once you've understood the motivations and viewpoints of the two historical figures, identify how each one would respond to the three ethical issues provided."
- Extend the concept to other areas: "How does this idea apply to the expansion of the railroads during the 1800s?" or "How is this portrayed in the Kingdom Protista?"
- Work with advanced resources: "Using the latest schematics of the space shuttle flight deck and real interviews with professionals at Jet Propulsion Laboratories in California, prepare a report that . . ."

- Add an unexpected element to the process or product: "What could prevent meiosis from creating four haploid nuclei (gametes) from a single haploid cell?"
- Reframe a topic under a new theme: "Rewrite the scene from the point of view of the antagonist," "Re-envision the country's involvement in war in terms of insect behavior," or "Retell Goldilocks and the Three Bears so that it becomes a cautionary tale about McCarthyism."
- Synthesize two or more unrelated concepts or objects to create something new: "How are grammar conventions like music?"
- Work with the ethical side of the subject: "Does the good in genetic engineering of humans outweigh the bad?" or "At what point is the federal government justified in subordinating an individual's rights in the pursuit of safeguarding its citizens?"

When evaluating truly proficient students, we often look for insights above and beyond what was requested in the original assessment prompt. McTighe and Wiggins in *Understanding by Design* suggest the following "look-fors" when watching for insightful responses.

"Look-fors" When Assessing Insightful Students' Responses
- Other ways to look at and define the problem
- A potentially more powerful principle than the one taught or on the table
- The tacit assumptions at work that need to be made explicit
- Inconsistency in current versus past discussions
- Author intent, style, and bias
- Comparison and contrast, not just description
- Novel implications
- How custom and habit are influencing the views, discussion, or approach to the problem to date (2004, p. 82)

Sample Tierings of Tasks

Remember that we are successively tiering, which means that we change the complexity or challenge of tasks more and more subtly each day. We might start out with dramatic tiering, then slowly pull back until we don't tier at all.

For example, we may provide a group of students with specific instructions to use a very structured format with strict parameters to perform a task. The next day, however, we ask them to do the same task but this time they set their own parameters based on agreed-on evaluative criteria. On a third day, they do the task but they are given a choice of formats instead of working with a mandated one. While there's no general rule of thumb dictating the number of gradations needed for successful tiering, it's enough for teachers to keep in mind our students' gradual movement toward autonomy. Here are two examples.

Example A
Grade Level Task:
- Draw and correctly label the plot profile of a novel.

Advanced Level Tasks:
- Draw and correctly label the general plot profile for a particular genre of books.
- Draw and correctly label the plot profile of a novel and explain how the insertion or deletion of a particular character or conflict will impact the profile's line, then judge whether this change would improve or worsen the quality of the story.

Early Readiness Level Tasks:
- Draw and correctly label the plot profile of a short story.
- Draw and correctly label the plot profile of a single scene.
- Given a plot profile of a novel, correctly label its parts.
- Given a plot profile with mistakes in its labeling, correct the labels.

Example B
Grade Level Task:
- Correctly identify five different types of clouds from given pictures. In writing, explain how they are different from each other.

Advanced Level Task:
- Correctly label the five basic cloud types in given pictures, then using your understanding of those types, identify clouds in given pictures that seem to be made up of more than one type. Explain your thinking in writing.

Early Readiness Level Tasks:
- Match the type of cloud in the picture with its name; explain your thinking in writing or orally.

Tomlinson's Equalizer

Carol Ann Tomlinson (1999) recommends teachers use an equalizer to examine and adjust the challenge level of assignments and assessments. The equalizer is a series of nine continuums, similar to the scale one might use for a school's climate survey of staff and students. The teacher considers the nature of every assignment or assessment in each area:

- Foundational to transformational
- Concrete to abstract
- Simple to complex
- Single facet to multiple facets
- Small leap to great leap
- More structured to more open
- Clearly defined problems to fuzzy problems
- Less independence to more independence
- Slower to quicker

These are not either/or descriptions. Because each aspect is on a continuum, there are varying degrees for each one. For example, for the first one, we can use an assignment that is leaning toward foundational, but still retains some element of transformational experience or insight. Looking down the list for further examples, we recognize that assignments can have relative independence, structure, and abstraction, not only absolutes of each one. We can plot our assignments on each continuum and see whether they are really achieving what we're seeking to do with students, then make adjustments as necessary. We can also use the equalizer another way by plotting the kind of assignment we want to provide our students, then design an assignment that meets the posted criteria. Either way, the equalizer is a very concrete and useful hook on which to hang tiering efforts. For a full explanation of each continuum, including examples, take a look at Tomlinson's 1999 book, *The Differentiated Classroom: Responding to the Needs of All Learners,* and Northey's *Handbook on Differentiated Instruction for Middle and High Schools* (2005).

Learning Contracts

One vehicle for tiering assessments is a learning contract. Learning contracts allow students to work at their own pace and on skills or in content areas that best meet their needs and interests. While the teacher may decide what objectives will be addressed, the student has an opportunity to negotiate the time ine for completion and how to obtain and demonstrate mastery. In most learning contracts, there is a combination of teacher- and student-designed tasks that, together, fulfill the expectations of the unit.

Some contracts indicate working behaviors as contractual stipulations. For example, depending on the grade level, a math learning contract with several content and work completion requirements may also require students to:

- Work without bothering others
- Use an indoor voice
- Avoid interrupting the teacher when he or she is teaching
- Bring two sharpened pencils and ample paper supply to class every day
- Refer to the posted classroom options list when stuck on something and the teacher isn't available to help at the moment

Checkpoints are also listed on most learning contracts. These are dates and descriptions that indicate when each item will be submitted for teacher assessment. Checkpoints serve two purposes: 1) They help the teacher assess student progress and possibly change instruction as a result, and 2) they keep students dedicated to the tasks and learning.

The contract must clearly list the student's responsibilities, the teacher's expectations, and the consequences for not living up to those responsibilities and expectations. In some contracts, there may be a space for both teacher and student to evaluate the success of every task. In addition, some contracts list opportunities that enable students to go beyond the basic requirements of the contract, if interested. They also have spaces for dates and signatures, signifying agreement to the contract's stipulations by both teacher and student. It's wise to provide a space for parents' signatures as well.

A learning contract is an alternative experience, not to be taken for granted by students (see Figure 5.1). If a student breaks any portion of the contract, then it becomes null and void at teacher discretion, and the student must return to what the rest of the class is doing if it's different from the contract's expectations. Because a contract's tasks are done in lieu of the regular class's tasks, it's important for teachers to make sure everything the rest of the class is learning is provided in alternative contracts negotiated by students.

Learning Menus

These are like using multiple drop-down menus in a favorite word processing package, and using one or more of the options from each menu. Students are given choices of tasks to complete in a unit or for an assessment from a predetermined list of options. It's fun to put choices in restaurant menu style, complete with appetizers, entrées, side dishes, and desserts. Entrée tasks are required, but students choose only one from any of the tasks listed in the appetizer section, and two from the side dish options. For enrichment, they may choose any one of the options in the dessert section. As long as we make sure any of the combinations students might choose achieves what we're after, the choice is up to students.

Figure 5.1 Sample Learning Contract for a Secondary Science Class

Student: Class/Subject:
Teacher:

The student will complete the following tasks by December 10:
A. Build and maintain a healthy terrarium for four weeks that contains all the elements listed on the accompanying direction sheet.
B. Explain in writing how each element influences the health of the terrarium.
C. Read and take notes on Chapter 13, "Habitats and Biomes," in the *Life Science* textbook using one of the five note-taking techniques we've learned this year.
D. In writing, answer the questions on pages 137–139 at the end of Chapter 13, and design one more analysis question for the chapter and answer it.
E. View the video, "At Home in the Biome," and create a matrix graphic organizer that identifies the five biomes described in the video according to: water sources, climate, typical flora, typical fauna, geographic location, and sample food chain.
F. Identify five limiting factors for a local habitat's carrying capacity and one action per factor that our community can take to remove those factors from limiting the habitat.
G. Write a personal mission statement about your dedication to protecting our natural resources. It must include your definition of natural resources, why it's important to protect them, and what specific steps you'll take to keep them healthy for generations to come.

Enrichment Options:
■ Create a Web site or public library display that accurately portrays the food, water, space, shelter, and arrangement for any three animals, each from a different biome; include a statement as to why it's important to understand elements of an animal's habitat.
■ Create a poem or artistic performance (fine or performing art) that expresses the interconnectedness of the food chain or web of life. Specific elements of the energy transfer cycle must be included.

Checkpoints:
The student will submit one or more of items A through G for teacher assessment on each of the following dates (negotiated with the student):

■ Item A: Date:
    Teacher Evaluation:
    Student Evaluation:
■ Item B: Date:
    Teacher Evaluation:
    Student Evaluation:
■ Item C: Date:
    Teacher Evaluation:
    Student Evaluation:
■ Item D: Date:
    Teacher Evaluation:
    Student Evaluation:

continued

Figure 5.1 Sample Learning Contract for a Secondary Science Class *(continued)*

■ Item E: Date:
   Teacher Evaluation:
   Student Evaluation:
■ Item F: Date:
   Teacher Evaluation:
   Student Evaluation:
■ Item G: Date:
   Teacher Evaluation:
   Student Evaluation:

Checkpoint Enrichment Options:
■ Item: Date:
   Teacher Evaluation:
   Student Evaluation:
■ Item: Date:
   Teacher Evaluation:
   Student Evaluation:

While working on these tasks during contract time, the student will:
■ Use time wisely
■ Ask questions when he or she doesn't understand something
■ Avoid bothering other students
■ Come to class prepared with two pencils, plenty of paper, rough drafts of writings, and textbook
■ Speak in a quiet, indoor voice
■ Stay seated unless obtaining materials or information for contractual tasks
■ Not work on homework from other classes

Contractual Consequences:
All grades earned on each of the contract's tasks will be used to determine [the student's] official grade for this unit of study. If any portion of this contract is not achieved in the time and manner specified, it becomes null and void at teacher discretion. In such instances, the student may be required to end all contractual tasks and return to what the rest of the class is doing without complaint.

Acceptance of Contract:
Student Signature: Date:
Teacher Signature: Date:
Parent Signature: Date:

   Will differently tiered groups have different menus from which to choose? Probably. Can we use one menu, but alter the choices differently tiered groups are allowed to make? Sure. Will some students ask for exceptions to those rules, wanting to do something different than we prescribe, perhaps something on another group's menu? Yes. Is this okay? Yes, as long as their suggestions achieve the same goals. We don't have to nail ourselves to our own ideas. Students acting on their own ideas are motivated to do the work, and sometimes, their ideas are better than ours.

Tic-Tac-Toe Boards

Students are given a tic-tac-toe board of tasks to complete, and are asked to choose one from each category, or perhaps any three in a row horizontally or diagonally that make a successful tic-tac-toe threesome.

Task 1	Task 2	Task 3
Task 4	Student Choice (Task 5)	Task 6
Task 7	Task 8	Task 9

Here's a board that uses Gardner's (1991) multiple intelligences.

Interpersonal Task	Kinesthetic Task	Naturalist Task
Logical Task	Student Choice (Task 5)	Intrapersonal Task
Interpersonal and Verbal Tasks	Musical Task	Verbal Task

To adjust for levels of readiness, we can provide more than one version of a tic-tac-toe board to differently tiered groups, and we can adjust the number or pattern of the assignments. For example, a student might be better served to choose one task from each row, not one from each column. In the next example, we can also provide different criteria along each axis of the board and ask students to respond to specific patterns we choose for their readiness levels.

Geometry	Summarize (Describe)	Compare (Analogy)	Critique
A theorem			
A math tool			
Future developments for a given topic			

Early readiness level students might be asked to do two from the summarize column and one task from any other column, whereas more advanced students may be required to do two from the critique column and one from either of the other two columns.

Cubing

Ask students to create a three-dimensional cube out of foam board or posterboard, then respond to the topic of learning through each of these prompts, one for each side of the cube: *describe* it, *compare* it, *associate* it, *analyze* it, *apply* it, *argue* for it or against it. To adjust the level of challenge, choose more or less sophisticated topics to which students respond, use different prompts, or use fewer of the preceding prompts; and on the empty faces of the cube, ask students to draw or portray through magazine cutouts what they recorded for those selected prompts.

We can also make higher- and lower-level complexity cubes and provide them to readiness-tiered groups of students. Each group rolls their own level of cube like rolling dice (tossing it in the air and letting it land also works), then each group member must interact with the chosen topic according to whatever face is on top of the cube once it stops rolling. In some situations, we ask everyone in the group to respond to every prompt on the cube, orally, in written form, or in some other fashion. Advanced readiness groups have cubes with more advanced prompts; early readiness groups have cubes with less advanced prompts. Yes, there will be times when we allow tiered groups to share cubes and make responses accordingly. Be open to that option.

Bloom's Taxonomy lends itself very well to cubing activities. Each face of the cube asks students to interact with the topic through one of Bloom's levels of understanding:

- Knowledge—Students can recall and cite content they remember.
- Comprehension—Students demonstrate their understanding of a topic.
- Application—Students use knowledge and skills in a different situation.
- Analysis—Students break down topics into component pieces and analyze them in the context of the whole.
- Synthesis—Students bring together seemingly contradictory aspects or topics and form something new.
- Evaluation—Students use all the other levels to judge the validity, success, or value of something, given specific criteria.

Summarization Pyramid

Another suggested structure that's easy to tier is a summarization pyramid. It's instructionally accordion-like because we can adjust the levels of the prompts for tiered groupings. Great prompts for each line of the pyramid include: synonym, analogy, question, three attributes, alternative title, causes, effects, reasons, arguments, ingredients, opinion, larger category, formula/ sequence, insight, tools, misinterpretation, sample, people, future of the topic.

_____

_____

_____

_____

_____

_____

_____

Frank Williams's Taxonomy of Creativity

> *"In four minutes, give me as many different equations as you can that use exponents only and to which the answer is twelve."*
>
> *"Categorize the given set of objects in at least three ways, with no one category consisting of less than three objects. Once completed, recategorize the objects in at least three new ways."*
>
> *"Design a simple or complex machine that replicates the motions of an insect's appendages."*
>
> *"Take any idea you've heard today and make it better."*

The first creativity task pushes students to think fluently. They are getting their minds revved for thinking about many different things. The second asks students to think flexibly. They are looking at things from more than one angle, noting patterns, thinking with dexterity. The third one asks students to be original. Play, innovation, and ingenuity are the stuff of real ideas and products. The last task asks students to build on other ideas. Elaboration can be a tough skill to teach, but it comes when we give students permission to free their minds—to let go of preconceptions and limitations.

Fluency, flexibility, originality, and elaboration are the first four levels of Frank Williams's eight levels of creative thinking. While the first four of the taxonomy are cognitive, the last four are affective in nature. Depending on where students are intellectually and emotionally, we can use this taxonomy to reframe learning experiences to meet their needs. Here are the descriptions of each level of the Williams taxonomy (see Forte and Schurr 1996) with an example science assignment for each.

- Fluency—We generate as many ideas and responses as we can.
  Example: Choose one of the simple machines we've studied (wheel and axle, screw, wedge, lever, pulley, and inclined plane) and list everything in your home that uses it to operate; then list at least two items in your home that use more than one simple machine in order to operate.
- Flexibility—We categorize ideas, objects, and learning by thinking about them in diverse ways.
  Example: Design a classification system for the items on your list.
- Originality—We create clever and often unique responses to a prompt.
  Example: Define life and non-life.
- Elaboration—We expand on or stretch an idea or thing, building on previous thinking.
  Example: What inferences about future algae growth can you make given the three graphs of data from our experiment?
- Risk-Taking—We take chances in our thinking, attempting tasks for which the outcome is unknown.
  Example: Write a position statement on whether genetic engineering of humans should or should not be funded by the United States government.
- Complexity—We create order from chaos, we explore the logic of a situation, we integrate additional variables or aspects of a situation, we contemplate connections.
  Example: Analyze how two different students changed their lab methodology to prevent data contamination.
- Curiosity—We pursue guesses, we wonder about varied elements, we question.
  Example: What would you like to ask someone who has lived aboard the International Space Station for three months about living in zero gravity?
- Imagination—We visualize ideas and objects, we go beyond just what we have in front of us.
  Example: Imagine building an undersea colony for 500 citizens, most of whom are scientists, a kilometer below the ocean's surface. What factors would you have to consider when building and maintaining the colony and the happiness of its citizens?

RAFT(S)

RAFT stands for *Role, Audience, Format, Topic* (or *Time*). The teacher provides a short menu of choices for each one of these attributes of a student's task, and the student chooses one from each column to create a unique task. One of the motivating factors is that students get to choose their own assignment, of course, but we can also make it compelling by tiering the choices. For example, we can provide an early readiness group with choices that are natural combinations so that any combination of attributes (role, audience, format, and topic or time) would be a straightforward experience with little ambiguity. We can also limit the number of choices so that students don't feel overwhelmed. For the advanced readiness groups, we can provide menus of options that would yield more abstract or diverse combinations. Pulling together what they've learned for the sake of the unique assignments they've created for themselves stretches students beyond what's expected in grade-level assignments.

The following is an example for an early readiness group.

Role	*Audience*	*Format*	*Topic*
A southern orphan living under a train depot	President Lincoln at the White House	A personal journal entry	Reconstruction of the United States
A southern colonel who has returned to the South to find that his plantation burned to the ground	A group of Civil War veterans gathered at a cemetery to remember a friend	Personal monologue	Why the South tried to secede from the Union
A northern industrialist	School children ten years after the Civil War ended	A set of drawings	The abolitionists
Harriet Tubman	A news reporter doing a story	A speech	Abraham Lincoln's presidency

To increase complexity further, we can replace one variable of the task—the "T" in RAFT can stand for "time." Instead of a chosen topic, the same topic is assigned to everyone, but students get to choose the role; the audience; the format; and an interesting time period such as fifty years in the future, during the potato famine, in ancient Sumer, or during the modern day.

Here's a similar experience to the one described on the previous page—this time for an advanced readiness group. In this task, all students must respond to the same topic—"How will (or did) the country rebuild itself after a war?"

Role	Audience	Format	Time
The mayor of Vicksburg, Mississippi	Congress	Rap or song	Two years before the war ends
A Japanese immigrant living in the United States, building railroads	A group of Civil War veterans gathered at a cemetery to remember a friend	Editorial letter in major newspaper	May 18, 2010
A northern industrialist	A group of European politicians of the 1800s	Political cartoon	During the McCarthyism of the 1950s
Robert E. Lee (chosen for his complex views, reflecting both North and South arguments)	Mrs. Bixby, who legend says lost four sons on the battlefield (Lincoln's famous letter referring to her ". . . sacrifice upon the altar of freedom")	PowerPoint presentation	Two years after the Civil War, during the Reconstruction era

Rick Stiggins (2000) recommends RAFT(S) as the way to go, with the "S" standing for "Strong Verb" or "Strong Adverb." This fifth column of choices is a list of compelling verbs and/or adverbs that set the tone of the piece to be created, adding another dimension to the task.

Change the Verb

"Describe the fall of city-states in ancient Mesopotamia."

After reading this prompt, can you feel the exhilaration of students raring to get started? It's a stampede of excitement!

Okay, maybe not.

Sometimes our prompts don't compel, and sometimes they don't meet developmental needs of students. One way to resolve both of these issues is to change the verb. Consider some of the following verbs:

Analyze . . .	Construct . . .	Revise . . .
Rank . . .	Decide between . . .	Argue against . . .
Why did . . .	Argue for . . .	Defend . . .
Contrast . . .	Devise . . .	Identify . . .
Plan . . .	Classify . . .	Critique . . .
Define . . .	Narrate . . .	Compose . . .
Organize . . .	Interpret . . .	Interview . . .
Expand . . .	Predict . . .	Develop . . .
Categorize . . .	Suppose . . .	Invent . . .
Imagine . . .	Recommend . . .	Generate . . .

These verbs energize prompts, providing both motivation and complexity as necessary. Here are some great prompts with strong verbs that might serve as tiered options:

- "Argue against socialism as the way to run government" (instead of, "Explain socialism").
- "Rank the following objects in order of importance to the protagonist of the novel: an innovative idea, law, hope, and family; then tell me how the ranking would be different for the antagonist of the novel" (instead of, "Describe the protagonist and the antagonist").
- "Interview the mantissa of a logarithm (the decimal/fraction part) about its role in a logarithm" (instead of, "What's a mantissa?").
- "Generate a set of effective guidelines for reuniting North and South Korea; base it on: 1) lessons learned from other countries' unification such as Vietnam and Germany, 2) your knowledge of the specific issues in North and South Korea, and 3) your understanding of communism, democracy, and other forms of government" (instead of, "How can North and South Korea reunite?").

One-Word Summaries

Quick, give me one term that best describes grading practices in the early twenty-first century.

. . . Cutting-edge? . . . Evolving? . . . Stagnant? . . . Controversial? . . . Frustrating? . . . Enlightened? . . . Responsive? . . . Politically influenced? . . . Outdated? . . . On-target? . . . Pedagogically sound? . . . Commonsensical? . . . Chaotic? . . . Practical? . . . Impractical? . . . Research-based?

Now choose one of these terms and argue for or against it as a good description of early twenty-first century grading practices.

Does it matter which one we choose? No. With any of the words and with either of the two choices (supporting or refuting), we're still analyzing critical attributes of grading practices in the early twenty-first century. The professor succeeds in getting us to interact with the information. If this is used as an assessment, the professor gains valuable insight about our understanding of the content and issues. The basic idea with this assessment is to invite students to defend or attack a particular word as a good description of a given topic.

We can tier this activity by providing different groups with different words to use, some more directly descriptive of the topic and some more indirectly descriptive. We can also allow students to choose a focus word from three words provided or to generate a word on their own. We can push for extended explanations or not, or we can change the way students complete the task— orally, written, artistically, individually, or in partners or groups.

Great Questions to Discuss with Colleagues

If you get the time, practice tiering assessments and assignments. For an individual topic, create one assignment or assessment that meets the standard task and one that is tiered above or below the standard. Once done, critique them with someone else in your discipline to make sure they account for all you want to teach and that they are developmentally appropriate.

Great tiering questions to discuss with colleagues include:

- Are we supposed to hold them accountable for everything? If we don't, isn't that just taking things off their plate and is that okay?
- How do we assign equitable grades when different tierings are used?
- Do we let all students try the more complex assessments if they want to, even if they're not ready?
- Do we let advanced students "get by" by doing less complex work occasionally?
- Can students occasionally negotiate the level at which they are asked to perform?

Closing Thoughts

Tiering is one of those teaching skills that gets easier every time you do it. Quickly then, design grade-level and above grade-level interactions for each of the following topics:

- The Marshall Plan
- Prokaryotic and eukaryotic cells
- Cosines
- Newton's three laws of motion
- Impressionism
- Soccer skills
- Analysis of the poems of Wallace Stevens

Your mind is already churning with possibilities. Use any of the formats in this chapter on which to hook your ideas, or make up your own tiering strategies. The point is to get good at it and to think in terms of tiering every time you sit down to design a lesson. In my own classes, I automatically tier for grade-level and above grade-level tasks and assessments, regardless of what the pre-assessments tell me. It keeps me pushing toward challenging material, not just getting by. When pre-assessments indicate the need to respond to below grade-level readiness, I'll add those ideas.

Through tiering, we teach more effectively. Differentiation is always most effective with developmentally appropriate curriculum and strategies. It is a disservice to students, to their families, and to schools to not tier when it is warranted. No one learns faster or better with material and tasks not geared to where they are mentally. If we're out to teach well, we'll tier. Sure we push students a bit; however, but we are mindful of Vygotsky's Zone of Proximal Development, where students are comfortable being pushed and, within which, they learn the most. Adjusting the level of challenge is one more craft we learn in the art of differentiation. It's worth pursuing it with colleagues.

CHAPTER 6

Creating Good Test Questions

Evaluate this item as a good test question, then read student Raul's think-aloud about it that follows.

Question 13: What is the best way to describe the Renaissance Age?
a. all of the below except "d"
b. a period in which all the great artists lived
c. an age of widespread feudalism and rampant religious "correctness"
d. an age that turned scientific and artistic pursuits toward mankind instead of the church
e. an age of rebirth
f. none of the above

Raul's thinking as he responds:

It could be "d" and "e," but also "b," but isn't that just my opinion, not really a fact? Am I supposed to circle the one with the most correct information? Maybe there's one word that's incorrect, and my teacher wants to see if we're smart enough to catch it. Wait, it can't be "b" because other great artists lived in other time periods. Now we're getting somewhere . . . Uh oh, wasn't there worry over "correctness" in the Renaissance as well as the Middle Ages? Okay. Skip this one for now, and see if answering some other question might give me a clue to answering this one . . .

Such multiple-choice questions as the one just listed have no life in a successfully differentiated classroom. They do not assess students' knowledge and skill. They assess the extent to which students can guess what's on the teacher's mind and respond in a way the teacher thinks they should. Tests shouldn't play games with students' success. Every test question should be important enough to ask and clear enough to answer.

There are many successful test questions that don't waste students' minds or time while also helping us determine a student's mastery, and some of these are even efficient to grade. Let's take a look at what goes into making successful questions.

Use a Variety of Questions/Prompts

Mix traditional and not-so-traditional questions and prompts. Traditional items include: matching, true/false, fill in the missing word, multiple choice, definition, essay, and short answer. Not-so-traditional items include: analogies; drawings; diagrams; analyzing real-life applications; critiquing others' performances or responses; demonstration/performance; integrating more than one topic; exclusion brainstorming; and deciphering content clues that, when put together, reveal a secret message or conclusion.

In addition, we want to mix "forced choice" items with "constructed response" items. Forced choice items are questions and prompts that require students to choose from responses provided by the teacher, such as true/false, matching, and multiple choice. The student does not need to generate the information himself or herself. Constructed response items are questions and prompts for which students must generate the information themselves and apply it in the manner in which it is requested. Examples of constructed response items include opportunities to interpret graphs; write short essays; write short answers; do drawings; or make up analogies, mindmaps, or flowcharts.

By using a variety of questions and prompts, we get a better picture of students' mastery. Some of them will be able to reveal what they know through one format very well, while other students will shine through another. If assessments are supposed to help us get accurate information about mastery so we can adjust instruction accordingly, we want to give students every chance to provide valid renderings of their proficiency.

We can turn more traditional test questions into innovative versions as our students' needs warrant. For example, "Define the Latin word root *terra*" is a traditional test prompt. To push students further, try this: "In the spaces that follow the prompts, write what you think each real or nonsense word basically means. As long as you capture the essence of the root words, the answer will be correct."

Terratempo— _____
Zotox— _____
Noveloc— _____
Lithjector— _____
Sophipsychia— _____
Thermalmaria— _____
Photophobia— _____
Protophytop— _____
Patripathy— _____
Magnijuris— _____

Or students can be given combinations of several common nouns and asked to "coin new words for each combination that incorporates all the nouns listed, using Latin roots and prefixes only."

Include items for which students must generate or purposefully manipulate information. Simply reporting what has been memorized isn't always a sign of understanding and long-term retention, which are our goals. It's easy to parrot information; it's masterful to apply, critique, evaluate, or create it.

Make It Efficient for Students

Provide a "T" or an "F" for students to circle on true/false questions. This way there will be no questions about how to interpret sloppily formed T's and F's. Students' true intentions are clear, and it's not as tiring as writing out the full words may be for some handwriting-challenged students.

For matching activities, write the definitions on the left and list the words to choose from on the right. This way, students read the sentence-length definitions on the left and then scan only the single-word lists to find the correct response, not whole sentences of definitions. It's tiring to first identify a single vocabulary term, then read every single sentence in a long list of definitions, especially if you have a learning disability in reading. Tired students don't produce accurate test results, so let's do everything we can to keep them from getting tired.

It's also helpful to keep matching items on the same page. Flipping pages back and forth gets confusing. Mistakes happen. In addition, keep matching portions of tests to about eight items or less. Beyond eight, it becomes a bit of an endurance test; and once again, it can become confusing and more of a clerical exercise than a thoughtful task that reveals students' mastery.

Nolen and Taylor advised teachers to keep the blanks in fill-in-the-blank items close to the end of the sentence or stem. This prevents reading comprehension issues. In addition, they say that any omitted words that students have to figure out, such as we might use in a cloze or fill-in-the-blank exercise, should be significant (2005, p. 221). Otherwise, it's too confusing, the answer can go in too many directions, and we won't be assessing what we think we're assessing. They add that it's wise to ask students to explain multiple-choice responses in short answer follow-up questions right after the question (Nolen and Taylor 2005, p. 206). Responses to such questions reveal mastery and non-mastery.

Make sure to highlight key words, such as *three, most, least,* and *not,* so students don't lose sight of the expectation while forming a response. This isn't making it easier; it's making sure the student reveals what he or she knows.

Double Recording of Test Responses

If you're using a multiple-choice, true/false, one-word answer, fill-in-the-blank, or matching format, ask students to fold their answer papers in half vertically and number the lines exactly the same on both sides of the fold. As they respond to the prompts, they record the answer in the same location on both sides of the fold. For example, if "86.2" is the answer to number 4 on the test, they record that answer on the number 4 blank on each side of the vertical fold (see Figure 6.1).

When students finish the test, they cut or tear the paper down that fold and turn one half in to the teacher. They keep the other half. When everyone is finished, the teacher reviews the answers to the test while students reference their copies of the answers. Students get immediate feedback on how

Figure 6.1 Example of a Double-Recording Answer Sheet

Name: Name:
Date: Date:
Period: Period:

1. _____   1. _____

2. _____   2. _____

3. _____   3. _____

4. _____   4. _____

5. _____   5. _____

. . .   . . .

20. _____   20. _____

they did on the test instead of waiting until the teacher has graded it. Using this approach means students in earlier classes carry around the test answers the rest of the day, of course, which means we'd have to change the sequence of questions for multiple classes; but it's worth doing in order to be timely with our feedback, and it's fairly easy to do in our computer age.

By the way, secondary English teacher, Susan Clark recommends: "When students grade their own papers, ask them to use highlighters or markers so there is no temptation to quickly change answers."

Avoid Confusing Negatives

In general, when assessing students in fifth through tenth grade, we should avoid using response choices that are meant to make students stumble over wording or logic: "All of the above except C and E," "Which of these is NOT associated with . . . ," and "None of these." At those grade levels, such questions don't assess students' mastery. Errors on these items are related more to reading, logical thinking, and worrisome nerves than students' understanding of content. In the last two years of high school, however, dealing with such negative responses is less confusing and can reveal accurate information about our students' understanding of topics. It's okay to incorporate a few of them on tests. Be judicious in their use, however. It's respectful and ethical to remove any question that is unjustifiably complex, used only to see whether students are reading directions or able to think in a contorted manner. Straightforward questions are respectful and useful.

Make Prompts Clear

In his book, *Test Better, Teach Better,* Dr. Popham says, that the less students have to guess the more they can achieve (2003, p. 94). He's correct. If it's a "guess what's on the teacher's mind" test prompt, the assessment becomes a nightmare, and any grade earned is close to meaningless.

"Describe the Renaissance" is an inappropriate essay question. Students don't know where to go with their responses; they don't know what is expected. Truly, the teacher that assigns such a prompt has no one to blame but himself or herself if the student fails in his response.

The effective teacher provides the intended parameters, clarifying for students what is expected. These parameters may include, but are not limited to: a clear example of what's expected, a suggested number of examples that must be included to support the student's claims, approximate length of the essay or project, and a suggested amount of time needed to complete the task. The teacher may want to include the relative point values of every component to be assessed so that the student knows where to spend most of his or her energy. Based on Popham's urging, here's the Renaissance prompt revised for clarity.

> In 250 to 400 words, describe the rise of intellectual life during the Renaissance. Include in your discussion a brief statement of the impact of any *five* of the following events and people:
>
> ■ Translating the Bible into English
> ■ The development of the Gutenberg press
> ■ Leonardo da Vinci or any one of the inventors/artists of the period
> ■ Shakespeare, Cervantes, or any one of the author/poets of the period
> ■ The works of any one of the humanist philosophers (Machiavelli and Thomas More, among others)
> ■ The Reformation
> ■ European exploration and expansion to the rest of the world by any one of these: Cortez, Magellan, Pizarro, the Mayflower
>
> This essay is worth thirty points. Each of the five aspects whose impact on intellectual life you describe successfully is worth five points. The remaining five points will be earned by following proper essay format, including a well-crafted introduction and conclusion. This should take no more than forty-five minutes.

In writing our prompts, however, we also need to make sure we don't give away the answer, as in multiple-choice questions that have grammar clues in the stem. For example, using grammar knowledge alone, not our knowledge of landforms, we can correctly answer this test prompt:

> The picture above depicts an example of an:
> A. peninsula
> B. guyot
> C. plateau
> D. estuary

"An" goes with the starting vowel sound in "estuary." If students knew this, they wouldn't need to think twice about their response. If this happens, stop the stem a word earlier, and place the articles in the potential responses:

> The picture above depicts an example of:
> A. a peninsula
> B. a guyot
> C. a plateau
> D. an estuary

Popham wisely points out that some teachers put too many factors into their true/false statements and students don't know which part is the intended response portion. Here's an example:

True or False: We are able to breathe on Earth because plants produce oxygen and we exhale carbon dioxide.

This is sort of true, but not completely. We get some oxygen from other sources on Earth, and our capacity to breathe has more factors than just the presence of oxygen (like pressure, other gases present, our anatomy, to name a few). A better prompt to assess students' knowledge is:

True or False: The only factor affecting our ability to breathe on Earth is the abundance of oxygen-producing plants located here.

This version of the prompt removes distracting information. It focuses the student on the one factor the teacher wanted to assess. The score of this test item will yield useful information. Make true/false statements completely true or completely false.

Keep It Short

Two or three will do. We don't need ten similar questions when we can see in two questions whether or not a student understands the concept. It's not a perseverance test. If there are subtle differences that must be assessed, include enough problems or prompts to assess students' proficiency accurately, of course, but less is usually more. If we want to know whether students know how to plot points on a four-quadrant graph, for example, we give them enough ordered pairs (coordinates) to land one in each quadrant, plus a few that place points along both axes, just to make sure they really understand the concepts. We don't give them twenty.

Be Careful of Timed Tests

Author and assessment expert Ken O'Connor reminds us that, "Timed tests are great underminers." He explains that ". . . no one professionally would ever try to collapse their knowledge into one hour of intense performance" (2002). He's right. The idea of timed performances or tests of mastery is a construct of schools, not the working world. This is not to say we shouldn't teach students to be efficient and expedient, but more times than not, we are assessing students on the extent of their skill and knowledge development, not how much they can cram into a small sampling in a narrow window of opportunity at this early hour on a Tuesday morning in late April. On the few occasions we're assessing fluency or automaticity with ideas, timed tests may be useful, but even then, the result may be inaccurate because students' angst regarding the approaching sound of the buzzer may negatively impact their thinking. It's worth giving serious consideration as to whether time restrictions on tests enhance or impede those tests' ability to reveal what we are seeking about students' levels of proficiency. In most cases, the restrictions impede accurate data collection.

Include Common Errors as Candidates for Responses

Including common errors in responses from which students choose an answer increases the validity of the grade. Students really know their material if they can discern the differences. For example, the answer to a science question could be "rotation," but "revolution" is also on the list of possible choices because the two are commonly confused. The word "weight" could be substituted where "mass" is the correct term to see whether students catch it. Other examples include math answers that vary from one another by one place value and graphs with multiple misinterpretations in the mix of possible responses. In matching responses, provide more choices than questions, and include a few that are similar to one another.

We're not being sneaky by doing this. Spend time ahead of the test explaining that such problems will be on it, and give students ample opportunity to practice spotting subtle errors and unreasonable answers prior to taking the test.

Put Some Fun into Test Questions

Incorporate students' names and their cultures into the test items. Instead of "If a community playground needs enough small gravel to fill a swing set area with the dimensions $40' \times 65' \times 1'$, how many cubic feet of gravel will this require?" how about, "Abdul is building a rectangular, practice hockey rink for his championship-winning, Mighty Anoles hockey team. How much water must he pour into the containing walls and then freeze, if the solid ice is 1.5 times the volume of the liquid water, and the dimensions are $100' \times 50' \times 2'$?" Students will look forward to the test just to see their names in print or the occasionally outlandish tasks they are doing in its scenarios.

Offering a pun, sharing a topic-related riddle, doing a parody related to the topic is okay once in a while. Humor relaxes students, even if they moan and groan over the puns. Here are some example comments used on an anatomy test: "Did you find the humerus in this test-erus?" or "This is just the tibia the iceberg," and "Grades will be announced to-marrow."

Even with humor and using students' names and their cultures, we never stray from substance. We keep our testing goals in mind as we make such insertions. Instead of "Describe the main character of the novel," we pump it up with, "Create the lyrics to two verses of an [insert name of popular rock star] song that accurately portray what the main character is feeling during this chapter." Instead of "For what did Frederick Douglas fight?" how about, "Give two similarities and two differences between the civil rights policies of our current president and the principles put forth by Frederick Douglas." Believe it or not, students appreciate meaty tasks more than drudgery tasks. Just make sure they have had plenty of practice with similar prompts prior to the test.

Make Sure Questions Assess What You Want to Assess

Sometimes we get so creative and complex that we stray from our goals. To start designing your questions, go back to the essential understandings or questions you've established for the unit of study and design ones that elicit substantive responses to those understandings. There's no need to be tricky; cut to the chase and ask students exactly what you're trying to teach. Here's an example:

> *Objective:* The student will be able to state the difference between osmosis and diffusion clearly.
> *Test Prompt:* What is the difference between osmosis and diffusion?

Straightforward questions often serve us best. Sure we can increase complexity and the compelling nature of test questions by changing the verb as mentioned earlier, but it's always important to be clear about what we're assessing and to get accurate information about a student's understanding. If an interesting new verb or prompt elicits a clear, accurate rendering of mastery, use it. If not, still use it to see students stretching themselves with the topic, but also ask that straightforward question in another prompt.

Make Questions Authentic to the Instruction

If we teach a procedure or concept one way, we test that way. We don't call for an approach on a test question that wasn't practiced by students extensively during our lessons. Our test questions should be reliable and valid indicators of what was experienced by the students.

If we allow students to use calculators while they practice math problems, we should allow them to use calculators on the test as well. If students are taught to use the writing process in their essay writing in class, they should be allowed to use the writing process in their class writing tests and for standardized tests at the state or provincial level. If students are taught in a nonconstructivist manner—for example, by teachers explaining a topic through lecture then asking students to practice the information—we cannot test those students using constructivist prompts in which students gather their own meaning their own way. Such experiences are not authentic to what the students experienced and the grade earned wouldn't be accurate.

Format Tests for Efficient Grading

If you're not using the double-column answer test mentioned earlier in this chapter, still ask students to record their answers on an answer sheet. If we teach more than one period of a subject, we only need to make one class set when we give a test. When we grade such tests, we have to carry home a much smaller set of papers—the answer sheets only, plus one copy of the test. As we grade, we don't have to scan through the test pages looking for the answers—we just run our eyes down the answer sheet.

There are two big problems with this, of course: 1) students don't have the questions in front of them when we return their papers, and 2) students don't always copy answers to the answer sheet correctly.

To solve the first problem, we photocopy enough copies of the test to give them out to students when we return their papers. It makes no sense to use a color-in-the-bubble test that is easily graded but offers no insight to students. What does a score of 18 out of 25 teach a student who cannot reflect on the test prompts and his or her responses to them? This may require a lot of paper, but find a way to give students copies of the tests when returning the answer sheets. If we can, save a lot of trees and photocopying costs and post the questions on the class Web site after the test has been given. It doesn't matter that next year's students see the questions in advance. They can do that with paper copies, too. What matters is that the questions are good enough to ask.

To solve the second problem, ask the student to pause at the turn-in basket before inserting the test and go over it one more time, connecting the intended answer with what he or she wrote on the answer sheet. For students with learning disabilities, ask them to write the answers on the test booklet, then help them copy responses to the corresponding blanks on the answer sheet. This is not cheating, and it leads to efficient grading.

We can make our multiple-choice, matching, or true/false questions have responses that create a pattern when recorded, too. This makes for easy grading. For example, an answer pattern might be, "dabadabadaba" ("daba" three times in a row). We can quickly see a letter that's out of the sequence. Of course, the moment our test answers reveal a pattern, we have to throw a curve ball so that students don't just record answers according to the pattern. For example, here's a successful answer pattern for true/false responses—TFFTTFFFTT—and here's an unsuccessful pattern—TFTFTFTFTFTF.

Use Smaller Tests Over Time

In order to get an accurate rendering of students' mastery and support the emphasis on formative assessment mentioned earlier, smart teachers give multiple, smaller, and focused tests over the course of the grading period, instead of one large test at the end. They do this for two reasons. First, that one day of testing at the end of the grading period can have a zillion factors negatively impacting students' performances. Testing is already a snapshot-in-time inference of a student's skill development. Why skew our interpretation further by limiting the opportunities and angles with which students can share what they know? If "all our eggs are in one basket," they can be crushed, never to be recovered, by one clumsy act. Grades are too important to students and their families to not diversify the portfolio from which decisions are made.

Perhaps more important, the more curriculum we put on a test, the less reliable that test grade is in providing specific feedback to students and teachers regarding what it is assessing. In one test, students may define vocabulary, make connections, analyze concepts, demonstrate memorized material, apply knowledge to new situations, and sift text for salient ideas—all in multiple content areas, and only if they interpret the directions for each prompt correctly. If we use longer tests that assess more than one skill or content area, it is wise to record more than one grade at the top in order to more accurately reflect the students' achievement and increase the usefulness of the grades.

One last caution: If students are asking us to hurry up and give them the test before they forget the material, are we teaching for long-term learning? Are students learning the material for the sake of the test alone? If so, what can we do to help them see the material's significance beyond the test? What makes students perceive their learning as fragile?

The brain can reach a saturation point where it feels like it has no more room for storage. We talk ourselves into this condition every time we sit and listen to a lecturer drone on for hours. Coherence weakens, neurons are pruned, and ideas get mixed together. If we're nearing our saturation point for material on which we will be held accountable, we get nervous. To alleviate some of this anxiety, it's appropriate to provide frequent opportunities and motivation to process and permanently store the information in our minds. Preparing for a test provides both.

Include Two Special Questions

First, on the tests themselves, ask students, "What did you think would be asked on this test but was not?" and as appropriate, provide the follow-up prompt: "How would you answer that question?" These questions are not necessary, of course, if students have received a copy of the test at the beginning of the unit, but it makes a great question if the students haven't already seen the test.

Second, include a question that at first sounds reasonable, but on closer examination, is impossible to answer. You'll get a good sense of a student's understanding by how he or she responds; that is, by deferring the response as impossible and explaining why, or by attempting to answer by bluffing through the response. Tell students such a question exists and not to be surprised by it, and give students plenty of experience responding to such questions while teaching the unit.

Tier Questions as Warranted

If some students focused on a different number of objectives or a different level of instruction during the unit, offer assessment questions of varying sophistication in each section of the test, and ask students to answer only the questions identified for their level. An alternative is to design one large test with all the questions, then circle the particular questions you want individual students to answer.

Is it okay for early readiness students to attempt the more complex questions? Sure. Ask them to answer their own level questions first, however, before attempting the more complex ones. Of course, successful responses to the more complex questions would require an altered scoring approach. They would also indicate a need to change your instruction.

Differentiated or not, it's wise to record the learning outcomes or standards the test is assessing at the top of each. If we level or tier tests in any way, we reflect that in the amount or wording of standards recorded. Recording the standards at the top of our tests keeps us and our students focused on the learning, not just the number of problems correct and incorrect. It also helps us keep track of students' achievement.

We may also want to consider how we sequence test items. Some of us prefer to start with relatively easy questions early in the testing sequence.

This gets students warmed up for the more complex responses required later, we reason. Others prefer to mix up the challenge index by placing test items requiring complex responses early in the test or by spacing them evenly throughout, rather than lumping them all at the end. This helps keep a proper attitude toward the test items, we think; and students don't get overwhelmed or intimidated by the complexity of the last questions, nor are their minds tired just when the going gets tough. We tell students in classes in which we do this to move beyond a test item that has them initially stumped, because something in later items might strike them as helpful in solving it.

Either approach can be successful, but test fatigue and item intimidation can be formidable. From my own experience, it is preferable in most tests to spread the challenge throughout, not clump it at the end. Note that assessment expert Rick Stiggins disagrees with this practice, however, calling instead for arranging items from easy to hard (Stiggins et al. 2004, p. 151).

Closing Thoughts

Increasing or decreasing rigor (or preferably, "vigor") in testing does not mean changing the number of tests or test items. It refers to increasing or decreasing the complexity or challenge of the required responses—tiering. We've discussed multiple ways to tier assessments, but three important factors must guide test design.

First, we make sure the question formats don't impede students' successful demonstration of mastery. Anything that might thwart a student in his or her response, such as confusing negatives, tiring matching arrangements, and prompts or answer choices that force students to play "guess what's on the teacher's mind," is immediately discarded.

Second, we level tests and quizzes for students' readiness. All differentiated instruction begins with a fair and developmentally appropriate curriculum, which includes assessment. Students won't learn any faster or better by being pushed to respond to assessments that are not geared for their developmental level. If they're ready for that advanced "pushing" by the teacher, that's great—it's developmentally appropriate.

Just as we might do when forcing a square block into a round hole, something will have to be removed from the student if the assessment format doesn't fit the child's needs. The student's mastery and motivation are diminished by forcing the fit. Instead of doing better, the student may do worse in the long run, failing the test and believing he or she is not capable. We will spend more time and energy overcoming that negative situation than we would spending time designing appropriately leveled assessments.

Does this mean we might increase our record-keeping, such as keeping one gradebook with grades, but another record book of standards and benchmarks achieved? Yes, though some electronic gradebook programs can do this for you. Does it mean we might need to re-examine our district's report card format or provide a supplemental report card that more accurately represents that student's achievement? Yes.

Finally, we need to get feedback to students in a timely manner. That means we design our tests and quizzes to be graded efficiently, and we make sure students get copies of the tests and quizzes with their answer sheets so they can learn from their mistakes. Some of our tests and quizzes will be in constructed response formats that are impossible to grade quickly, however, especially if we teach more than one hundred students. Quick feedback is still important though, so we try to make tests and quizzes short, such as one-page writings, five sample problems, and oral explanations, so that students get the feedback they need. Feedback is not only information that is used by students, but it's also motivational.

CHAPTER 7

The Relative Nature of Grades and Their Definitions

I made a list of all the major skills I wanted the ESL high school students to develop and rewrote those into standards I wanted them to achieve. I grouped the standards by general themes, and assigned overall percentages to each theme and thence to each standard within each theme. My "gradebook" became an AppleWorks document listing the standards, with a column for each student listing her current level of achievement on each standard covered during that particular term. Assignments were graded using whatever rubric or rubrics fit. Every three weeks or so (we do interim reports with advisors as well as sending home comments at midterm and the end of the trimester) I would recalculate each [student's] current standing in the course. It was somewhat tedious, and certainly far from perfect, but it did a better job of relating each student's grade to what she was actually able to do than any other system of grading I've used before.

—Bill Ivey, secondary educator

There are some aspects of teaching that we keep in cages in hopes they will never escape. Collectively, they are the "elephant in the room" that everyone can see but no one mentions for fear of reprisals. Grading practices are often this elephant. We don't share our concerns with our own grading approach or that of a colleague's often, and we don't spend time with each other determining the meaning of a C, an A, or discussing what constitutes a 3.5 on a rubric.

The day is upon us, however. It's time to talk about grades, grading, and report cards openly, if we haven't before, questioning assumptions, embracing alternatives, and focusing on the promise of what teaching and learning can be. How we interpret and implement grading practices has a dramatic impact on how we differentiate instruction, and vice-versa: differentiated instruction directly impacts our grading policies.

As uncomfortable as the idea might seem, we have to accept the fact that summative grades as we now use them have little pedagogical use. Imagine, for example, a list of what one teacher has taught during the last grading period: four-quadrant graphing, graphing inequalities, isolating the variable, accounting for two or more variables, multiplying binomials, logic problems, slope, and *y*-intercept. The grade on one student's report card: B.

What does this grade tell us about a student's mastery of these eight topics? Very little. We've aggregated so much into one little symbol, it's no longer useful. Class after class; week after week; grading period after grading period; year after year; with a 4- or 100-point scale; with traditional report cards, then new ones, then traditional ones again. We scramble every time and in every format to boil everything that occurred in a student's journey toward understanding our disciplines (while also assimilating society and his or her role in it) down to a single symbol in a tiny box on a piece of thin paper that may or may not make it out from the crumpled darkness of the book bag—and only if parents ask for it.

We can do better.

The relativity of grades is easy to spot. Read the sample student essay that follows and give it a grade. Before you take another breath, your questions start forming: What grade level is this? What is the student's background with the topic? Is this from an advanced student, a struggling student, or a student from somewhere in between? According to what criteria shall we grade the essay? Try, if you can, to push these questions to one side and grade "blind" to all the particulars.

The prompt to the student:
Write an essay that provides a general overview of what we've learned about DNA in our class so far. You may use any resources you wish, but make sure to explain each of the aspects of DNA we've discussed.

Student's response:
Deoxyribonucleic Acid, or DNA, is the blueprint for who we are. Its structure was discovered by Watson and Crick in 1961. Watson was an American studying in Great Britain. Crick was British (He died last year). DNA is shaped like a twisting ladder. It is made of two nucleotide chains bonded to each other. The poles of the ladder are made of sugar and phosphate but the rungs of the ladder are made of four bases. They

are thymine, guanine, and cytosine, and adenine. The amount of adenine is equal to the amount of thymine (A=T). It's the same with cytosine and guanine (C=G). The sequence of these bases makes us who we are. We now know how to rearrange the DNA sequences in human embryos to create whatever characteristics we want in new babies—like blue eyes, brown hair, and so on, or even how to remove hereditary diseases, but many people think it's unethical (playing God) to do this, so we don't do it. When DNA unzips to bond with other DNA when it reproduces, it sometimes misses the re-zipping order and this causes mutations. In humans, the DNA of one cell would equal 1.7 meters if you laid it out straight. If you laid out all the DNA in all the cells of one human, you could reach the moon 6,000 times!

Now that you've finished reading the essay, give it a grade. Come on, what do you think?

> *. . . An A? No, not quite; it's a little scattered and there's no conclusion. How about a B? Well, there is a lot of jumping around, I'm not even sure the content is correct, and this is one long paragraph, not an essay. Maybe just a C+. That seems safe enough for now. What if this is from an advanced high school student who wrote this on the bus this morning but was given three weeks to do it? The grade should be lower, then, maybe to D level. Maybe it's just a rough draft, not the final version. Then again, what if it's from a third grader? It's pretty good if it's from a third grader . . .*

This student's response has been offered to a number of teacher groups to grade, and it earns a range of grades from A to D upon first read by most of them, from A to F by the rest. The interesting thing is that almost any essay results in the same response from teachers—varied grades. If we provide the necessary background to the student's response—grade level, grading criteria, student's profile, version number—the grade range among teacher groups remains A to D in most cases.

After close examination we see that some of the material in the student's writing about DNA is not correct—what we can do with technology and the explanation of mutation, in particular. There are other issues with the writing as well: extraneous information not pertinent to the topic, simple sentence structures, disjointed flow—few transitions, no paragraphs, and no conclusion or connection back to the main topic.

Now reconsider the response in light of the following descriptions of four different students: Do any of the descriptions justify an adjustment in the grade you gave it earlier?

- The student is new to this country and is learning English for the first time. He worked on the response for three weeks, and had the assistance of an ESOL teacher in the room with him as he worked on it. He did five drafts before this one. It is the first essay he has ever written.

- The student is identified as profoundly gifted in language arts and science for this grade level.
- The student did not meet any of the checkpoint deadlines for completing the response, never having outlines, drafts, or anything to assess in an ongoing manner. It seems to have been done the night before it was due.
- The student has several learning disabilities, one of which is in written language. This response reflects four weeks of hard work, some of which was additional work after school.

Ask yourself: What adjustments did you make or not make in the grade and what was your reasoning? Our answers to these questions reveal our basic beliefs about grading's role in teaching and learning in a differentiated classroom.

If we make no changes in a grade as a result of significant insight regarding a student's background, it might mean that we think the curriculum supersedes the student. Society has deemed this material important to learn at this age level, and it is in the student's best interest to be held accountable for the same, immutable response as everyone else. The student will only learn if his or her feet are put to the fire, so to speak. Our role is to present the curriculum and provide that tough, real-life accountability, and there is only one way to express declarative truth about our unit on DNA.

On the other hand, if we adjust a grade according to a student's background, it might indicate that we serve students before, or at least while also, serving the curriculum. Students thrive because teachers bend a little here and there to teach in ways in which students can best learn and so remain hopeful about their prospects. In this approach, the teacher's role is to figure out which ways students best learn and then to provide it, mindful of goals society deems appropriate for students to achieve at this grade level.

Are we afraid, however, that adjusting grades based on student information is somehow weakening the curriculum and thereby, the student's mastery of course content? Sure, but we're in it for the big picture—students learning the material, not just having it tossed in their laps and told to make sense of it on their own. Also, if we focus on the now, the moment in front of us, we'd lose sight of the multi-year nature of skill and content acquisition. Some students taking longer than others, some students needing to process the information more personally/vividly/consistently then others, and some students needing multiple attempts and getting subsequent feedback in order to learn—all are justifiable options if our goal is for students to learn the material. There's no loss to our cause, and in fact, students will flounder if we don't differentiate. We might as well differentiate and increase the chances of content and skills being learned to a greater degree. If our goal is something else—pure accountability, passing along the curriculum, a pretense of "rigor," or "By golly, I'll shape them up" mentality—then we run a greater risk of failure. We also realize that we grade some students in light of their personal backgrounds, but with others, we do not. Grades become increasingly relative this way.

The fact that a range of grades occurs among teachers who are grading the same student product yields important observations:

- Effective assessment can only occur against commonly accepted and clearly understood criteria consisting of frequent and extended communication among like-subject teachers.~
- Teachers have to be knowledgeable in their subject area in order to assess students properly.
- Grades are more often than not subjective and thereby likely to be more distorted in their accuracy than teachers realize.
- Grades are not always accurate indicators of mastery.

As a final task in looking at the subjective nature of grades, consider what a great teacher would write to a student about his grade on the preceding essay.

The teacher interprets the grade for the student—what would he or she say? Feel free to choose any of the student backgrounds just described to which to respond. A potential opening line might be, "Miguel, the grade you earned on this essay is a _____. This grade indicates . . ."; if you have the time, write a grade interpretation right now.

When you're finished, describe the process you went through to create the interpretation for the student. You might consider the sequence of actions you took, which part was more difficult to do, which parts could be misinterpreted, whether you had enough evidence for the interpretations, whether parents would have an accurate picture of the child's achievement on this essay, among other points. It's not trivial. These are not questions for an obscure graduate course on grade analysis. These are the questions of reflective practitioners who want their assessments and grades to be useful to themselves, their students, and their students' parents.

The stresses associated with grading student products, especially in diverse classes, spur dreams of grade-free classrooms in all of us from time to time. Jennifer Beahrs, an American teacher working in a school in the United Kingdom that does not use grades, comments on what life is like without having to grade students:

To be honest, I am doing more assessing and honest evaluating than I ever did in the States. Every night, I collect and "mark" their math and writing based on the objective from the lesson, so I always know exactly what they know (or have a really good idea)—and I teach based on what they know. Last year, I felt I got way too bogged down on their grades and wasn't thinking enough about what they really know!

Secondary teacher, Paul Bogush, says:

. . . [R]esearch points to the fact that when a task is graded (or even if you earn money for a task), eventually the quality and quantity of the work declines. This goes for preschoolers and art, to factory laborers and assembly lines. I try my hardest to get rid of grades in my classroom and slowly wean kids off them from the moment they enter in September. Doing work just to get a grade, or hearing teachers say, "Do your homework or I will give you a bad grade," "You need to study so your average will raise to a B," or "If you forget your text, you lose two points"—all of those things are just a sad form of coercion.

Bogush continues by citing author Alfie Kohn:

To read the available research on grading is to notice three robust findings: students who are given grades, or for whom grades are made particularly salient, tend to (1) display less interest in what they are doing, (2) fare worse on meaningful measures of learning, and (3) avoid more difficult tasks when given the opportunity—as compared with those in a non-graded comparison group. Whether we are concerned about love of learning, quality of thinking, or preference for challenge, students lucky enough to attend schools that do not give letter or number grades fare better. Where grades are still given, students benefit from a concerted effort to make them as invisible as possible. The more they can forget about grades, the better the chances they will be engaged with ideas.

Including these comments is not a call to abolish grades, much as Alfie Kohn (2000) would have us do. Most teachers agree on at least a limited justification for grades and grading as they are currently used. These comments are more of a wake-up call to avoid becoming complacent regarding the role of grading in teaching and learning. There are more than a few high schools that do not use grades at all, however. Students receive feedback, not grades, and parents embrace this. In the United States, these are usually private or charter schools. Interestingly, grading expert Ken O'Connor writes: "Very few colleges disadvantage students in admission decisions if they do not have a class rank or GPA information . . ." (2002, p. 208).

In my own experience, more and more colleges are not asking for class rank. The representatives with whom I spoke said they don't find it significantly predictive of a student's performance in college. They still want the grade-point average, however, though we might suggest it not be weighted as heavily as it would be if teachers were more accurate in their grading.

We can see the subjective, relative nature of grades on many levels. Grades are even influenced by their placement in the turn-in basket. Educator and assessment expert, Dr. Tom Guskey, reports:

> *Research has demonstrated . . . that good work is evaluated much more favorably when it follows poorer quality work than when it precedes it. If the good paper follows two or more papers of poor quality, the biased advantage is even greater. . . . Knowing this, students who wish to enhance their grade could simply make sure they place their paper beneath that of a poorer performing classmate. (1997, p. 34)*

A bottom line here is that we place a bit too much emphasis on one mark or grade in our society. Grades are inferences, personal interpretations on the part of the teacher, not infallible truths about students' mastery. We err when we attach too much self-worth and celebration to so fleeting a moment, so inaccurate a tool, so subjective an overworked teacher's judgment. Grades are fragile things on which to base so much. It's worth keeping them in perspective.

Defining Grades

Ask teachers from the same grade level and subject to define each of the symbols they use for grading, including A, B, C, D, and F, or their cousins such as O (Outstanding), G (Good), S (Satisfactory), N (Needs Improvement), U (Unsatisfactory), as well as checks, check-minuses, and zeros; there will be substantive differences in at least a few of their definitions. We bring to our grading practices our life experiences and biases, and these will be different from others'. Assuming that we prefer consistency among our grading approaches, what can educators do to better align definitions?

First, we can define each mark for ourselves and discuss our definitions with one another. What does an A really mean when it comes to our unit on ancient civilizations? What is B mastery in our unit on an author's use of metaphor? In his book, *Transforming Classroom Grading,* Robert Marzano (2000) reminds us of the eye-opening report from the federal government's Office of Educational Research and Improvement in 1994 in which students earning A's and B's in impoverished schools had the same level of mastery as C and D students in affluent schools when tested on the same material in the same manner.

What happened here? Were teachers' expectations in the impoverished school less than in the affluent school? Did they think they were being kind by lowering expectations? Did the teachers just not have an accurate frame of reference because they had never worked in affluent communities? Did administrators miscommunicate grade definitions?

It's not something we're proud of, but many of us are guilty of adjusting our grade expectations based on socioeconomic status of our students. Most of us do it inadvertently, but some do it on purpose. In my own case, I worked for a number of years in a low-performing school with a significant number of students on free or reduced lunch, as well as a couple of violent gangs and some wannabe gangs. I later moved to a school in which those subgroup percentages were dramatically smaller and I realized how much my expectations for students had plummeted in that other school. I attributed the lower expectations to being nice, which on reflection, seems to be a cover-up for the fact that I was just plain tired of fighting all the battles. I was making it easier on myself by making it easier on the students and their families. It really did seem, however, that it was kinder to not expect as much from them. After all, I reasoned, they have so much on their plate—look at the great strides they've made despite their poverty and troubles. As I look back on it, I cringe.

For most of us, we subjectively determine evaluative criteria. This may or may not be justifiable with you, but it's good to know which way the wind is blowing locally and nationally and to decide on whether it's preferable to have consistency. Truly, it is preferable to be consistent.

When most of us were growing up, C meant our work was average or normal. This is not the case anymore. In most school districts across North America, B is the new average. C now equates to "less than preferred." Many of today's parents look at a C and ask their child in a concerned "What happened?" tone, followed quickly with a call or e-mail message to the teacher about getting additional assistance for him or her. This is not a recent phenomenon. Even in the early 1980s, my students' parents were equating a C grade to "Something's wrong with my child." Of course, some parents celebrate a child's finally earning a C after a string of D's and F's; it's grounds for homecoming and extended family are invited to dinner. Times are changing, however, and what is considered "on grade level" or "normal for a child of this age" is changing, too. We have to spend time in conversations with our colleagues to identify what we mean by such designations.

Of course, that's also the rub: What is normal for one child may be below or above normal for another. It is very arbitrary to say that during the second week of November all students will have gained full proficiency with a particular principle in physics or fully appreciate Atticus' responses to Scout in Harper Lee's *To Kill a Mockingbird*. Every one of us learns at a different pace. It flies in the face of all we know to be good and true about human learning to hold students to the same pace of learning and mastery as their classmates. Recognizing the fallacy of equal-pacing-for-all pushes us to adopt differentiated practices. It still boils down to a universally accepted and developmentally appropriate standard of learning, and a clear understanding of what each level looks like.

An A in some classrooms means the student meets 100 percent of the criteria for proficiency. He learns all the material well, so he gets the highest grade possible. In some classrooms, however, an A is only given to those students who exceed the standards. Just meeting the standards only earns a student a B.

Moosa Shah, a life science teacher at Rachel Carson Middle School, says that an A is reserved for those students who ". . . explain the 'why' of the intended question. But there's a lot of a teacher's professional judgment in grading those responses." High school chemistry teacher Kathy Bowdring defines an A as being exemplary, demonstrating understanding beyond most state standards. "Standards of learning," she says, "are usually baselines, and mastering just the baselines is not an A in my class."

This can be shaky ground: The student masters everything listed in the course description and standards of learning, yet the highest mark he can earn is the one indicating "Almost excellent." Ethically, we should have laid out specifics on how to earn an A, and those criteria should have been the minimum standard for everyone. When pushed to define what it means to exceed the standard, many teachers and administrators use such phrases as, "The student uses more breadth, depth, and style in his products" or "She works harder than others," or "He takes initiative and does more than the directions require"—all of which are nice, but they tend to be nebulous, guess-what-will-impress-the-teacher approaches. These descriptions rely on subjective opinions on the part of teachers and students' luck, charisma, maturity, and ability to "read" the teacher's intent. As described before, some of these approaches also distort the accuracy of the grade as valid indicators of mastery.

If a state's standards are baselines as Bowdring observes, it makes sense to require students to exceed them in order to achieve an A. What constitutes evidence for exceeding the standards, however, must be made public and clear. Students should know exactly what's expected to achieve excellence. In education, it is rarely wise to keep expectations for high achievement a secret. It serves no one and frustrates everyone.

On the other hand, it may serve communities and states well to increase the expectations for A-level standards so students are all striving for what we consider to be excellent learning, not just pretty good learning. If we raise standards, however, it's critical to give students the specific tools to achieve those standards. Such tools are provided in successfully differentiated classes.

D and F grades provoke further discussion. Educator and author Doug Reeves once said that a D is a coward's F—the student failed but the teacher didn't have the courage to tell him (2002). If we accept the notion of grades as accurate indicators of mastery, his statement makes sense. Reeves and others have also indicated that anything less than a C grade should be considered temporary. Such work is less than desirable and therefore should be unacceptable. Some of us negotiate grades, however. We tell a failing student, "If you do really well on the end-of-year test or on this final project, you'll squeak by with a D, which will allow you to advance to the next level." The problem with this, of course, is that anyone earning a D doesn't have the proficiency necessary to do well in the next level of the course. No one is fooled, yet it's so easy to rationalize.

In light of this and other concerns with failing grades, some school districts consider using a grading scale of A, B, C, I, in which the *I* stands for "Incomplete." The teacher's message to the student with the incomplete label is clear: "You will not receive credit for something you have not mastered, but I will hold out hope that you can and will master it." If a student doesn't demonstrate mastery within a specified amount of time, the grade often becomes an F for record-keeping purposes. While it seems appropriate to have gradations of proximal mastery (A, B, C; Excellent, Good, Fair), levels indicating "limited proficiency" (or a D grade) and "no proficiency" (or an F grade) send the same message—the student is struggling, and something must be done.

Taking the idea further, former Rachel Carson Middle School assistant principal Sue Howell suggests "A, B, and 'You're not done'" as something to consider. It allows students to see themselves as a work in progress, and it keeps them moving toward mastery rather than settling for anything less than full understanding. She adds, "We're always in dress rehearsal, preparing for a performance." Initially a more traditional grader while in the classroom, Howell says she became interested in this approach after working with neuroscience experts at the Krasnow Institute for Advanced Study at George Mason University in Virginia, a group of researchers dedicated to understanding the brain and intelligence. Howell thinks that the more we explore the connections between cognition, neuroscience, and education, the more we'll change what we do in the classroom, and that includes turning to more effective grading practices like the grading scales just mentioned.

English and language arts teachers often sit together with anchor papers to determine what constitutes each level of a rubric or grading scale. They agree, for example, on the criteria necessary for a 4.0 expository essay and the degrees of achievement within that 4.0 descriptor that would constitute a 3.0, 2.0, 1.0, and 0, as well as gradations within each one. It's just as important for teachers of other disciplines to do the same. Our eyes are opened in such conversations. Some of us find content we had been elevating to great importance in our classes is not even mentioned in others, and content we merely surveyed with students that was analyzed in depth in our colleagues' classes. Whatever we discover, we feel like we're back on track, though we may not have realized we were ever off track in the first place. It's empowering and worth modifying the master schedule and hiring substitute teachers so teachers can meet to hold such discussions.

Here's another perspective regarding grading that we alluded to earlier: Most teachers connect grades to criterion-referenced assessments; that is, students' knowledge and skill are evaluated against specific standards. Curiously, though, we often use "Above average," "Average," and "Below average" when defining grades. Here's the problem: *Average* is a norm-referenced idea; we're comparing students against each other.

We're hypocrites when we do this. We claim to be about standards and what individual students learn, but fall right back into comparing students with one another when it comes to grading. How can a grade defined normatively be used to accurately and fairly portray a student's criterion-based mastery? It can't, and we look foolish doing so. In differentiated classes, we need to be "on the same page" when it comes to instruction, assessment, and reporting achievement (grading). Let's define grades based on our intent with students, not something outside of that intent that does not hold up under scrutiny.

Middle school science teacher Bobby Biddle defines a grade as "the level of progress from nothing to mastery, the extent to which a student has acquired the skills and information." Notice the lack of comparison with others.

High school teacher Bowdring says that a B is when ". . . you can spit it back to me, you can memorize the information." She gives a C to students who understand the generalities but do not grasp the nuances of the topic. She adds that there are necessary gradations below C, as we move toward F, that require the use of D. She feels that the more we aggregate into fewer grading levels, the less we can differentiate among students and the more we're willing to accept as indicative of each grade level—suggesting that by limiting the number of possible grades that can be earned, we actually diminish the meaning of the grade and the usefulness of its feedback. When it comes to differentiating grades, she sees mastery as absolute: "Either you have it or you don't," she says, then adds, "but some kids don't have the same tools as others, so we have to take that into account."

Both of these teachers' definitions hold up to scrutiny and are based on their intent with students, though I would disagree with Bowdring's assertion that we need more gradations in the failure zone in order to differentiate for students. Bowdring does make a good point when she adds that teachers should look at grade definitions seriously:

I fear we're on a grade inflation roll these days. Colleges have to offer more and more remediation classes because high school students are going to college with less and less mastered for their high grades. Teachers have to hold students accountable for the material so those grades mean something.

Two Final Concerns. First, when grading, do not draw a "frowny" face next to a low grade as if communicating what you think of the student's performance on the task. Nolen and Taylor report that ". . . those who . . . receive a frowny face . . . are only further shamed" (2005, p. 179). If feedback is supposed to be helpful, we can't shut students down from listening and engaging in that feedback. The frowny face is really nothing more than the teacher venting, but it keeps students from hearing our message.

The second concern is teachers who declare on the first day of class that all students have an A and that all they have to do is hold on to it. Grading policies in which students start out with 100 percent and can only drop or have their status chipped away through bad decisions and immaturity, such as poor planning, little self-discipline, lack of preparation, and being tardy to class, seem inherently negative. It's like telling students, "You're all wonderful now, but I'm going to document your fall." It's similar to recording "−12" at the top of a test instead of "88/100," emphasizing deficits over achievement. The teacher who starts off the grading period with everyone at the highest grade possible can't help but note even more acutely students' digressions within their not-yet-formed maturity. Yes, we want to teach students to not make mistakes, but it seems inappropriate to limit recognition of academic achievement because of immature emotional/social growth. Let's tell students instead that we assume they will build their learning and achieve mastery throughout the grading period, and let's show them their newly achieved milestones every time they occur.

Some teachers think students will fail at integrity because we didn't attach integrity to academic grades, but we give students feedback on integrity in many other ways. They will gain integrity by our careful attention to substantive and clear feedback. Perhaps we can pursue something that looks for students' growth over time, not their mistakes over time. We're out for students' success, not how they fall short. We can send a clear and unequivocal message that correlates high grades with mature behaviors—showing up on time, coming prepared, participating—without resorting to grades to teach those behaviors.

Students need feedback and lots of it, but grades are not the best forms of feedback. Grades by their very nature are post-learning, and we want students to learn. That means we can't spend a lot of time using grades as learning tools. Instead, we do a lot of formative and specific feedback along the way, regarding what has been accomplished thus far. To teach those bigger messages of life, we talk about them, we do think-alouds, we read stories about them, we ask students to give testimonials about them, we affirm students, we have one-on-one talks, we model those sentiments, and we help students create calendars of completion. At every step we hold up a constructive mirror so that students can see how they are developing. There's hope.

CHAPTER 8

Why Do We Grade, and What About Effort, Attendance, and Behavior?

This coming year, our principal wants us to build in an attendance component in our grade—25 percent—students will start with one hundred points, and lose ten for every absence. I understand why—we had kids who missed sixty days this year, and still managed passing grades. However, this skews the grade away from whether or not the objectives of the course were met. Should we fail a student who meets our objectives just because he was absent? But on the other hand, if you think of school as the child[ren]'s "job"—they would not hold the job if they were gone that much from work. I am torn.

—Cossondra George, secondary teacher

We can teach and students can learn, even brilliantly, without any sort of grade being in the picture. It happens all the time. Consider those mini-epiphany moments students and teachers experience in their studies; they most often do not relate to whether a student will be graded on a task. Imagine these scenes: the class when a student realizes via a peer critique that he or she needs to make a concluding sentence to connect the supporting evidence of a paragraph back to its main idea, the time when a student successfully titrates a solution in chemistry class, or when a student blends white paint faintly across a downshaft of yellow light to soften the sunbeam that spills through an opening in a window's curtain in a painting of a summer afternoon. Or how about that first grader making the

Grades as motivators breed depend-
ence, reduce risk-taking, creativity,
and value.

—Rick Stiggins, educator and assessment
expert

leap from word+word+word as reading to reading words in clusters and drawing meaning from the enclosing punctuation marks? Grades were not only unnecessary, they would have been in the way.

So why do we grade students? Most teachers say that they grade students because they are required to do so. This response suggests most teachers see grading as a "necessary evil" rather than a positive function. Why is this? Perhaps it's because grading can be tedious, making teachers feel like they're drowning in a sea of papers, projects, and accountability. With their teaching and grading, teachers have to be fair, brilliant, diplomatic, patient, foresightful, and immediately responsive to 180 students, their parents, and administrators.

This is tough to enjoy. One stack of three- to four-page papers from 180 students, for example, can take more than twenty hours to grade at seven minutes per paper, only ten hours if we spend half that time per paper. How are teachers supposed to do this during their fifty-minute planning period each day, along with assessing the other assignments they've given, writing lesson plans, returning parent phone calls, writing college recommendations, completing teacher narratives about students up for local screening committees, attending committee meetings, sponsoring clubs and sports, ordering supplies for next year, standing in line to photocopy enough copies of the geometry review packet for next week, fixing the computer that keeps freezing, finding that copy of that other resource book that will better meet the needs of Keisha in second period, and eating lunch? Grades and grading philosophies can be contentious, and because teachers are so stressed about many aspects of their jobs, they view negatively anything that threatens to add to their already overburdened schedule. Besides all this, evaluating others and their work is difficult. It takes a mental and emotional toll.

In their more contemplative moments, however, teachers delve deeper and find reasons for grading. Their responses can be boiled down to these six:

- ■ To document student and teacher progress
- ■ To provide feedback to the student and family, and the teacher
- ■ To inform instructional decisions

- ■ To motivate students
- ■ To punish students
- ■ To sort students

Notice the dividing line between the top three and bottom three. The first three reasons seem the most useful and worthy. They work. Those three roles for grading enable us to live up to the promises of schooling, helping teachers teach and students learn. We need to document, provide feedback, and guide our decisions on a regular basis in order for students to achieve in our classes.

The bottom three reasons, however, cross a line. When we grade to motivate, punish, or sort students, we do three things: we dilute the grade's accuracy; we dilute its usefulness; and we use grading to manipulate students, which may or may not be healthy. The bottom three reasons tend to take us away from our goals as teachers, but we use grades in these ways to function in our schools. It's not always wise to do so, and it's worth noting why we are grading students.

We don't want to become mired in playing games with grading, such as when we negotiate with students that if they do the task, they'll get a high grade regardless of what they learn, and that if they don't do the task, they'll get a low grade regardless of how purposeful the assignment was to their learning. Suddenly we're emphasizing compliance, not learning, and we're off course.

A surprise to some: Low grades push students farther from our cause, they don't motivate students. Recording a D on a student's paper won't light a fire under that student to buckle down and study harder. It actually distances the student further from us and the curriculum, requiring us to build an emotional bridge to bring him or her back to the same level of investment prior to receiving the grade. Guskey and others have documented this effect (Guskey and Bailey 2001). Given this, imagine a student earning a string of poor grades—how motivated will he or she be?

High grades also have issues. Alfie Kohn says that high grades have a little bump in motivation—students who earn an A want to earn another one. This is short-lived, according to Kohn, works only on the part of some students, and is extrinsic, meaning it doesn't help students' intrinsic motivation to achieve success later.

Here's a working premise for the remainder of this chapter's discussion.

A grade represents a clear and accurate indicator of what a student knows and is able to do—mastery. With grades, we document the progress of students and our teaching, we provide feedback to students and their parents, and we make instructional decisions regarding the students.

If we accept this premise, the rest of our discussion will make sense; however, some of the currently popular grading practices become questionable.

For example, should we incorporate behavior, attendance, or effort into an academic grade? If the grade represents the number of days students attend school in addition to what students have mastered, it can no longer be used to accurately document mastery, provide feedback, or guide instruc-

Finding the balance between challenging students and encouraging students is difficult, I know. Some policy makers are concerned that too many teachers are taking the easy way out, in the sense that, instead of searching for ways to reach kids that don't respond to traditional methods, they grade the kids on "effort." This keeps down the F's on the grade reports, but it can result in passing kids along from grade to grade until they get old enough to disappear.

—John Norton, educator and moderator, MiddleWeb listserv

In the past I have been an absolute stickler for handing in work on time with exceptions on a case-by-case basis. I had in my mind that I was promoting excellence by doing that. . . . Over time I realized I was sending the message that timeliness was more important than learning. There are many deadlines that I miss for paperwork and the like simply because I am too busy or something came up that needed to be attended to first. That is real life. While I push my students to turn work in on time, I'd rather have the work than not because the work I assign is designed to teach and practice important concepts we're working on. I [now] post students' missing work outside their homeroom doors, and they have done a far better job of turning it in—and getting current work turned in on time.

—Ellen Berg, secondary teacher

tional decisions. Sure, some schools, particularly high schools, use the lure of passing grades to get students in danger of dropping out to attend class. High schools in Fairfax County Public Schools in northern Virginia, for instance, have a policy that three unexcused absences from a class results in an automatic F. While this policy keeps some would-be class-skippers from checking out early every day, the F may or may not be an accurate portrayal of the student's mastery of course content.

Instead of toying with grades in ways that lead to false indicators of mastery, middle and high schools can pursue other options: analyze their structures and programs to see whether they're meeting the needs of modern students (Do they have a fully developed vocational program? Does poverty play a role in this student's lack of success?); examine the extent to which teachers differentiate instruction, which often increases motivation; examine whether their teachers are trained in adolescent pedagogy; examine students' personal lives, if necessary (Is he or she getting enough sleep and eating well? Is he or she depressed? Is there a problem with substance abuse? Is there something dysfunctional in the family?); and examine the extent to which teachers connect with families and members of the community to get students to participate in school.

Dr. Mel Levine was correct when he claimed in his 2003 *New York Times* best-selling book, *The Myth of Laziness,* that laziness is a myth. When a student manifests what seems to be laziness, successful teachers realize there is something else going on. Laziness doesn't exist. Knowing that, teachers of students who are frequently absent keep searching for what works.

If we incorporate behavior into the grade, we run afoul of our intent to keep grades as accurate indicators of mastery. Imagine this feedback to a parent: "Your son's grade, Mrs. Wilson, indicates what he knows and is able to do, in addition to all the days he was polite to others, participated in group discussions, did not steal others' property, maintained an organized notebook, and brought his pencil to class." With baggage like this attached, the grade is no longer functional. We might as well not grade academics.

Let's explore the question of incorporating participation, effort, and behavior into grading a bit further.

Grading Participation

Many school subjects lend themselves to evaluating a student's participation: drama, physical education, band, orchestra, chorus, speech, public speaking, conflict resolution courses, among others. In these subjects and all others, however, we must consider whether students' participation is a technique used to learn the standards, or if participation is the standard itself. If participation is merely an avenue a teacher travels with students in order to arrive at mastery, then it is inappropriate to grade it. Mastery refers only to what students know and are able to do regarding the standards or learning outcomes, not the routes we take to get there. If participation is the actual skill being taught, then it's appropriate to grade it because it is the mastery we're seeking.

    If we think that in a particular subject participation is gradable, then we have to agree on a standard of excellence for participation. What should be considered? The criteria will be different for different teachers and in different subjects. Possibilities include: the student's willingness to participate; courtesy toward others; attentiveness; how he or she balances listening and talking; timing; avoidance of incendiary language; the extent, relevance, accuracy, and substantive nature of his or her contribution or remarks; the manner of his or her contribution and whether it was matched to the intended audience; whether he or she incorporated proper resources, references, and protocols; and whether the student has grown over the course of the year in the application of any of these criteria. Grading can get subjective and complex very quickly.

    It may be advisable for teachers to give feedback on participation, but not to include it in the formal, end-of-grading-period grade. For example, even in drama class where participation is a huge part of the experience, there are universal concepts we want students to master. Proper voice inflection at the proper time might be one. We grade the extent of the students' skill development—the capacity to inflect voice at just the right moments in a dialog or monologue, but we don't grade students on the fact that they stood up and tried to inflect their voices. This is analogous to grading students in world civilization classes on whether they took the test. We grade the matter of the test (mastery), not the fact that they took it (participation). In music classes, do we grade the fact that students performed for us, or do we grade the skill displayed in their performances and perhaps their growth in that skill? We grade the skill and growth. It's the same in physical education—we don't

> Many classes must include participation grades, and even many activities in core classes are about participation—not necessarily the same thing as class discussion. What about the band student who knows how to read music and can answer 100 percent on "paper" tests but cannot perform due to lack of practice, off-task activities in class, etc.? What about physical education classes? Should students not have to participate, but just take a test to see whether they know the rules of various games and physical activities? Should choir students not have to perform, but still get an A if they know all of the words to a song? Should everyone in my fiber testing lab get an A even if they stood around and constantly talked about social events, and just copied the results from the others in their group? . . . In many subjects and activities the process is primary—and participation is vital.
>
> —Margel Soderberg, secondary teacher

grade the fact that they played soccer for thirty minutes as heavily as we do the skills and growth they demonstrated while playing.

It might be easier to liken participation grades to work habits or homework grades. We allow them up to 10 percent influence on the mastery grade at the end of the grading period, but anything more than that unduly influences the final grade's accuracy in terms of what students know and are able to do; and in differentiated classes, the grade must be accurate to be useful.

Determining the extent of a student's participation isn't always easy, either. One student's full-bodied, maximum-intensity participation is another student's disinterested glance compared with what he or she can do. Once again, it's subjective. Sure we can tally the number of interactions a student makes, but the interactions are the medium through which they reveal mastery, not mastery itself. By limiting but not eliminating a participation grade's influence, we provide enough feedback on participation to be helpful and enough grade impact to be motivating for students.

Having said this, do we sometimes bend the rules for certain students? Yes, we're human. Is it wise to do this? Sometimes.

Secondary educator, Cossondra George, once shared this:

> *I have F. in class . . . who is always participating, always knows what is going on. A very enjoyable student to have in class. However, due to F.'s home situation, he does very little homework, and struggles socially at school. He is frequently suspended, absent, etc. . . . I cannot fail this young man simply because he turns in little outside class work to me, even when his percentage falls below the magical 60 percent. He is too much an active learner in my class. That is where "participation" comes into a grade.*

In this case, Cossondra found another way for F. to show his mastery. She gave him every opportunity to reveal his understandings via his active learning in class. Homework wasn't an avenue that worked for this student, so she chose a different route that wouldn't limit the expression of his knowledge. This is responsive teaching.

If, however, she gives him high marks just for speaking in class, regardless of the mastery levels demonstrated, she will have to record on the report card that the grade earned is based on a modified curriculum. The grade does not reflect the same level of competence in the subject as others of the same grade. This may be the best thing Cossondra can do, and it's also accurate.

The greater gift is to record accurate grades, not ones "fudged" by artificial elevation due to our sympathy for a student's home life. The reality, however, is that sometimes students are limited by their living/growing conditions and we have to consider that when grading. If we do, we mark it on the report card or in the cumulative folder for others to reference as they interpret the grade. Despite the harshest conditions at home, we must portray a student's academic development accurately. If we can find alternative routes to demonstrate that mastery, we choose them.

Sometimes teachers elevate the importance of participation in an academic grade in order to stimulate students. Teacher and principal Bill Ivey says:

> *Speaking as someone who hardly ever spoke out in class until my second year of grad school (although I was always thinking and was always on-task), I learned so much more when I finally started talking—for me, anyway, there was a major difference between merely suspecting something might be true and actually putting the idea out for others to hear and confirming that one way or another. Additionally, if a student is not participating in a discussion, that is a valuable viewpoint which is missing and the whole class is diminished. It's sometimes hard to get that concept across to students, and especially to well-meaning parents who are sticking up for their kids. I do understand and support the concept that class participation takes on many forms, and I have written standards for my classes which attempt to define class participation as both a mental and a vocal process. But in the end, what's best for a class and every individual student in it is for everyone's voice to be heard, and I think it's legitimate to make that part of the grade.*

Former principal and now education consultant, Chris Toy, has an interesting take on whether or not to grade participation:

> *. . . a great quote by Einstein: "Not everything that can be counted counts, and not everything that counts can be counted." I happen to believe that teaching our children "ways of being" matters. I won't go as far [as] to say that it matters more than academics because academic learning is certainly at the core of schooling. But to insist that affective traits, such as attitude, participation, effort, cooperation, must relate directly to a content rubric is, in my opinion, trying to count something that is not countable. I do believe that no one should be penalized for thinking and working quietly. It's not about being the center of the class. It's about showing up on time, with the tools and attitude to get the work done.*

Alternatively, we may be penalizing students who don't like to speak up when we offer bonus points or high grades to the whole class for participation, even though we know these students won't be able to achieve it. Remember, the course description does not state, "Participation in class" as one of its standards or benchmarks. It's a little disingenuous to require it for successful grades, and grading participation in class discussions creates angst for students who want to do well but who are developmentally not ready to do so. Why put them in a pressured position of not being able to achieve something that everyone else can do readily but is not an indicator of mastery for the course? I've had a number of students over the years who feel like they've failed when they haven't earned a high grade in everything. To purposely set up a compelling goal (bonus points, a high grade) that everyone else can easily earn but they cannot seems to be a penalty of sorts.

Just making expectations or policies clear to students doesn't always mean that it's fair to invoke them. Students have to be given the personal tools to achieve those expectations as well, and that includes time, reflection, and feedback. Also, the expectations and policies have to be developmentally appropriate for the students' readiness level. Does this mean we don't push students to do things they're not comfortable doing? No. We push students all the time, stretching them all we can. The difference is when we start evaluating their stretching exploration and recording those evaluations as permanent indicators of mastery—a grade.

Of course, some of us use participation to tip the scales one way or the other for a student with a borderline grade. Educator Deborah Bova says:

> I have always considered classroom participation (a really subjective assessment) as the "make or break" scenario. If the child has a grade that is an 87 percent and participates consistently and in a positive way, I will push the grade up to the 88 percent which is a B–. I have never used participation to take away from a grade unless it is an oral presentation which is lousy and the grade is lousy and that affects the average. I believe participation can influence in a positive way, but should never detract from academic accomplishment.

Grading Effort and Behavior

What about effort being woven into an academic grade? In order to answer that, someone first needs to tell us how to measure effort objectively. We don't have a commonly accepted, legally justifiable, nonsubjective method for measuring how hard or sincerely someone is working. We can provide anecdotal evidence and list the amount of time and resources students spend on a task, but identifying personal effort levels objectively eludes us. Yes, we can chart work habits in order to provide feedback and develop positive behaviors as true habits, but we do not have an accurate yardstick for effort. Comparing some students who went all out on a project with those who did just the bare minimum to satisfy the requirements is a subjective call. One student's outstanding effort is another student's quickly thrown together, scribbled page. Declaring the extent and impact of students' efforts with authority can be difficult to defend.

We know there is a very high correlation between academic success and effort, behavior, and attendance. These are valued work ethics too, and the correlations work in almost all cases, but not all. When we mix ancillary criteria that are not meant to serve as indicators of mastery with assessments that are meant to serve as such, we can't trust the results or make decisions based on such criteria.

Karen Gruner, a chemistry teacher at St. John's Literary Institute at Prospect Hall, says: "One of life's tough lessons is trying hard and failing. It does no kid anywhere any good to give grades based on trying hard or behaving nicely because sooner or later they hit the wall of not having the knowledge the grade implied."

Some teachers will argue, however, that if we don't weave effort into the academic grades, students will fail to learn the correlation and they won't adopt such positive behaviors. Chris Toy comments:

> *It can't be just the academic standards. What makes all of us unique and so amazing goes way beyond our academic knowledge. It's got to be the whole of what we want and need kids to know in order to be successful and to realize their full potential.*
>
> *Someone said, "I agree that effort, preparedness, timeliness should count for something, but I'm not sure it is in their grade." I say, why not? Could any of us have their potential reduced by not demonstrating these things? I think we do kids a disservice if these are not reflected in what we expect them to be able to do. Would any of us keep our jobs if we could not or consistently refused to work, be prepared, or show up on time?*

Toy is correct. In a perfect world, we could find a way to incorporate all the factors that matter in an assessment of a student, and the report of that assessment would be accurate and useful for everyone.

In that world, however, we wouldn't be limited by trying to quantify the unquantifiable. We are imperfect beings trying to objectify the subjective. In addition, the high stakes placed on grades as a guarantee of a student's precise mastery of something, and as tickets to success and stature, increases the pressure behind the square peg being jammed into the round hole. The current system doesn't allow for healthy and responsive grading practices that meet everyone's needs.

On the maturation side, we don't want students to think that just because they worked hard yet failed, they should get something for it. As adults, we are fired if we fail to produce what is requested, no matter how hard we've worked or how cooperative we were. So the student who works hard but

I believe that items such as "being a caring, positive, contributing member of the community," while certainly appropriate for inclusion in a school's mission statement, are not appropriate for state standards. Why? I would have a problem with measurement of this attribute. The middle school student is inherently "me centered." Do I grade on something the student has little control over—their rate of maturity? Can I legislate caring members of any community? Are they really just reflections of their home life at this stage?

—Marie Bahlert, secondary teacher

earns a D gets a D on the project, test, or report card, not a C for being mature or diligent.

In addition, we teach self-discipline and hard work in many ways, not just through report card correlations. For example, students learn more about the connection between self-discipline and higher achievement if we help them reflect on their use of time and the resultant quality of their work. If we leave it to the grade to speak for itself, it won't. The causal relationship between worry over low grades and a student's subsequent self-discipline isn't as strong as we think. It's our commentary with the grade, not the grade itself, that makes the difference.

We can also affirm hard-working students publicly, share stories of hard work leading to success, and help students keep calendars of completion. We can show students examples of poorly done work completed without regard to self-discipline or deadlines, and we can show examples of work done well and completed with integrity. We can model the message by carefully preparing our lessons instead of always teaching off the cuff. We can emphasize formative checkpoints over summative ones, again focusing on what we do en route to mastery, not just post-learning punishment or rewards.

Students who excel and receive recognition and more choices as a result of their hard work will create another positive pressure to work for some of their not-so-motivated classmates. It's never easy, but there are many ways to teach self-discipline, and incorporating effort into a mastery grade isn't the most useful way to advance that message or increase the utility of the grade.

Montgomery County in Maryland is tackling head-on the issue of separating effort from achievement in grades. Consulting teacher, Paula Schmierer, says:

> [We are] . . . moving to a standards-based report card system. . . . There is a clear separation of work behaviors (learning skills) from academic ability—they are recorded and reflected separately on the report card. They always were recorded separately, but until now, not everyone separated them out for academic grading purposes. It is forcing teams or departments to dialogue about student learning and that has been a good thing . . . for teaching, for learning, and for parents knowing what the grade truly means.
>
> There has had to be a mind-shift for many folks on this. . . . Learning skills definitely can play into the grades of many students. But when you separate the content skills knowledge from those behavioral skills, teachers have to take a look at why the student whom you think should under-

stand the material isn't performing as you thought. Perhaps there's something else going on with that student.

Finally, close analysis of how we report effort, academic proficiency, and other aspects of students' growth is evolving teacher by teacher, school by school. It's worth entering the conversation. Note teacher Susan Bischoff's comments, recently posted on a teacher-leader listserv:

> *In my experience, late/missing work is rarely caused by a simple decision not to do the work, but teachers often treat it that way. You're teaching your kids they can be successful when you insist on their success and accept nothing less. For some teachers, that translates into a zero-tolerance policy (ZERO-tolerance; get it?).*
>
> *I've found that once I've enabled success, the child more often than not responds by gradually becoming more independent in [his or her] success. So, you're teaching responsibility rather than simply punishing kids for not demonstrating it.*
>
> *On the other hand, I do admit I have a hard time philosophically giving an A when there is a lot of late work/retries. It does frequently happen. My hand SO wants to change that A to a B but I live with it. The other side of the report card and the comment area lets me tell the rest of the story. So, yes, I do believe that academics must be separated from work behaviors.*

We had a little social experiment last year. In one school the principal deducted 10 percent for each day late teachers were in turning in their recertification points and extra duty pay forms at the end of the year. You know when we're so busy and things just slip through. (They were restored of course.) But the message was loud and clear and fostered much discussion . . . that building has now adopted a policy for not penalizing student scores for being late. The expected onslaught of late work never happened.

—Marsha Ratzel, secondary teacher

Chapter 11 has more ideas on how to grade late work.

If grades are most useful to students, parents, and future teachers when they are accurate, it makes sense to question any action that distorts their final declarations of mastery. While important to life and learning, teaching techniques, such as class discussions and active participation, as well as student efforts to come to know course content and skills, are not demonstrations of mastery themselves; they are routes to that mastery. Referencing students' skill development with these techniques and experiences makes accurate declarations of mastery difficult to determine.

Chris Toy and others make good points about the value of incorporating participation and other nonacademic skills into an academic grade, but doing so would change the meaning of a grade beyond its tenuous objectivity used to standardize learning and also change it from how we've defined grades here. It would further strain the already thin attempts to objectify the subjective. Those nonacademic factors are inherent in the student's academic achievement and corresponding marks; they lead to those marks. It seems counterproductive to muddy the waters further by doubling their influence (grading those characteristics while students are learning and also weaving them into the final graded assessments), and overtly entangling a teacher's subjective insertions regarding nonacademic factors into a grade. Specific feedback on these factors should be communicated to students and their parents, but it should remain a separate column on the report card.

CHAPTER 9

Ten Approaches to Avoid When Differentiating Assessment and Grading

If we want to differentiate instruction and assessment yet also provide helpful feedback, document progress, and inform our instructional decisions, we must do everything we can to make sure the grades students earn at any level are accurate renderings of mastery. This requires critical examination of some commonly accepted but often inappropriate grading practices. Let's examine the top ten practices to avoid when differentiating instruction and assessment.

1. Avoid incorporating nonacademic factors, such as behavior, attendance, and effort, into the final grade. (See the rationale given on this in the preceding chapter.)

2. Avoid penalizing students' multiple attempts at mastery.

Not allowing multiple attempts at mastery is another way of saying we don't allow work or assessments to be redone for full credit. Many of us have said the following to students: "You can redo the test, but the highest grade you can earn on it is a B out of deference to those who studied hard and achieved an A the first time around," "For every problem you go back and correct, I'll give you half a point of credit," or "You can retake the test, but I will average the new grade with the original one."

   If we hold such a philosophy and a student has been giving sincere effort during the unit, we are holding the student's development against him or her.

I would be alarmed if more than 75 percent of my students were failing because I would think I had missed the mark somehow. So that begs the question, at what point do I begin to wonder where I've not succeeded in my responsibility? Am I satisfied with a 75 percent mark? Or an 85 percent or a 95 percent for having my students pass my class or pass that test?

—Marsha Ratzel, secondary teacher

This is an unfair stance. The truth is, not all students are ready to receive what we have to offer, nor are they ready to learn at the same pace as their classmates. Even adults learn at varying paces from one another. Adolescents and young adolescents have amazingly varied rates of learning—they are all in dramatic transition. What sticks with one student won't stick with another, and even within the same student, there is tremendous inconsistency. A student who always "gets it" early in the unit or year suddenly has trouble with something else later in the year, and it's not clear why.

The fastest growth spurt in human development is from age zero to two. We change more during this time physically, emotionally, and intellectually than at any other time outside of the uterus, and the pace of development of any one portion of the mind or body is different from person to person. Given this, it would be rather absurd, even abusive, to demand that all young humans recite the alphabet in the eighth hour of the fifth day of the tenth month after the second year of their lives. Most toddlers are not in school, however, so this variance doesn't pose any grading concerns.

Now, advance forward to young adolescence and adolescence, which is the next most dramatic transformation physically, emotionally, and intellectually of our lives. Ages ten to eighteen rival ages zero to two in terms of how much we change. It is just as absurd, even abusive, to demand that all 180 students we teach demonstrate 100 percent proficiency with 100 percent of the test in this exact test format at 10:00 A.M. on this one Tuesday in the second week of October. How arbitrary and without justification it is to declare that the third of February is when everyone will be at the same point in their mastery of *The Federalist Papers,* and there's no chance earlier or later to demonstrate and be given credit for full mastery.

Imagine the negative impact on a student who needs another route, a few more examples, or another few days to process information before successfully capturing Boolean logic or a geometry proof. The teacher who teaches the unit of study but then tests the student before he or she has mastered everything makes a common and an understandable mistake. We can't know the perfect time to assess every student's level of proficiency. This isn't a problem, however, because we use that feedback from the initial assessment, reteach or assist the student, and allow him or her to try again. We're out for students' success, not just to document their deficiencies.

The ineffective and unethical response, however, would be to get in the way as the child strives to learn and demonstrate understanding to the fullest extent. The teacher who denies the option to redo tasks and assessments in order to reach the standard of excellence set for students has to reconsider their role: Is the teacher in the classroom to teach so that students learn, or is he or she there to present curriculum then hold an assessment "limbo" yardstick and see who in the class can bend flexibly and fit within its narrow parameters?

Reality check: Middle and high school teachers can't teach children individually all the time. We could never give each student a test on a different day according to when he or she is ready. We teach the masses. In order to not lose our sanity, we have to make and hold some deadlines. That's fine, but when it comes time to generate the letter grade that will declare mastery or lack thereof, we have to respect the student's individual development and consider that everyone learns at a different pace and in a different manner and, perhaps more important, that these variances are not setbacks, negative, or punishable.

Education expert, Dr. Nancy Doda, puts it succinctly: "We don't want to admonish students for not learning at the same pace as their classmates. We don't want it to become, 'Learn or I will hurt you.'" When we hold students to one moment in one particular day of the school year to demonstrate mastery in a topic, we are telling them that they must learn at the same rate, to the same extent, and with the same tools and resources as their classmates, or they will suffer. This isn't teaching.

If we really want students to reflect on their mistakes and revise their thinking and/or performances, they have to know their efforts will count. If we want them to heed our feedback on their work, they have to know that it can be used to improve their status. Nolen and Taylor make the case well in *Classroom Assessment:*

> *Feedback that is given on an assignment that can't be revised or that is not clearly and specifically related to future work is unlikely to be seen as useful by the student. Policies that give only partial credit for revisions are little better than no-revision policies—why should the student spend time and effort revising something if the best he can hope for is a slight improvement in the grade, despite the fact that he now understands how to do the work? (2005, p. 60)*

Nolen and Taylor remind us that teachers who are focused on students' growth and mastery usually allow work and assessments to be redone. They say that teachers who are primarily focused on how students do in comparison to others, a limiting reference for differentiated instruction teachers, usu-

The only thing that counts for the grade on the report card is how students do on assessments. I try to have several different types of assessments for the students so kids who bomb tests can be successful. I also allow students to retest as many times as they need to, to show me they know the concept or skill. All other aspects of grading I address in the comments section of the report card. This includes the amount of assignments they complete (or don't complete), absences and tardies, behavior issues, etc.

I was nervous about the change, but I saw kids who had failed until seventh grade being willing to take a risk and try on some assignments. Instead of a grade, I wrote feedback to let kids know what improvements were needed and what they were doing right. As the year went on, I got more classwork and homework turned in than I ever did when it was part of the grade. I saw kids become more confident in their abilities, and grades reflected what the kids could do. I was amazed at the difference! I know how I'll be grading next year.

—Lisa Pierce, secondary teacher

Retesting: When my principal challenged me to consider the implications for those who weren't playing the system, I tried it. After seeing how many kids went from failure to success (or degrees of success), how it promoted a culture of self-improvement, and how it reduced test anxiety, I had to admit she was right [about allowing retesting]. While I do see students who take advantage of retesting situations (and I deal with those as they present themselves), there are also a large number of students who benefit from multiple opportunities to "get it." It's the re-exposure and practice that happens during the rewrite process that is the magical ingredient . . .

—Brenda Dyck, educator and author

ally do not allow work and assessment to be redone. In addition, Nolen and Taylor write:

> *If the purpose of grades is to communicate achievement, teachers are likely to give students full credit when revisions or retakes demonstrate better achievement. . . . The rationales behind various partial-credit strategies are similar to those behind various late-work policies. "It's not fair to those who did a good job the first time around," "It's a throwback to proponents of norm-referenced grading." . . . If grades are meant to stand for the students' level of competence at the end of the quarter, semester, or year, teachers must ask themselves, "Does it matter how quickly they reached competence? Does it matter if it took extra feedback or a second revision? (2005, p. 301)*

In a differentiated classroom, teachers often allow students to redo assessments for full credit. Chapter 10 takes a closer look at what this means for teachers and students.

3. Avoid grading practice (homework).

Homework is never to learn material the first time around. Successful teachers don't give homework unless their students have already mastered the concepts. If students have a partial understanding of something and we ask them to practice or rehearse the material in the homework assignment that night, we are doing them a disservice. They will learn it incorrectly, and it will take ten times the emotional and intellectual energy to go back and undo "bad" learning. This is a side effect of confabulation.

Confabulation is when the mind seeks the big-picture connections of something it has learned, and when it doesn't find all the pieces of the puzzle, it makes up information or borrows from other memories and inserts false information into the holes of missing understanding. The worst part is that the mind convinces itself that this entire picture is the original learning. It has difficulty detecting what was true and what was confabulated for the sake of the big-picture requirement. No matter what we do as teachers, our students' minds will be trying to create the larger contexts in which all content and skills fit—regardless of whether we provide it.

Rethink homework if it is a major reason kids are failing.

—Eileen Bendixen, secondary teacher

Your brain is trying to make connections right now as you read these words: You're thinking about whether confabulation is true, whether it fits with what you know already, how it compares with other cognitive theory information you've received over the years, how you will categorize it in your mind, how you will use this knowledge when you work with particular students, who among your colleagues might be interested in hearing about this, and where the author is going next with this information. If you were a student of mine and we had several days together to interact on this topic, we'd be able to prevent a majority of misconceptions that arise in your thinking, and we'd tackle confabulated learning to the ground. Two of the greatest allies in the battle against confabulation are frequent assessment and revision of instruction.

Take this idea back to homework, assessment, and grading: Homework is given after students have mastered material. It's assigned so that students can practice, reinforce, elaborate, prepare, and extend their understanding, not to learn something "cold." We are skating on thin ice when a student says he doesn't understand something and we respond, "Do the homework assignment. It will be made clear to you."

Does this mean we occasionally give different homework assignments for different students, or take away homework entirely one evening for a subset of students? Sure. What is fair isn't always equal, and we're out to be fair and effective as teachers. The next night's homework for these students who didn't master the topic today includes material asking them to practice today's concepts as well as tomorrow's concepts. The rest of the class won't get this kind of homework tomorrow night. As long as we make a practice of extending this offer to everyone and students don't perceive that we significantly increase or decrease someone's workload over the course of a week, they'll accept the different requirements and timing.

The following brief descriptions establish a rationale for this premise: In differentiated classrooms, we don't grade homework. Homework is practice, not a demonstration of mastery, and letter grades are saved for declarations of mastery. Letter grades are given post-learning; homework is assessed *while* learning. Be clear, though: We must give feedback on homework, and we give feedback on homework without using grades. If we feel we need to grade the collective homework for a grading period in order to coerce students into doing it, a small percentage is the most we should apply. More about this later.

No adult would put up with being graded on his or her route to come to know a concept. Imagine an education professor who teaches a complex teaching approach and tells us that he will visit our classrooms in one month to evaluate our proficiency with it. "You have one month to practice this," he tells us. One week into that month, however, he shows up to see how we're doing, gives us some feedback, then adds, "I'll be using my observations of you today in your final grade at the end of the month." Many of us would cry foul in such a situation because we were just beginning to practice the concept; we weren't ready to demonstrate full proficiency.

This is analogous to putting a letter grade on a student's math homework. We taught students how to determine faces, edges, and vertices on eight different three-dimensional solids on Tuesday, and the student practices it that night. How fair is it to grade that student's practice with it? Wouldn't the grade be more ethical and accurate by first processing the practice attempts with the student, then giving more practice experiences, exploring the concepts further, providing more practice, building the student's automaticity with the concept, then finally declaring that tomorrow he or she will be assessed officially on the concepts to determine level of mastery?

If we grade students' practice or their steps in coming to know a concept, the final grade is not accurate. It does not represent pure mastery. It represents what the child knows and is able to do as well as all the practice attempts and immature understanding of the concepts along the way. We don't do this in the "real" world of adults where we're always given the highest grade that represents our mastery. Past, occasionally inaccurate explorations are not held against us. We should afford the same courtesy to young adolescents and adolescents.

The most important response to a student's homework assignment is feedback, not grades, and grades in general are poor forms of feedback. Some teachers claim, however, that students will not do homework assignments if they are not graded.

This notion is false. There are many ways to make homework compelling without resorting to grades, but those ideas are beyond the purview of this book. If readers are interested, let me recommend the works of Robert Marzano (1992, 2000), Ken O'Connor (2002), Neila Connors (2000), and Harris Cooper (2001) as well as the chapter dedicated to the topic in my own book, *Day One and Beyond* (2003).

I ran across a teacher in New York state a year ago who counts daily quizzes as 50 percent of the final academic grade. These quizzes have a few questions, and they are completed during the first few minutes of every class. They are based on the previous night's reading. The teacher claims that students won't do the reading unless they know they will be quizzed on the material the next day, so those grades count heavily in order to motivate reluctant students.

I asked this teacher what his grades represent. He said, "Mastery of the material." Then I asked him whether the grades on these quizzes represent mastery of the material or just that students did the reading—a work habit. He said they indicated both.

I disagree. After students read something, they need time and expertise to help them process the information. At a minimum, the teacher should have helped them interpret and apply the information learned in the previous night's reading and given them more practice with the material before ever considering a formal assessment for mastery. The teacher's grades don't reflect what students know and are able to do. Fully half of the grade's declaration in this situation is based on whether a student did what was asked, not what he or she understands. The grade can no longer be used to document progress, provide feedback, or inform instructional decisions.

Daily quizzes that are announced in advance and given to make sure students do homework are more likely to invite students to cheat than to be declarative assessments of learning. They are more about compliance than standards. We may or may not agree with this sentiment for each of our quizzes, but it makes sense to reflect on their use: Are we giving this quiz to keep students "on their toes" and working, or are we giving the quiz to assess student learning and provide feedback? Is it both? Do we give quizzes in order to catch students making mistakes with their time and learning, or to truly aid their growth? And, of course: Is the quiz going to yield accurate information about students' proficiency? In reality, it's normal to use quizzes as both cattle prod and thermometer, but we should lean toward the thermometer.

What if there are other factors impacting a student's ability to complete homework assignments? Some of my students over the years have been in charge of their younger siblings because their parents worked four jobs between the two of them. The parents didn't arrive home every evening until after ten. My students in those families were in charge of dinner, bathing little brothers and sisters, and laundering their clothing, as well as discipline and making sure everyone's homework was done. By the time everything was done, they were exhausted. Some even worked in local businesses after school prior to going home to those responsibilities. The eight pages of reading about the Spanish-American War, the sinking of the USS *Maine,* and the rise of yellow journalism that I assigned students to read and summarize for homework pales in importance under such conditions.

John Buell, coauthor of *The End of Homework: How Homework Disrupts Families, Overburdens Children, and Limits Learning* (2001), reminds us that homework is unfair to impoverished children. He says they do not have the tools, resources, and school focus required to make homework a useful learning tool. Quite often, they are in survival mode, not able to think beyond how to get food, clothing, and medicine for themselves and their families, let alone contemplate the symbolism and character dynamics in F. Scott Fitzgerald's *The Great Gatsby,* a novel to which they have trouble relating as it is. This isn't to say impoverished students shouldn't be taught these things or that they should have serious intellectual requirements for them lessened to any degree. In fact, for many impoverished children, it is the highly challenging intellectual pursuits, and the stories of other cultures and people, that provide momentary escape from the palpable despair of daily poverty and impetus for surmounting their conditions. Highly challenging, academic work has been proven over and over again to be among the most powerful ways to respond to children of poverty. Wright's *Black Boy,* Conroy's *The Water Is Wide,* and Meier's *The Power of Their Ideas* provide clear examples.

What this means is that instead of just presenting and documenting students' failures, teachers must remain vigilant for responsive teaching. If something isn't working because of the student's context, we change the tasks, tools, resources, assessments, or environment to build valid success. Buell infers that teachers who mandate homework and penalize impoverished students who don't complete it well or at all are being insensitive. He says there is no solid evidence to support the current emphasis on students doing large amounts of, or even daily, homework.

Whether we agree with Buell based on our own teaching and learning experiences doesn't matter as much as questioning our status quo does. By doing that, we purposefully expose our own thinking every year and pose the question: Is this homework assignment, and our requirement that it be done, in the best interest of my students' growth and learning? If not, what can I change to make it more helpful?

Given all of this, how much should homework count in an overall academic grade? Very little. Most school districts suggest 10 percent. Any more than this dilutes the accuracy and thereby, usefulness, of a final grade. Ten percent is enough to serve as a carrot in front of the horse's mouth or a stick on the horse's back side, if that's what we think we need with our students, but it's not so much that it would distort declarations of mastery in most cases.

Homework here refers to tasks assigned to students who have already mastered the material. These are check-and-zero assignments such as answering questions on a worksheet, solving practice problems, reflecting on a current event, and/or creating flashcards for vocabulary words. Remember, homework's purpose is to practice, reinforce, extend, and prepare students, never to learn material for the first time. Homework is only assigned if students have a good grasp of the material already. If they don't, the homework is not assigned, or an alternative assignment that requires students to practice only those aspects they have already mastered is provided.

4. Avoid withholding assistance (not scaffolding or differentiating) with the learning when it's needed.

Imagine the situation in which a few students are struggling to make sense of text and the teacher provides a matrix or similar graphic organizer to help structure their thinking. Using the prompts from the organizer, these once-struggling students are now able to identify and organize salient information; they learn well. When it comes time to take the test, they are competitive with the best thinkers in the class.

Is this fair? Yes.

Are the grades for all students in this class accurate renderings of what they know and are able to do? Yes. The limitations to learning have been removed.

If we did not allow students to use the supporting organizers, yet still administered the same test, the struggling students would not have a chance. They would have floundered once again, and the grades written at the top of their tests would not indicate what they were capable of achieving. In the example mentioned in an earlier chapter of a student who needs glasses, we deny that student a fair and accurate rendering of mastery when we remove the glasses in the misguided attempt to be equal. Again, what is fair isn't always equal.

If we want grades to be accurate indicators of mastery, then we have to remove any barrier to students coming to know the material, as well as any barrier to their successful demonstrations of mastery. To not do either of these tasks makes any subsequent grades earned false; they are based on mis-information, and the grade is no longer valid or useful. Barriers in instruction and assessment include inappropriate testing formats, requiring all students to learn at the same pace as their classmates, using the same tools with all students when different tools are needed by some, inflexible teaching, and narrow focus curricula, among others.

By the way, is it appropriate to offer those same graphic organizer to all students if we're going to offer it to a few? Sure. Remember, the most professional thing we do sometimes is to get out of our students' way. Truly, some students won't need them, but some will. Using them doesn't make it easier, it actually pushes students farther than they would be pushed without them.

5. Avoid assessing students in ways that do not accurately indicate their mastery.

Okay, let's stop here and assess everyone who is reading this book. I'd like you all to express what you know about differentiation, grading, and assessment through a six-minute interpretive dance. You have three days to prepare the dance. You must be accurate, you must incorporate three major concepts within each of those areas, and you must cite all your sources properly.

Some readers would find this task intriguing, even motivating. Many others would be appalled. They'd ask for extensions, special resources/tools, coaching, alternative formats, or they might even pursue unethical means to pass the assessment. Many would lose hope. Welcome to the world of students who learn differently. A regular, no-nonsense, traditional test can stir the same reactions in many of our students.

Consider the following word problem:

Each new military jet costs 7.8 million dollars. The government wants to purchase eleven of them but has only 83 million dollars to spend. Will they be able to purchase all eleven jets?

Which operation(s) should students use to solve this word problem? Multiplication and subtraction. How do we know this?

Seriously, how do we know this?

Most of us probably have a picture in our minds: An image of a plane with "7.8 million dollars" written over it. Then maybe we realize that all we have to do to solve the first part of this problem (yes, we realize there will be more than one part) is to add 7.8 million dollars to 7.8 million dollars to 7.8 million dollars to 7.8 million dollars and so on. Just as soon as we imagine this, however, we realize that this repeated addition is the same as multiplication which is much faster. Then we start searching for which numbers to multiply, and based on our understanding of the picture in our heads and what we think the problem is asking, we choose to multiply 7.8 million and eleven. Whatever this total is will be compared with the 83 million dollars, which is done by subtracting. We'll note the difference, revealing whether we are over or under the stated budget, then answer the question.

Clearly, this is more of a reading comprehension problem than a math problem. We can't even begin to solve this problem until we have a clear picture of the situation's logic and what's being asked of us, and that can only be captured if we read the problem correctly.

Now imagine a student who is brilliant in math, but new to this country. His English proficiency is very low. He cannot form a picture in his mind from the word problem itself, but if explained to him orally, he could accurately multiply the larger numbers and compare them with the $83 million budget, arriving at an accurate answer. The test format as it is does not allow him to reveal his true level of proficiency with the mathematical concept.

There are many students who don't speak the "language" of the assessments we give them: the highly interpersonal child asked to work alone for hours at a time, the writing/reading learning-disabled child asked to make sense of advanced text without any of his or her normal tools or strategies for success (a focusing T square, a graphic organizer, listening to the text on tape, being able to read the words aloud, using an AlphaSmart® to make a response, or being given an extended time period), the impoverished child asked to determine the appropriateness of a budget for an extended European vacation. With all three students, the teacher's assessments as stated will not result in an accurate rendering of mastery. Each student's performance will be distorted by the assessment format or approach. The grades earned are useless to the teacher and the student.

If a child doesn't write well, yet understands diffusion and the role it plays in animals and plants completely, why would we give an assessment that requires a written essay on diffusion and its roles in plants and animals? It would be more a test of essay construction than of diffusion. For those of us who cannot play the violin, we would be hard-pressed to express a novel's theme through a violin performance, yet this is very similar to what we are asking students who can't write well to do when we assign thematic essays in content areas. As students, we would say the test is unfair. We'd claim that we knew the novel's theme, just couldn't get it across to the teacher. If we teachers, then, are assessing students' essay writing, then we use essays as assessments. If we are assessing something else, however, then we consider using an alternative format in lieu of the essay or, at the very least, in addition to it.

Let's be clear: Essays are excellent assessment tools and are worth assigning for their own sake because they teach students rhetoric and reasoning that transfer to many other subjects and to life. When it comes time to consider the accuracy of a grade, however, we must be sure that the assessment format reveals the truth about a student's proficiency. If not, it should be scrapped for something more accurate. With every assessment, we must consider what we are trying to test, find the most accurate way of revealing what students know. Anything else is subterfuge.

One alternative format that teachers often misuse as a way to differentiate assessment is artwork. They ask students to draw their personal responses or to do art-heavy projects such as travel brochures, maps, cartoons, posters, dioramas, pop-up books, mobiles, and sculpture. Interactive notebooks can entail major artistic efforts from students as well. Some teachers see these tasks as innovative and revealing of students' mastery.

While they can be helpful instructional strategies and revealing for some students, they are not so for many. When students with little or no art skill learn of these assignments, they wither. They spend the majority of their efforts on the artistic aspects while subordinating their exploration and expression of accurate mastery; the medium becomes a barrier to success. I've seen interactive notebooks, for example, that took students hours to generate, but the majority of the time was spent in detailing and coloring their illustrations, not processing the ideas themselves. Just as any of us would do, these students worry most about what they cannot do. If we want them to focus on the content and skills of the unit, why would we cause such angst or add to their workload?

Artistically portraying content is a powerful way to learn material and should be used regularly as a learning tool in the classroom. When it's time to grade a student's mastery of that same material, however, artistic proclivities or lack thereof will affect what he or she can portray. Heavily artistic projects used for final declarations of mastery should only be used with students who have developed art skills; otherwise, students who lack those skills will receive inaccurate grades. Artistic skills can include aesthetics, eye-hand coordination, spatial thinking, visual arts, and kinesthetics, among others. These are excellent tools for all of us to learn. That's just it, though—we're learning them, we haven't mastered them. That makes it difficult for some of us to use them when being evaluated. In a differentiated class, we may assign art-laden processes to help students come to know material, but we rarely mandate that all students use art skills to demonstrate mastery.

Does this mean we don't grade our students' political cartoons? No. It means we teach them all cartooning skills to improve their competence, and we complement their demonstrations of proficiency with other assessments, such as written analyses and quizzes, and what they contribute orally.

6. Avoid allowing extra credit and bonus points.

"Mr. Terwilliger," David asked. "I didn't do so well on that written, political cartoon analysis. I need to do something to raise my grade. Could I do a poster or something on cartooning for extra credit?"

"'Sorry, David," Mr. Terwilliger replies. "I'm not a fan of allowing students to do extra credit to boost their grades. You can't substitute posters and other things for most assignments because I give assignments with a specific purpose in mind. In this case, how does doing a poster on cartooning teach you to analyze political cartoons in writing, or prove that you can?"

David looks down, his face crumbling in early panic. "It doesn't," he laments.

"I tell you what," his teacher continues. "You can go back and redo the written analysis until you meet the high standard of excellence set for it. What do you say?"

David looks up, not appeased, but not completely lost. "I don't think I can do any better. I worked on that for a long time, and all I got was a D+. I don't know how to do it differently."

"Well, look at it as your first attempt. You have more feedback now. Let's take a look at what still needs improvement. I'll work with you as you rewrite. You'll get it."

David thought for a moment before speaking. "Okay, but I don't know how I'm going to do this and keep up with my regular work. I have a baseball tournament every night this week."

Mr. Terwilliger nodded. "It's not insurmountable. Let's see what we can work out."

Many teachers offer extra credit as a way for students to improve a low grade. They think it gives students hope, and if the student is willing to take the initiative to do something a little extra, he should be rewarded by the addition of more points or a raised grade.

Some teachers also offer extra credit as incentive to students to stretch themselves, pushing beyond the regular unit of study. They might announce to a class, "Anyone who wants to earn an extra twenty-five points can do so by analyzing the current political climate for environmental protection programs and compare it with the political climate for such programs in the mid-

1970s. What's changed, how are we affected today, and what is the likely climate for environmental protection programs twenty years from now?"

These seem relatively safe and routine strategies, but we need to be very careful with extra credit offers. Anything that has enough points attached to it to alter a grade's accuracy in terms of what students have mastered should be avoided. For example, if a student demonstrates a C level of mastery, he or she shouldn't be given an opportunity to artificially inflate that grade with other work that doesn't hold him or her accountable for the same benchmarks or learning outcomes as the original assignment. Substituting a poster for an essay, for example, wouldn't cut it if teaching essay writing. Life science teacher Shah says it well: "How can you do the extra when you haven't done the regular?"

On the other hand, if the teacher is simply looking for a way for a student to express what she knows about pinocytosis, it doesn't matter what test format is used. In another example—conducting a real interview with an adult expert in the field of study, the student would not adequately apply the same skills and content by summarizing an interview news show, mentoring others in interviewing techniques, or creating a library display or PowerPoint presentation on interviewing skills. If we're assessing interview skills, she conducts an interview, and with the student, we analyze it and eventually evaluate her proficiency with interviewing others.

Though we might consider alternative routes to demonstrate mastery as we first design our unit, the choices for the final offering are made after serious contemplation. There is a purpose to each one. If a student can muster an alternative assignment that accounts for everything we are seeking, we can give that alternative serious consideration.

Bonus points on tests call for the same caution. If the student falters in his or her demonstration of mastery with the regular test items, but overcomes those scoring losses with points from a bonus section, then we have to reconsider whether the new, bonus-inflated grade really represents what the student knows and is able to do. This is especially a concern if the bonus questions or prompts are unrelated to the test's topic, such as the spurious bonus questions used by some teachers: "What's Mr. Terwilliger's favorite sport?" or "What famous person died on this day in 1989?" or "What was the score of last night's Orioles game?" or "Who's buried in Grant's tomb?"

If the bonus problems allow students to demonstrate the content and skill proficiencies required in the regular test items, then it's probably okay to use the bonus-inflated grade, but it begs two questions: If the bonus questions require the same skills and content as the regular items, then why are they not a part of the main body of the test? And, if the student can respond to the bonus questions that require the same skills and content proficiency as the regular test items, why couldn't he or she do the regular ones to show proficiency?

To offer extra credit as a way to compel students to push themselves is okay in most situations, within limits. If we find students getting interested and pushing themselves only when the extra credit options are offered, however, we may need to rethink our lesson plans. Students should be challenged and stretched by the regular lessons, not just the extra credit experiences. We need to keep our minds open to the possibility that advanced students need to have a higher operating level in most of their work, not just the occasional extra credit opportunity. If we find students progressing only during enrichment or advanced, extra credit experiences, let's meet those students' needs by turning those types of extra credit experiences into the standard operating procedure for them every day.

Are there times when bribing students with extra credit might be okay? Sure. If we live near Washington, D.C., for example, and the Smithsonian Institute announces that one evening next week an archeologist who has just returned from doing field research is going to hold a seminar and announce a major new find, we entice students to attend the briefing at the Baird Auditorium at the National Museum of Natural History and report back on the exciting new discoveries. We promise things like, "I'll make it worth your while in the gradebook." This may only mean turning one or two zeros in the homework column into checks, but students are a bit more interested in pursuing the extra credit experience and it doesn't affect a grade's overall accuracy.

Educator Chris Toy offers an idea that seems to be a sensible way to offer extra credit while also keeping the grade accurate:

> *Our math teachers use the method of having the highest grade for the basic assignment be ninety-eight points, or an A. Challenge points go to students who extend their work above and beyond the basic project. What is needed for challenge points is well defined by the teachers ahead of time. Challenge points are available to every student on every graded assignment, including homework. It's interesting to see the cross section of students who make the attempt. It's not always the best and the brightest.*

Science teacher, Bobby Biddle, says:

> *I don't allow students to come up to me and ask for extra credit opportunities, but I'll put extra credit opportunities on tests and assignments here and there, usually about something challenging, just enough to be motivating, but not distort the grade. Of course, when Duke beats North Carolina, I put one extra point on every student's test automatically.*

Biddle has also been known to use extra credit to substitute for a student's lowest grade. "Every kid can have a bad day," she says.

Susan Clark, an English teacher at the same school, gives extra credit via books with higher Lexile numbers (see www.lexile.com for many of such books):

> *Students have to read a certain number of pages per week. We have the Lexile numbers for each book. Lexile numbers indicate the challenge level of the reading. If students read books with higher Lexile numbers indicating greater challenge, they get more points for reading the book.*

7. Avoid group grades.

Many of us from time to time have done something similar to this: We've told students in groups that we will select one notebook from each group at random and grade it. Every group member will get the same grade for their own notebook as the one representative notebook earns. We then give the group time to compare notes and get everyone's notebook up to speed so that whichever one we choose, the group will look good.

Pretty reasonable, right? Maybe not. What does that grade tell us about any one of the students in that group? Little to nothing. How does that grade guide our next steps? It doesn't; it's not an assessment.

Most teachers consider it unfair to give entire groups of students the same grade based on one group member's performance or on the whole group's performance on a task. This makes sense. Grades that are given to whole groups like this don't reflect an individual student's achievement or growth, and therefore can't be used to document progress, provide feedback, or inform instructional decisions. Group grades are often a form of coercion used by teachers to compel students to work with members of their groups to learn the material, at least superficially. Since they are not accurate indicators of mastery on the part of any one student, and that's what grades are supposed to be, they undermine the legitimate use of grades.

In addition, group grades tend to create unhealthy peer pressure among classmates, often generating negative feelings toward immature and/or unmotivated members of the group who did not work as much as others, or who had trouble achieving to the same level. Some students can glide through a group task doing little or no work, but earning the same high mark as those who did all the work and made the group score well. For the ill will they often engender and the antithesis of grades and learning they promote, group grades are wisely left off the differentiating teacher's menu of best practices.

Does this mean cooperative learning activities are inappropriate? No. Cooperative learning is an outstanding teaching strategy. When we use it with our students, however, we're mindful that it is a technique used to teach students about a topic, not a demonstration of proficiency in that topic itself.

For one reason or another, we may assign grades to a cooperative learning product and everyone in the group gets the same grade. That doesn't mean the grade has to be fully influential in the end of the grading period declaration of mastery, however. We can use the grade as a minor feedback or documentation symbol in the moment of the lesson, but the discerning teacher takes time after the lesson to decide whether the grade earned in the cooperative learning task was a grade indicating mastery of the topic being studied or of proficiency with the cooperative learning process. If it's associated more with the process, we drop the grade's influence on the final grade because it is not a statement of mastery. With cooperative groups, we strive to grade students individually, and we set up the positive interdependence such that no student receives a lower grade for another student's lack of achievement.

8. Avoid grading on a curve.

Grading on a curve means that the teacher gathers everyone's scores on a given assessment, then arbitrarily sets a cut-off for the number of each letter grade to be dispensed for that assessment. For example, in a class of thirty-two students, the top five scores, whatever they are, might earn an A, even if they are in the 80 percent zone. The next ten grades below that are reserved for all B grades; the next ten for all C grades; the next five for the D grades; and the last two, whatever they are, for the F grades. Moving left to right, from lowest to highest grade, that makes a pretty nice, positively skewed, bell curve—2, 5, 10, 10, 5. We can rest easy that we've done our job when we get such a nice grade distribution, right?

No. Grades that are used for documenting progress, providing feedback, and guiding instructional decisions are criterion-referenced. That is, they are based on the student's demonstrations of knowledge and skill scored against a set of established criteria. The students' achievement is put in terms of mastery of standards. Norm-referenced grading is comparing students against others in their grade level or age group. There's no reference to mastery; it's about standings, not standards.

Grading on a curve is extremely distorting as a reference of mastery. A student can achieve a 70 percent mastery rating, for example, but get an A because his or her score is among the top three scores of the class. In terms of mastery, however, he or she is a D student if 70 percent is a D on our school's grading scale. This kind of grade yields nothing useful to the modern, highly accomplished differentiating teacher. All we can conclude from such grading is that some students do less well than others. There's nothing in that statement that helps provide feedback to specific students nor decide where to go next in the lesson on the Cartesian plane.

Guskey reminds us that grading on a curve also moves us farther away from one of our teaching goals—collaboration. He writes that grading on a curve

> *. . . makes learning a highly competitive activity in which students compete against one another for the few scarce rewards (high grades) distributed by the teacher. Under these conditions, students readily see that helping others become successful threatens their own chances. (Guskey and Bailey 2001, pp. 36–37)*

He furthers his argument by quoting from Johnson and Toauer (1989) who found grading on a curve to mean the following:

> *High grades are attained not through excellence in performance but simply by doing better than one's classmates. As a result, learning becomes a game of winners and losers, and because the number of rewards kept are arbitrarily small, most students are forced to be losers. . . . (Guskey and Bailey 2001)*

To be honest, I almost did not mention grading on a curve in this book. It is slipping from our lexicon in most school districts, for it seems to be an obsolete practice indicative of less enlightened times. We've progressed as a profession, or so I thought. In fact, some new teachers have to ask what we mean when we mention curve grading in conversation.

Unfortunately, several universities, including a few ivy-league schools that set much of the tone for academics in America, have departments that recently reinstituted grading on a curve. They claim they need to sort students, increase their dedication to studies, and create more accountability. Grading on a curve does the first of these inappropriately, and it does neither of the remaining two. Universities should reverse their decisions to allow grading on a curve.

9. Avoid recording zeros for work not done.

Zeros skew the grade to a point where its accuracy is distorted. Teachers using the 100-point scale who do not replace a zero with a fifty, sixty, or seventy to equalize the influence of all grades earned end up recording inaccurate grades. This is true even when students do less than the upper-F level, too. Once a student has crossed over into "failure," delineating degrees of failure doesn't help anyone, and it lessens the usefulness of the grade. This is controversial for most teachers, however. A more detailed rationale is presented in the section in Chapter 11 entitled "Record a Zero or a Sixty?"

10. Avoid using norm-referenced terms to describe criterion-referenced attributes.

If grades are standards-based, reporting what students know and are able to do, they declare mastery of a student's learning, not how he or she is doing in relation to others, such as we would get when talking about a student being average or not. The use of mastery criteria to identify relative "averageness" makes no sense in the standards-based classroom. For more on this, see the discussion of grade definitions in Chapter 7.

CHAPTER 10

Conditions for Redoing Work for Full Credit

I allowed my students to retake exams, even those who scored in the nineties. However, I added an extra step. At the bottom of their page, I required them to explain to me the types of errors they made and how they were able to correct them: "What did you do wrong to get this grade? How did you correct the problem?" Many times they just made calculation errors. I truly believe that students do learn at different rates and who's to say that they are all ready to test at the same time? For that reason, I let them retake tests anytime they requested it. Yes, I had a lot of paperwork at first, but after awhile, it actually decreased. Students began analyzing their mistakes before turning in their tests. We also practiced analyzing their errors during homework/classwork checks.

—Melba Smithwick, secondary math teacher

In a successfully differentiated class, we often allow students to redo work and assessments for full credit. There are a number of stipulations and protocols that make it less demanding on teachers and more helpful to students, however. Let's take a look.

All Redone Work Is Done at Teacher Discretion. Redoing work is not to be taken for granted. In my classes, I ask parents to sign a form that outlines this and other protocols for redoing work at the beginning of the school year. This serves as due process, and I can reference it when a parent complains that I did not allow his or her child to redo an assignment. If I get a hint that the student has "blown off" a four-week project until the last three days, or boasted to classmates that he or she will just take the test the first time as an advance preview and then really study for it next week because, "Mr. Wormeli always let's me redo tests," I will often rescind the offer and discuss the situation with the student.

I use the word *often* here because one, universal, always-respond-this-way declaration is inappropriate in many grading and teaching situations. In many cases there are extenuating circumstances, and in differentiating classes, we do what's developmentally appropriate for students, not just what the rules dictate.

If it's a character issue, such as integrity, self-discipline, maturity, and honesty, *the greater gift may be to deny the redo option.* We have to weigh that choice every time we consider allowing students to redo work. Also, if a particular student is asking to redo work more than twice a grading period, there may be another problem that needs to be addressed. We may need to modify our instruction, coach the student on time-management skills, confer with the parents, look at the student's schedule outside of school, or get some guidance from a school counselor because of a difficult emotional issue the student is experiencing. The rule of thumb, then, is to consider the extent to which students abuse the policy by becoming chronic redoers. If they abuse the system or repeatedly ask for a redo, we need to modify the system. On most occasions, however, our first response is to be merciful. One of the signs of a great intellect is the inclination to extend mercy to others, and all successful teachers are intellectual.

How We Would Want to Be Treated as Adults. This is another criterion to consider. There are many times in which we've had something due for a committee, an administrator, or a graduate course, but we were too overwhelmed, tired, neglectful, or immature in our planning to finish the task in time. Good reasons or not, we are very grateful for that committee chair, administrator, or professor who smiles and says, "I understand; that happens. Have it for me Monday, and we'll be fine." As long as we don't make such delays habitual, it's usually not a problem, and we're still held in high regard. The world can be an unrelenting whirlwind of criss-crossing priorities and urgencies. It's getting harder to make the most efficient choices and stay in good health, mentally, emotionally, and physically. Offering compassion to others in the midst of this is not only effective, it's refreshing.

Ask Parents to Sign the Original Task or Assessment and Request the Redo Opportunity for Their Child. This keeps them aware of what's going on. It also prevents the student from begging, "Please let me study this during lunch then retake the test in the afternoon. I can't take this grade home to my

Dad." The earliest moment students can redo tasks or assessments is the day after receiving the original assignment or assessment. Such a time period helps you decide how you want to conduct the redo, and it forces the student to form and execute a plan of studying.

Reserve the Right to Change the Format for All Redone Work and Assessments. There are times when it's not worth students' going through the whole project or assessment from the beginning for a redo. For time and sanity's sake, we may just want to assess the student orally and record the new grade right away. Instead of a student redoing a large, complex culminating project on the use of imagery in poetry, for example, I might call the student to my desk and ask him or her to find five uses of imagery in each of two different poems, then to explain how the poet used the imagery to invoke feelings and thoughts in readers' minds. I might ask the student to give me the technical terms we use to analyze poetic imagery, then I might ask him or her to generate a few lines of poetry that incorporate two of those types of imagery. In ten minutes, I've reassessed my student, and I record the new grade in the gradebook. Kathie Nunley in her interesting book, *Layered Curriculum* (2001), offers compelling reasons for doing this sort of assessment.

If the assessment is a forced choice test and students can easily memorize answer patterns, giving the students the same test again is not an option—we have to change the assessment. Tell students that up front but that you will inform them of any changes from the original assessment format when they make their redo requests.

If the test is a constructed response format in which students generate the content, skill, performance, or process from their own mind and body, then it doesn't matter if they have a copy of the test in front of them while they study or if the redo version is the exact same test. If they memorize their responses—intellectual or physical—we still win; the student learned the material and that was our goal.

Ask Students to Create a Calendar of Completion That Will Yield Better Results. It is disrespectful to you and to the student for him or her to spend considerable time restudying the material only to get the same grade or lower. If you can, sit down with the student for a few minutes and work out a successful study plan. Get practical, too: "What will you need to do on Thursday so you can turn this in to me on Friday?" After the student responds with several suggestions, you continue, "What will you do on Wednesday so that you can do these steps on Thursday so you can turn this in to me on Friday?" Later say, "What will you do on Tuesday so that you can do the steps on Wednesday so you can do the steps on Thursday so you can turn this in to me on Friday?"—always working backwards to the present day.

Most students don't have the time-management and task-analysis skills to finish the redo material while keeping up with current work. They need adult guidance. It's developmentally inappropriate to give students a deadline of three days from today to finish the work to be redone, as well as the current work, without guiding them on how to do this, and then admonish them for being irresponsible when they show up with only a quarter of it completed. "You should have used your time more wisely," you scold. "All the rest of these assignments are zeros."

This response is abusive. Most students need interaction with an adult to create a successful calendar of completion. This is also true for students who were out sick or on vacation and are doing make-up work by a certain date. Compassion goes a long way and isn't soft. It's tough and requires serious thinking.

Creating a calendar of completion means we *set a date by which time the redone work is submitted, or the grade becomes permanent.* This is usually one week after the original assignment is returned in my classes, but extenuating circumstances can change that.

Redos and Grades. If a student studies extensively yet still earns a lower grade on the redone work, we can take several actions.

Reconsider the student's earlier, higher grade. Was it a fluke? Was it a valid indicator of mastery? Something is wrong when a student's mastery decreases over a few days' time. In such cases, we need to investigate what happened by reexamining the responses on the earlier assessment and interviewing the student. We may need to reteach the material to the student, while also assessing our lesson plans to make sure we're teaching so that students carry the correct information forward, not just to have presented the curriculum. We don't just admonish the student for not studying and move on.

When it comes to what grade to record in the gradebook—the higher or lower one—choose the higher grade. In most of life, we're given credit for the highest score we've earned. Many lawyers, driver's license holders, accountants, teachers, and engineers appreciate this policy.

Don't average the first and second grade together, either. This is not an accurate rendering of mastery. An analogy with the Department of Motor Vehicles works here: Imagine I'm going for my driver's license in a state that requires a grade of 80 percent correct on the written exam in order to pass. On the first attempt, I earn 20 percent. This isn't very good—stay off the sidewalks, I'm driving! After studying a bit, I go back and earn 100 percent on the written exam. I'd get my license, correct? Sure. If we averaged the two scores, however, I wouldn't get my license, and I'd have to muddle through a string of 100 percents to finally get my license. We don't do this to stable, secure adults; why should we do it for humans in the morphing?

The only time lower scores start to matter is when we get on in years or become infirm and our health keeps us from performing to the same level as we once did. In most school situations, this isn't a concern.

Do Not Allow Any Work to Be Redone During the Last Week of the Grading Period. This is another suggestion that helps as well. It is completely arbitrary and has no pedagogical basis; it just saves teacher sanity. Students usually get worried about their grades and pester their teachers during this time, but the teacher needs the week to finish grading anything outstanding and to determine final grades for the report card. It's difficult to keep up with students redoing work while preparing report cards, so give yourself this guilt-free time.

Ask Students to Staple or Attach the Original Task or Assessment to the Redone Version. Sometimes it's difficult to remember where individual students are in their redo journey. Seeing the original materials helps us determine student growth and keeps gradebook accounting clear.

Langley High School chemistry teacher and department chair Kathy Bowdring says that she does not allow work to be redone, but she does want to teach students the material they missed and give them every chance to succeed. Instead of asking students to redo tests, she asks them to do a post-test analysis of their performance. This is done on students' own time. Through the analysis, students examine and explain what they did incorrectly as well as the concepts being assessed. They also describe what they'd do differently the next time they are assessed on the material. To complete the post-test analysis, they are allowed to use the teacher, the book, notes, and any other sources they wish. The post-test analysis is graded by the teacher and averaged with the original test grade. Bowdring wants students to care about doing well with the test so she counts it along with the written analysis.

Moosa Shah, a middle school life science teacher, says he doesn't allow work to be redone either. He says

I have also struggled with the retake issue. On one hand, I'm very big on students being responsible and prepared the first time around. If they know the retake option is there, they are likely to not put forth their best effort the first time. On the other hand, there are the students who do try their hardest and still fail to grasp certain concepts. . . . I agree that the student who scored 93 percent should be allowed to retake if the student who got a 53 percent is allowed. If the first student wants to do even better, then who am I to stifle [that] interest?

However, they do need to have some accountability. I think the compulsory attendance at a review session is a great idea. You can't just show up and do a retake; you have to do something first that demonstrates your commitment. Otherwise one hundred kids might show up for the retake just to get out of something else.

—Rick Speigner, secondary math teacher

I truly believe that math is developmental. I don't think that all kids learn math at the same pace, or at the same time in their life. I think some kids need more practice, more time with a concept, more one-on-one conversations. If I believe that, then how can I possibly think that they are all going to be ready for the test at the same time? That is also why I give full credit for retests. I think that a student's grade should reflect what they know at the time of the report card, and if a student has mastered the concepts we have covered—no matter when, as long as it was during the reporting period—I think that should be reflected in his or her final grade.

—Kelly, middle school math teacher

the spiral nature of the curriculum is such that students will get more than one chance to both learn and demonstrate their learning of the material. "And besides," he adds, "I've set it up so no one assignment is going to bomb the student's overall average."

The decision to allow students to redo work that is poorly done or missing is a tough one. Teachers debate the merits of allowing redos in schools around the world. If we're basing our decision on the "real" world outside of school, then the answer is clear: Allow students to redo work. This may run counter to some teachers' assumptions that in the real world you don't get "do-overs."

Yet we do. Pilots can come around for a second attempt at landing. Surgeons can try again to fix something that went badly the first time. Farmers grow and regrow crops until they know all the factors to make them produce abundantly and at the right time of the year. People mark the wrong box on legal forms every day only to later scribble out their earlier mark, check the correct box, then record their initials to indicate approval of the change.

Our world is full of redos. Sure, most adults don't make as many mistakes requiring redos as students do, but that's just it—our students are not adults and as such, they can be afforded a merciful disposition from their teachers as we move them toward adult competency.

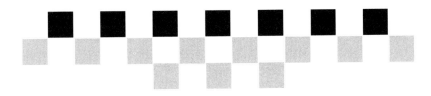

CHAPTER 11

Six Burning Grading Issues

Record a Zero or a Sixty?

A student does not turn in a project. You record a zero in the gradebook. When it comes time to determine the student's mark at the end of the grading period, you have to make a decision: Do I keep the zero or turn it into a sixty in order to make the grading scale fair? (Note: Some teachers choose fifty or seventy as the new value.)

Few aspects of grading cause as much consternation among teachers as this one. On the surface, it seems like the student could literally sit on his or her rear end and do nothing for an entire grading period and still earn sixties on all the tests and projects. It's wrong, we think, to give students points when they didn't do anything—in fact, it's cheating. This is a very understandable conclusion on the part of teachers, but it's incorrect.

When we turn students' zeros into sixties in our gradebooks, we are not giving students something for doing nothing. We're adjusting the grade intervals so that any averaging we do is mathematically justified but, even more important, that any grade we determine from the pattern of grades is a valid indicator of mastery.

Consider the intervals for each grade in the 100-point scale. In many classrooms, an A ranges from ninety to one hundred, a distance of eleven points. B's, C's, and D's have almost the same range, ten points each. When it comes to an F, however, there is a sixty-point range of possibility. A zero has an undeserved and devastating influence, so much so that no matter what the

I never give zeros. If an assignment is forever missing, it goes in my book as a fifty. That's an F–, punishment enough. Entering zero has devastating mathematical consequences on grade averages, often putting students into an irrecoverable position. Why bother to keep working when you know nothing you can do will bring that average up to passing? I want them working, not shut down.

If we entered grades as forty/A–, thirty/B–, twenty/C–, ten/D–, zeros would be OK. But, with ninety/A–, eighty/B–, seventy/C–, and sixty/D–, fifty is an F–. Entering zero in the gradebook is the equivalent of giving a kid a K–. For that reason, if a kid miserably fails a test—for example, a score of 35 percent—I put it in as fifty/F–.

Fifty/F– is low enough. If kids never turn in work, or consistently fail tests, they will still average an F and fail. But, if they just have a few bad days, they can raise their average with quality work and pass.

—Susan Bischoff, secondary teacher

student does, the grade distorts the final grade as a true indicator of mastery. Mathematically and ethically this is unacceptable. Figure 11.1 shows the negative impact of a zero on the 100-point grading scale.

Does a string of perfect papers for a grading period combined with one paper not submitted equate to a C+ level of mastery? No. The B+ is a more accurate rendering of what the student knows and is able to do as a total, which is what we are trying to portray with grades. In addition, if the zero was earned in the first half of the grading period or even just once in a consistent string of other grades, and we are grading on a trend because we want to be current in our evaluation of the student's mastery, we might even drop that one score and use the majority of grades, and the most recent, so the student earns an A for the grading period.

In Virginia Beach, Virginia, school board member Emma L. Davis argues against recording zeros for students who didn't do work or scored less than sixty on assessments using a 100-point system. She compares the practice to taking temperature readings over time.

Consider trying to find the average temperature over five days and recording eighty-five, eighty-two, eighty-three, and eighty-six, then forgetting a day and recording zero. The average temperature would be sixty-seven, a figure that does not accurately show the weather from that week. If those temperatures were grades, a student would fail after consistently earning B's and C's. (Gruss 2005)

A reminder: In differentiated classes, the grade must be accurate in order to be useful. We avoid any practice that would decrease a grade's accuracy.

The 4-point grading scale is also guilty of this concern, if we use it to calculate percentages. The zero we would use on the 4-point scale if the student didn't turn in the paper doesn't keep the student's percentage the same as would be obtained by using the sixty points we give the student's zero on the

Figure 11.1 Negative Impact of a Zero on the 100-Point Grading Scale

Test Scores for Six Tests	Percentage	Grade
0, 100, 100, 100, 100, 100	83	C+
100, 100, 60, 100, 100, 100	93	B+

100-point scale. In fact, the percentage on the 4-point scale when we incorporate the zero is the same as the percentage we record when using a zero on the 100-point scale. See Figure 11.2.

To reconcile this, we have to declare 1.0, not zero, as the failing and/or unscorable level on a 4.0 rubric. A 1.0 is what we record if a student doesn't do his work or gets less than an F on the test. If we use 1.0 as the bottom score of a 4-point grading scale, the resulting average is more in line with our goals of not penalizing a student's average beyond repair for one assignment not completed. See Figure 11.3.

When determining the overall grade using the 4-point scale, however, most of us use the mean—we add the scores and divide by the number of scores. When we do this, the zero does not have as devastating an impact on the overall grade as it does when turning 4-point scale scores into percentages (100-point scale). See Figure 11.4. To mitigate the undue, negative influence of a zero on the overall grade, teachers use smaller, rubric-size, grading scales.

While the B shown in the figure is closer to the student's actual mastery, given so many A's earned, it's not entirely accurate. Most of us grade on a trend and would record an A if this student earned this many A's in a row. We'd be looking at the median and mode, not the mean.

Of course, in both scales, we can record an I for "Incomplete" for the short term, and later record zeros or sixties, or adjust that scale to 1.0 for failure if the student doesn't do the assignment.

If the bottom line for a differentiated class is to make grades as accurate as possible, it makes the most sense to round zeroes and any grade less than a

Figure 11.2 Comparing the Negative Impact of Zero on the 4-Point and 100-Point Scales

Test Scores for Six Tests	Percentage	Grade
4.0, 4.0, 4.0, 4.0, 4.0, 0	83	C+
100, 100, 100, 100, 100, 0	83	C+

Figure 11.3 Using 1.0 as the Low Score on the 4-Point Scale

Test Scores for Six Tests	Average	Grade
1.0, 4.0, 4.0, 4.0, 4.0, 4.0	88%	B

Figure 11.4 Using the Mean on the 4-Point Scale

Test Scores for Six Tests	Mean	Grade
0, 4, 4, 4, 4, 4	3.3	B
1, 4, 4, 4, 4, 4	3.5	B+

sixty (or seventy) to a sixty (or seventy) when we average grades on a 100-point scale. If this is difficult to accept, then recording an I for missing assignments that later turns into a zero if not completed is probably best, though we may not choose to use the zero as we document progress, provide feedback, or inform our instructional decisions subsequently.

This is one more proof that grading scales and systems we currently use do not always support our teaching/learning goals. There's more than enough compelling justification to pursue alternative forms of feedback and record-keeping that don't require us to use less than desirable math manipulations to communicate student achievement. We're waiting for someone to step up to the plate and figure it out.

Potential concern: Some of us may be afraid that a student who earns a zero that has been adjusted up to a sixty can brag about how he can achieve those sixties without learning or producing anything. We're afraid other students will try it.

Think about this for a moment. In most school districts in which sixty and below is an F, this means failure. What sense does it make, then, for the student to claim to classmates, "Hey, check it out: I didn't do the project, and I still got an F," which is what he or she is declaring. The correlation between hard work, learning, and achieving success is still clear: If we act irresponsibly and/or don't learn, we fail, and failure is failure, no matter the degree.

Adjusting zeros to sixty is not giving students something for having done nothing. It's adjusting the grading scale so that it is ethically justifiable, so that each grade has an appropriate amount of influence on the student's summative evaluation and the grade can be used in decision making. Marking zeros as sixties still means the student failed; it's just using the upper, more constructive and recoverable end of the F range. If grades are to be accurate—and they have to be accurate in order to provide feedback, document progress, and inform our instructional decisions—then we have to adjust all zeros accordingly. An F does not state that the student is misbehaving or a cognitive "loser." It means only that the student failed to demonstrate mastery. The cause isn't important. Whether it was due to immaturity or lack of understanding, our response is the same: investigate and take action.

Grading Gifted Students

For some students, the regular classroom does not meet their needs. It is too slowly paced and too simplistic, or prevents them from using and demonstrating their advanced understanding and skills. They have the mental ilk and skill sets that go beyond what is typically found in children of their age.

Within this group, however, there are gradations of giftedness. Some are advanced beyond the regular classroom, but not so far as to be considered genuinely gifted, geniuses, or prodigies. Still, the regular classroom cannot meet their needs and something must be done. Then there are those students who are gifted in a single subject. They might be taking high school geometry in fifth or sixth grade, but they cannot write a basic paragraph or grasp the idea of checks and balances in our government. There are some students who are gifted in music, the arts, and sports, but when it comes to other courses, they flounder. Finally, there are those students who excel at everything, who need to be significantly accelerated, even to the point of skipping three or four grade levels. Though I disagree with some of its recommendations, the 2004 Templeton National Report on Acceleration, *A Nation Deceived*, makes a compelling case for considering such acceleration.

I think just giving [gifted students] that democratic feel to the curriculum also in and of itself makes differentiation happen. It also gives students a reason to care about what they are learning. In as much as possible, I've worked to let them have a voice in how we study the topics that are required by my curriculum. This helps them take ownership and helps those that are capable take the leadership role and, in some cases, step forward to share a personal interest or hobby that accelerates where the curriculum would have otherwise taken us.

—Marsha Ratzel, secondary teacher

For those students who go on to advanced grade levels or coursework, we grade them according to those upper classes' grading protocols; the profoundly gifted thirteen-year-old is graded against the same criteria as his sixteen-year-old classmates. On the other hand, for the students who remain in their current grade level but experience an enriched curriculum that better meets their gifted needs, teachers may find themselves in an awkward grading situation:

Do we give them an automatic A for the regular education material we teach because supposedly they have surpassed it?

Do we instead set more rigorous standards that go beyond the course description, then hold them to those standards? If we do, how is that justified to students and parents if they are kept in a regular education course?

What if these students are truly challenged and end up earning only a B or C on the advanced material? Will their report cards reflect the advanced level and we weigh the grades accordingly, or will they come across as B or C students in regular education studies?

Here's an eighth-grade American history teacher's dilemma with her own child:

My twelve-year old just finished sixth grade. She was in honors math and seminar (pullout program for gifted). She struggled with the math . . . and has now come to the conclusion that she does not want to be smart anymore, because it is too hard. She works harder than her friends do in all her classes, has extra work on top of it with seminar, and is expected from her parents to put her best into everything. When she slacks off and earns a B, she knows and we do as well, that she could have done better. It is hard to teach children the importance of doing your best when they do that and do not get the recognition they think they deserve in the form

of a higher grade. This is one reason why I dislike letter grades and the importance our society and historically, education, has placed on them.
—Carolyn Beitzel, Beverly Hills Middle School, Upper Darby, PA

Remember, in a differentiated classroom, we choose to do what's fair, not equal. In order to be accurate, useful, and fair, grades for gifted students will require special considerations.

One concern with gifted students in the regular education class is to make sure they have mastered all the material that the other students have mastered before or while experiencing the enriched curriculum. A high grade in an advanced curriculum means not only have these students done well with the advanced material, but they have also mastered the regular material. With these students we compact the curriculum to a shorter time frame, then do something different, often something connected to the unit of study that everyone else is studying, while the rest of the class continues with the regular unit.

We assess these students and provide feedback regarding their work with the advanced material; but for the assessment that impacts the report card grade, we focus on those regular education, essential understandings and their inherent content, concepts, and skills. We incorporate the more sophisticated material in the assessments, but now the problem becomes how to report their progress.

Ideally, we'd have sections of the report card dedicated to both grade-level and advanced material. Since most of us don't have such capacities on our school's report card, one response is to record the grade that reflects the highest achievement made regarding the grade-level material, then note the student's achievement with the advanced material in the comments section—assuming we have a place on the report card to make such comments. Some middle and high school report cards allow teachers to select narrative comments only from a preapproved list of options, and much of the time, those options do not accurately reflect the comments we want to communicate about all students. In such situations, then, it's helpful for the teacher or school to use an addendum to the main school or district report card in which the teacher can report the student's achievements in more detail. The addendum is stapled to or sent home with the regular report card.

This is what we do when students are in the regular classroom and get advanced work to do while in the class. For students enrolled in the honors version of the regular course, however, the best route is to grade them against those more challenging standards. The grade earned describes the proficiency with both the regular and advanced material, not just the regular material. The report card indicates the advanced material by listing the name of the class, such as "Algebra I Honors" or "Biology II."

The report card provides clear and accurate communication of the student's progress. If the current reporting format does not allow for that, we change the format or we add clarifying reports of our own design to help everyone involved have a better picture of the student's achievement. This is better than shrugging and saying, "Oh well. My hands are tied. I'll force the student's advanced experiences into the limited symbols and spaces on the regular card, even though someone's interpretation of those marks could be distorted by its format."

Weighting Grades

The issue of weighting grades as more influential than others when tabulating a final grade is important to consider. Marsha's comments below are correct in that teachers sometimes double-weight some components of instruction by weighting items for individual assessment grades then weighting them again when calculating final percentages for the grading period. We have to be careful.

For most of us, the more complex and demanding a task or concept is, the more credit we want to give students for having mastered it. Credit proportional to achievement is the rule. Following this principle, some school districts give more weight to grades earned in higher-level courses. Since the grades carry more weight, students are supposedly more motivated to enroll in those advanced courses in order to improve their grade-point average. Dr. Guskey, however, claims that, "We know of no evidence that shows [weighted grades] serve to motivate students to enroll in more challenging courses or dissuade students from enrolling in lower-level or remedial courses" (Guskey and Bailey 2001, p. 134). He adds that weighted grades are used primarily to sort students, to select students for placements on the honor roll, and to determine who will be valedictorian.

A grade needs to be accurate, and if an A in one class represents a much better and broader achievement than an A in another class, it should be noted in some way in the student's transcript. Whether the turbo-powered A should carry more weight in the overall GPA is another matter, however. In addition, each of us will weight different elements heavier than others, once again raising

> My fourteen-year-old took an advanced math placement course, worked her tail end off doing two hours of homework a day, plus working on projects over some weekends only to get B's all year, finally pulling it up to an A at the end of the year. Her GPA for the year was something like 3.85 and she pointed out that had she taken a regular math course, it would likely have been a 4.0. She understands that she learned and did more than the other kids, but still didn't think it fair that her grades didn't reflect the harder work she was doing. She also wasn't invited to the end-of-year awards night. Was she basically being punished for being smart? Just what do grades really mean anyway?
>
> —Roxanne, secondary teacher

> I could weight these categories if I wanted to, but I tend to think that weighting makes things messy and I choose not to do that with percentages. I do that by the number of items I pick to include in a category and it takes care of itself. Otherwise it seems to me . . . that you double-weight. If I give twice as many problems for students to solve and then I weight it by percentage, then I think I have doubly weighted the value of that assignment.
>
> —Marsha Ratzel, secondary teacher

I teach sixth-grade LD kids in math, reading and language arts. Each subject is graded differently because I . . . need to grade them according to their educational and IEP needs. For example, in math, they are graded this way: preparation/participation, 20 percent; binder, 20 percent; tests/quizzes, 20 percent; homework, 20 percent; projects, 20 percent. The majority of my students do not perform well on tests, so I count the projects the same weight; this gives them an alternative assessment to demonstrate knowledge and understanding. . . . I count being prepared with proper materials as crucial.

—Laurie Wasserman, secondary teacher

Is one of the contributors to the grading problem because we hold time constant over all students? If they learn at different rates, we ignore that because we have to hold time constant . . . we can't move them along to the new unit or the next grade until they have spent the requisite amount of time in grade level.

What if grades reflected learning and time was variable based on how well you could accomplish the learning objectives? . . . Each foreign service officer is given a rating based on their new language ability. When they reach a certain level of proficiency that matches the task they are going to do, they "graduate." Some people fly through, others take a little more time, and some take a huge chunk of time. What if our schools looked more like that and grades showed you where you were on finishing up with the learning you needed to go on to the next thing?

—Marsha Ratzel, secondary teacher

the cloud of subjectivity over our supposedly objective grading plan. Some of us weight grades according to what students need, such as Laurie Wasserman notes in her comment on the left.

We weight grades every time we count tests more than quizzes and quizzes more than homework. We also weight grades every time we grade students for following a particular process in addition to grading the resulting final products. Does the grade for successfully memorizing physics formulas and vocabulary beat the grade for being able to apply those same physics ideas and vocabulary to new and unique situations? It depends on what we deem more important, memorization or application. We can't achieve the latter without the former in many cases, but the latter is the more important outcome.

For now, most highly accomplished differentiating teachers are comfortable weighting grades on assignments or in gradebook categories according to the complexity and extent of learning achieved in each one. In a differentiated class, however, every student is given as many tools as necessary for advanced achievement and thereby, more weighted grades. No one is turned away from opportunities to experience depth nor the acknowledgments of those successful undertakings in a differentiated class.

Of course, weighted grades often result in higher grade-point averages on transcripts, with some higher than 4.0—the high point on most grading scales. To what extent, however, are those grade-point averages significantly predictive of future success in college or life? Sure there's often a correlation between a student's successful performance in high school and his or her subsequent success in college or life; however, past a certain point, the high GPA loses its ability to distinguish between students. Rarely can we identify a qualifiable or quantifiable difference in work products later in life for students earning 4.25 or 4.3 grade-point averages in high school. Any pay scale increases or awards earned by that 4.3 student as a result of such a score would be unjustified.

We all know individuals who had a 2.0 grade-point average in high school who matured while in college and graduated with a 3.0 or higher. Many of us were in this group ourselves. We also know students with a high GPA in high school who were put on academic probation in college due to lack of achievement. Colleges and universities realize this happens. More and more of them are looking for evidence of academic proficiency and commitment beyond just the grade-point average as a result. The GPA is not sufficiently predictive of future success.

Grade-point averages also help us identify class valedictorians. For what purpose, however, do we identify the one student in school with the most statistical fortitude when grades can be so subjective, relative, and prone to inaccurate accounting of students' mastery? And when it comes down to who is selected for all the accolades and honors, the differences between students are often a matter of tenths or hundredths of a decimal point. Is this the dubious criteria in which we place such high academic virtue?

Mastery and achievement are not that precise. It's impossible to delineate absolute achievement as more or less in such minute comparisons. When we select valedictorians, then, we arbitrarily anoint one student as more worthy of celebration and affirmation than multitudes of others, even those graded only one hundredth of a decimal point away. Even if they were a full decimal point away, the practice is questionable.

There is no value to the school or student body in identifying a valedictorian. Such a position to be filled does not entice students to work harder, and it often places unhealthy pressure on students who are already under enough stress. Let's find ways to celebrate everyone's achievements and milestones instead. It's time to retire identifying a class valedictorian and class rankings as conventional practices. They both serve little or no predictive or affirmative purpose, they cause more bad feelings than good, and they are the antithesis of a school's mission to nurture students and their potential.

Automaticity Versus Concept Attainment

When grading, teachers have to consider whether the grade accurately represents a student's automaticity with the subject or his or her coming to know the subject. *Automaticity* refers to how deftly and efficiently the student responds to the task. Here's an example.

> If we want students to determine the total area of three congruent parallelograms, and they are given the area of one of the two triangles that make up half of one of the parallelogram's total area, we'd like them to be able to solve this automatically. Students know that a triangle's formula for area is: (1/2)(base)(height), so doubling a triangle's area reveals one full parallelogram's area (base)(height), and tripling that one parallelogram's area is the answer to the problem.

A part of this solution requires that students know that all three parallelograms will have the same area because they are all equal in size and shape, per the description of the shapes as congruent. Putting the response efficiently, then, we'd like students to realize that if they're given the area of one of the triangles within one of the parallelograms, it's a quick matter of doubling that area, then tripling that new answer, to arrive at the proper response to the problem.

If students are just beginning to grasp such thinking, they may take more time to solve the problem, using drawings and written steps to guide their thinking. When it comes time to grade them, we'll have to consider whether these steps are allowable. They may reflect a student who is still in the concept development phase of his learning. This is what we mean when we consider automaticity versus concept attainment: Are there stipulations, considerations, angles of understanding that we must address or for which we hold students accountable while we grade?

Samples of Automaticity Versus Concept Attainment in Science, History, or Mathematics

Automaticity. Students consistently choose the proper graph for a given situation, plot the information efficiently, then use the information as a tool for their arguments or observations about a topic. They can also quickly point to errors in graphs, such as improper uses of a particular format (using a bar graph when a line graph better reveals the longitudinal pattern we are seeking), improper interpretations of data, and how an axis's improper intervals distort conclusions about the data.

Concept Attainment. Students are just beginning to learn the basics of different types of graphs—line graph, bar graph, pie graph, scatter plot, and box-and-whisker plot. They can recognize and name the types, format the graphs, plot the data, and answer questions about the data properly as well as extrapolate inferences about future events or other scenarios.

English/Language Arts Samples

Automaticity. Students can quickly identify what role any word plays in a sentence based on its location and relation to other words. In addition, students incorporate parts of speech and their roles naturally as they edit each other's papers:

"This part is confusing, Ravi, because there is no *antecedent* for this pronoun."

"Use the *adverb*, 'well,' not the adjective, 'good' after verbs."

"That's the wrong *conjunction* for here, Sonja. You're contrasting two ideas that are opposites of each other. You should use, 'but,' not 'and.'"

"Keisha, get rid of the *interjections*. They ruin the momentum and they are too melodramatic."

Concept Attainment. Students learn the nine parts of speech and how to identify them: noun, pronoun, verb, adverb, adjective, conjunction, interjection, objects, and subjects.

How do we know whether to go for automaticity or for concept attainment with a particular student or group of students? We examine the essential understandings within the standards we're teaching and assess the extent of their mastery by the student(s). We consider our own definition of mastery (see Chapter 2) and determine whether students live up to that description.

Something to consider: Differentiating teachers don't limit students' exposure to advanced or sophisticated material just because they haven't yet mastered the foundations. There are some math teachers, for example, who don't teach Algebraic methods and concepts to students who have yet to master the multiplication tables to fifteen. These teachers err in thinking that learning is mostly sequential—students being allowed to take the next step only when the previous one is passed.

Learning isn't as linear as we think; it's more episodic. Connections are made in students' minds in millions of ways we can't witness. The advanced ideas to which we expose students with or without foundations provide context and motivation for learning those basic ideas. Great differentiating teachers teach advanced concepts while also filling in the missing foundations in those students who need them. They let students use calculators when working with advanced ideas, for instance, but not when mastering their multiplication tables. Everyone at every level tries word problems, makes analogies, analyzes literary devices, investigates errors, finds evidence for claims, and thinks critically—all at their own pace and in their own way. As differentiating teachers, we don't limit students, we get out of their way.

For many units of study, the first year of learning the material is for concept attainment. The automaticity comes in subsequent years of application. Even in those lessons in which automaticity is expected during that first year of exposure, however, we can respond to both concept attainment and automaticity via formative assessments and feedback during instruction.

The key is to remember what we're going for as we design our assessments. If students are just attaining the concept, for example, we don't force them to do a large number of test items in a short time period. That would be a test of automaticity. Alternatively, if we're looking for students to demonstrate automaticity, we don't give them test items that focus purely on where students are in their understanding of individual aspects of the concept.

Grading Late Work

If a student turns in work a day late, most teachers grade the assignment, but lower the grade one full letter grade for being late. Two days late equals two letter grades lower. We continue with three and four days and lowering grades until it's a complete failure, and the student wonders, "Why bother?" Surprisingly, many teachers and parents continue to encourage the student to do the missing work even though it's still an F, as if doing the work would teach them the content. I disagree.

Driving an assignment into the ground like this doesn't serve anyone. While there should be consequences for not meeting deadlines, we can still spend time investigating the situation before arbitrarily lowering the grade. In addition, keeping up students' hope that hard work even after the deadline will deliver a positive response in the grade works. Very few students learn from experiences in which there is no hope for positive academic recognition for mastery obtained.

One of the first things to consider is whether the student's late submission of assignments is chronic or occasional. If it's occasional, then it's easy to be merciful: Let the student turn it in late for full credit. Teachers turn things in late all the time, as do workers in every profession. The idea that "You can't get away with turning work in late in the real world, mister" isn't true. Flights are delayed every day, cars are not fixed until the day after they are promised, and dentists often run a bit late as the day progresses. The student has earned our goodwill and flexibility with weeks or months of on-time performance, so we can extend the courtesy.

If it's chronic, however, it's time to teach the student about the power of being on time. There are many already-mentioned ways to do this, but because your colleagues do it and it seems reasonable, you may have to lower the grade for each day late. The problem, of course, is that this new grade is tainted and is no longer useful to the differentiating teacher.

In this situation, record two grades for the student: one that represents his level of mastery or performance regarding the material, and one that reflects the late penalties. For example, a student could earn an A/D. When it comes time to document progress and inform instructional decisions, use the accurate rendering of mastery, not the grade decreased by the tardy response. Your decisions and documentation will be useful.

Reconsider whether it needs to be a whole grade lower for each day late in order to be of consequence to the student. It doesn't. Take a few points off for every day an assignment is late, but not a whole grade. A whole grade lower is punitive, a few points off is instructive. The student will still learn, and you keep the experience from becoming a vicious black hole to both parties. Even more important, the grade stays close to being an accurate rendering of mastery.

No matter what, if a student is chronically late with assignments, we have to investigate. We don't simply admonish the student and record the F. There is something wrong. It could be the level of instruction, the student's home schedule, an emotional issue, lack of resources, cultural insensitivity, miscommunication, auditory processing issues, or something else. We help students advocate for themselves, not just hold them accountable. Student accountability without purpose is one reason why students drop out and schools fail. If students leave—physically or emotionally—there's no one to teach, and if that's the case, why are you wasting time reading this book? We teach and assess in ways that keep students in school.

Let's deal with late work in ways that lead to students' personal investment and to learning the material.

Grading Special Needs Students in Inclusion Classes

Grading in an inclusion class can be awkward if the regular education teacher and the special education teacher do not share the same philosophy regarding each person's role in the inclusion class. To ease grading issues, then, it's wise for inclusion partners to clarify and mutually agree on their roles and grading philosophies and for the school administration to clarify how grading will be done for special education students included in mainstream classes.

The most effective and accurate approach used by most of us who've been teaching inclusion classes over the years is to consider all students in the classroom as the regular education teacher's students, not some of them belonging to one teacher and some belonging to the other teacher. The regular education teacher has his or her eye on the mandated curriculum and each student's progress toward mastering it. The special education teacher may or may not have expertise in the class's curriculum—a definite advantage if she does, but not always realistic in every situation. The special education teacher brings expertise regarding how best to teach students with the identified needs as well as dedicated focus on the student's individualized education plan (IEP) goals. He or she informs the regular education teacher of those goals and works with him or her to make the accommodations necessary for the student to maximize achievement in the class.

When it comes time to complete report cards, philosophical agreement is critical. If it's not there, there's a lot of unproductive friction. For example, if the regular education teacher believes providing accommodations for special needs students dilutes the rigor of learning and accountability for those students, he or she will think any high grades earned do not equal the same high standards of excellence earned by regular education students who've also earned high grades. The regular education teacher will have trouble recording special needs students' high grades on their report cards. This teacher has an inaccurate understanding of differentiated instruction, of course, and would require professional development in that area.

The special education teacher may report that the student has demonstrated wonderful growth over the course of the grading and ask the grade to be high to indicate that growth. This brings up a major dilemma, however: Should the grade represent progress over time or should it represent the extent of a student's mastery of standards set forth for all his classmates at the grade level in this subject?

If the report card allows teachers to indicate that a grade needs to be interpreted in some way when reading it—that is, the grade does not indicate the same level of mastery as that same grade earned by other students—then the regular education teacher can relax: He's not giving a false A because it was an adjusted curriculum and the report card is marked as such. If this is not possible, however, the regular education teacher is going to be frustrated. For suggestions on how to handle this, see Chapter 14 on report card formats.

Both sides must agree on what is the healthiest approach for grading each special needs student in light of the long-term goals for him or her and the curriculum. For some, a less-then-perfect compromise is achieved when a student's personal progress against IEP goals is recorded only on a report card addendum, and grades on the regular report card reflect only how the child is doing against the standards set for all children. While this is accurate, it can be disheartening to special needs students because it is inappropriate to hold them accountable for standards that are developmentally unattainable. All differentiated instruction centers on developmentally appropriate curriculum.

A healthier compromise is a detailed discussion of the special needs student's progress between the regular and special education teachers. The regular education teacher identifies the standards that should be mastered by report card time, and the special education teacher indicates whether such standards are developmentally appropriate for the student. If they are, then both teachers look for evidence in the student's work products—oral, written, or otherwise. If the student took a different route via accommodations or differentiated instruction but still managed to demonstrate close to what regular education students were required to demonstrate, there's no problem. The student is graded against the expected standards for all students.

If the special education teacher indicates that the standards are developmentally inappropriate, then the student is evaluated against a different set of standards or modified curriculum, and both teachers identify evidence for accomplishment of those new standards. Of course, this conversation should have happened at the beginning of the grading period, but it also happens at report card time. It does no one—the student, the family, the teacher, or the school—any good to grade a student against developmentally inappropriate curriculum. Such a grade destroys hope critical to success, and the grade is useless for instructional planning, providing feedback, or documenting progress. Again, the question is not how to equitably assign grades, it's how to do what's fair and developmentally appropriate.

As with all difficult issues in education, solutions for grading come in two ways: through conversation and constant reexamination. While the comments about the various grading issues discussed in this chapter may help in some situations, they won't in all. Establish a climate and inclination in your building for this school year that allows teachers and administrators to explore grading issues constructively. Chapter 15 contains specific ideas on how to do this.

CHAPTER 12

Grading Scales

Two of the most popular grading scales used in secondary classrooms are the 4-point and 100-point scales. For this discussion, 4-point scales refer to the collective group of smaller grading scales, including 3.0 and 5.0. Scales based on 100 refer to any scale in which a percentage is obtained, including the grading approach whereby students earn specific amounts of points out of a larger total (such as earning 270 points out a possible 300) and then that number is translated into the equivalent percentage. While many teachers claim their particular discipline requires the use of a 100-point scale instead of a smaller scale, the case can be made for the 4-point scale as the more prudent choice in most assessments in all subjects. Let's take a look at the rationale.

First, the smaller the scale we use, the higher the inter-rater reliability. This means an A in Mr. Green's class represents the same level of mastery as an A in Mrs. White's class across the hall or across the school district. In order for this to happen, very clear and mutually agreed-on descriptors must be used. When we as teachers all agree on each point value's descriptor, we're more consistent in our grading. We will still elevate and de-elevate different aspects of each unit we teach, however, no matter how many clarifying conversations we have or how many promises we make with one another as colleagues, but it's a start. Smaller scales make individual distortions less likely, so if consistency is important, we'll use them more often than larger scales.

At first glance, one would think that smaller scales in which teachers use rubrics to make informed declarations of mastery would be more subjective.

We're interpreting the student's work rather than observing how the numbers add up to a grade. This is not the case, however. Larger scales, such as ones that use 100 or 300 points are more subjective. The smaller scale in which point values are correlated directly with clearly defined criteria keep us focused on the credible justification for each grade. In larger scales, it's easier for teachers to fudge numbers based on nonacademic factors, and in some cases, hide observations of mastery behind the grade averages.

For example, let's look at one classroom in which the lowest A average a student can have is a 94 percent. A student asks his teacher, "My average is a 93.4. Can't you just give me the A? I'm so close." The teacher replies, "You just didn't have that last ounce of 'umph' to get yourself over the top. This was pure mathematical calculation, and numbers don't lie. It wouldn't be fair. You'll stay with a B+."

The teacher in this scenario took himself or herself out of the picture. The teacher wasn't focused on mastery but on justifying a grade. In truth, it's easier to defend a grade to students and their parents when the numbers add up to what we proclaim. It's when we seriously reflect on student mastery and make a professional decision that some teachers get nervous, doubt themselves, and worry about rationalizing a grade. These reflections are made against clear criteria, however, and they are based on our professional expertise, so they are often more accurate. Sterling Middle School assistant principal Tom Pollack agrees. He comments, "If teachers are just mathematically averaging grades, we're in bad shape."

Marzano mentions considerable meta-analyses of educational studies that show that a grade based on frequent use of rubrics with clear descriptors results in a more accurate rendering of students' mastery at the end of the grading period, while basing a grade primarily on mathematical averages often distorts its accuracy (Marzano 2000, pp. 61–62). If this is true, it would seem prudent to use 4.0 rubrics all the time. This is difficult to do, however. Some tasks just lend themselves better to 100-point scales, such as a quick quiz in which students' scores are determined by observing the number correct out of the number possible. One could argue that a rubric could have been used for a short quiz, too, but there may not have been time to create a rubric, and we needed something quick to guide our next steps with students.

In order to create objective, accurate grades, then, we should use a rubric in the majority of our assessments, but not fret if we use pure, mathematical calculations as well. Our grades will still be fairly accurate, and we'll be able to sleep at night. Because rubrics take a while to create, revise, and use consistently, it may take two to three years before we are comfortable with them once we start using them regularly. Each time we create one and use it, however, it gets easier to do. Chapter 4 has ideas on how to design good rubrics.

By the way, when grading with a smaller scale such as we do when using rubrics, we can grade on a trend and use what Ken O'Connor refers to as the

Logic Rule (2002, p. 156). He says that if we see mostly 4's and 5's on a 5.0 series of rubrics across a student's row in the gradebook, for example, we are justified in giving the student an A for the grading period. If we see mostly 3's and 4's, a B is warranted. He suggests that it is not necessary to calculate every grade down to the hundredths decimal place.

Rick Stiggins et al. suggest something similar in his Decision Rule conversions (2004, p. 319). For example, Stiggins recommends:

> [If] at least 50% of the ratings are 5's and the rest are 4's, the grade is an A, [if] at least 75% of the ratings are 4's or better and the other 25% are not lower than 3, then the grade is a B, and [if] 40% of the ratings are 3's or better and the other 60% are not lower than 2, then the [grade] is a C.

It continues to D and F as well, looking at the general trend of 5.0 rubric ratings as the determining factor for the final grade, not the pure, absolute mathematical average of the scores. In short, most experts and teaching veterans agree that our decisions based on the consistency of evidence (the grade pattern) and our professional opinions via rubrics will generate an accurate appraisal and mark.

What happens when we grade students using a 100-point scale, but we keep our gradebook in a 4-point scale? We can still make the correlations. For example, if a student earns an 82 percent on a test, this is a C+ grade in some school districts. A C+ is a 2.5 on the 4-point scale, so we write the 2.5 in the gradebook. Whatever grade the average on the 100-point scale equates to is the grade we use on the 4-point scale; it's just written with the 4-point scale value.

Sample Scale Correlation

100-Point Scale	Grade	4-Point Scale
100–94	A	4.0
93–90	B+	3.5
89–84	B	3.0
83–80	C+	2.5
79–73	C	2.0
72–70	D+	1.5
69–64	D	1.0
63–0	F	0.0

What about the situation in which a student earns a B, but it's a high B or a low B? Over the course of an entire year, the difference will not be significant in terms of mastery, and mastery is what grades are based on, not averages. This isn't being dismissive, but the reality is that the difference in learning (mastery) between the high and low versions of one particular grade is not that much. In larger grading scales, for example, the difference between a B and a B+ is just a few points. How exact can we be when identifying a student's true mastery of something? Does a 0.01 (1 percent) difference in a grade-point average really mean a discernible, significant difference in mastery? No. It's splitting hairs.

There are some teachers who disagree with this. They claim that there are a large number of mastery points wrapped into each percentage point due to multiple and influential assessments over a long period of time, and that the difference of one percentage point can describe mastery or lack of mastery of a significant amount of material. If this is the case, then whittling grades down to their exact and relative values (offering 2.75's, for example) may be necessary. Each time we are tempted to do this, however, let's remember how elusive declarative mastery is, as well as how subjective we are in the micro-moment of grading each product from each student, and how we make it even more subjective when we aggregate a variety of data for a summative grade. And let's wonder whether having done this, even justifiably, will have any lasting impact ten years down the road. Yes, there are times when delineating minute levels of achievement within a letter grade matter, but there are many times such delineations are not warranted.

In most cases, the only time an exact grade-point average to the hundredths place becomes important is when we're sorting or ranking students, such as we might do when determining the class valedictorian. It's time to question the efficacy of sweating the decimals and ranking students for such things. Whether one student is 0.03 away from another child's score doesn't matter in the big scheme of life. To make such distinctions artificially pins a student's well-being to something superficial, and it deflates many other students' sense of worth. Is this what schools are about—to rank students and put them in their place?

It's dangerous to emphasize something in our schools that has no positive purpose for learning or living. While some of our schools use GPA differences to determine placement in advanced courses, we all recognize the need to rely on other factors, such as preplacement assessment tests, student products, and teacher recommendations, to get a sense of where the student is regarding the subject.

In addition, grade cutoffs and subsequent grade differences are arbitrary. In some states and provinces, the grading scale is: A = 80–100, B = 60–79, C = 40–59, D = 20–39, F = 0–19, which, mathematically, is similar to the 4-point scale. In other states and provinces, the scale is: A = 90–100, B = 80–89, C = 70–79, D = 60–69, and F = 0–59. In my own district, it's: A = 94–100, B = 84–93, C = 73–83, D = 64–72, and F = 0–63. The arbitrary nature of grading scales makes pure declarations of mastery impossible; everything's relative. Anything predicated on grades earned in those grading scales must be interpreted. We can make conclusions about a student's general trend toward mastery, maybe even make a direct inference, but absolute declarations of mastery? No. It wouldn't be accurate.

Teachers who tell students they've earned a high B or a low B aren't helping themselves or their students. Such statements create more resentment and grade myopia than they're worth. Do students who earn the low of a grade level feel motivated to try harder? No. Because true mastery is not an exact science, it makes no sense to try to turn grade representations into such.

Many school districts, including my own, do not allow minus-versions of grades (A–, B–, C–, D–). They aren't useful. Minus grades do not help us guide our instructional decisions and provide feedback, nor do they motivate a student to work harder when he or she receives one. The message students receive from minus grades is similar to: "You're a C student, but a loser of a C student, closer to being a D student." This doesn't make the student want to redouble his or her efforts during the next grading period. In addition, the few points' difference between a legitimate grade and its minus-version is often within the margin of error as we determine mastery; it's not an exact science. Because the positive return is dubious and it can actually damage efforts, it's wiser to remove minus-versions of grades from the grading lexicon. This isn't going soft on students by any means. Keep your standards high. It's recognizing the true nature of mastery. If the student is performing with less than a grade level's standard, have the courage to give a plus-version of the lower grade, not a minus-version of the current one.

Some teachers may struggle with changing numerical averages into opportunities for using rubrics. Although the rubric descriptions in Chapter 4 have more information on generating rubrics, an example here might help:

Task: Solve 2½ divided by 1¼ = ?
Student's Response: 2

100-Point Scale Grading Approach. The student wrote 2 as an answer. If the answer was wrong, we'd look at how he or she worked the problem, but may or may not give credit. The grade is based on the answer. If the student wrote 1.5, he or she would earn a zero for that problem but, more important, would not learn anything from the score.

4-Point Scale Grading Approach. A rubric would have been given to the student prior to the test. Universal "look-fors" would have been identified for the student to demonstrate. For the 4-point standard of excellence, the evaluative criteria might include:

■ The student recognizes the need to convert the mixed numbers into improper fractions for ease in calculating.

- The student understands the need to divide fractions by multiplying by the reciprocal of the second fraction.
- The student multiplies the two improper fractions correctly.
- The student simplifies the answer into lowest terms.
- The student double-checks his or her work to make sure there are no careless errors.
- The student arrives at the correct response.

The student is given full credit for anything from this list that he or she does correctly. If the student seems to understand everything and follows all procedures except for one careless error that results in an incorrect response, he or she might earn a 3.5 or 3.0 instead of the 4.0, but it's not an absolute zero. This is a more accurate rendering of mastery, and it's significantly more useful to the teacher and the student. Anything that needs improvement is circled on the rubric; the student learns something from the scoring of the problem.

"Wait a minute," some readers may say. In the real world, it doesn't matter whether we account for all these universals in the evaluative criteria and give partial credit for portions done correctly; the bottom line is whether the work was completed accurately. We can't give students the notion that they can follow only some of the proper procedures, get the answer wrong, and still be given credit for doing the problem.

These readers are right. Of course, it's not possible to teach such a message. Remember, though, more often than not students are in the concept attainment stage. We're not going for automaticity all the time. We don't expect adult-level competence at every turn. Students are evolving. Unless we're teaching twelfth graders, we can't constantly rally around the real world or college as justifications for all we do. To students, the world beyond school is very far away. We're preparing students to live this one week and month of their lives as competent citizens of our communities. They will still get the connection between success and getting the answer correct.

We're about student learning, and most often that comes from specific and timely feedback during the process of learning, not a tabulation of correct answers. If we're truly focused on mastery, then we'll want to do everything we can to provide that feedback, emphasizing formative over summative feedback as much as possible. Besides, those grades weren't A's. There was a penalty for not getting the right answer, so they were fairly "real world" in how we graded them.

Something else to consider: Smaller grading scales have a higher correlation with outside objective testing (Marzano 2001). If we want to know how students will do on those high-stakes state assessments we give every year, the majority of our classroom assessments during the year should use smaller, rubric-type scales instead of 100-point scales.

For many of us, we think grades based on rubrics are based more on a teacher's personal judgment or opinion than on pure mathematical calculations and are thereby subject to our moods and other potential distortions, making them less accurate. A teacher's personal judgment via a rubric seems to go against the data-driven emphasis we seek in many schools today. If we examine it further, however, we see that our decisions via rubrics are more informed—based on more data, not less—than can be achieved through pure percentage calculations.

An additional benefit of smaller grading scales is that students and their parents focus more on learning, not grades. We get off the grade-myopia train. If we consistently emphasize a learning outcome, standard, or benchmark in our oral and written comments in the classroom, students and their parents adopt the language as well. Instead of students responding that they have to get more problems correct on a test in order to do better in class, they list the concepts and skills they have to master to do well. Growth and achievement rally around listed outcomes, benchmarks, and standards. What a terrific outcome!

One caution: If we primarily use a 4-point scale, many students and their parents will equate the highest numerical value (4.0) with an A, the next highest value with the next highest letter grade, B, and so on. They will wonder why we just don't write A, B, C, D, and F if that's what they really are. No matter how much time we spend wordsmithing our descriptors or how much we emphasize them to students and parents, they won't pay much attention to the descriptors in a 4-point scale. They'll just look at whether the student earned the top, next to the top, middle, next to the bottom, or bottom score. Of course, we use 4.0 rubrics so that students and their parents will focus on the standards via the descriptors, but students and parents won't always do this.

If we want to avoid this natural tendency to bypass the descriptors and attach our own emotional baggage familiarity to each grade, we'll have to use 3.0, 5.0, or 6.0 rubrics. Using a scale that is one or two gradations less or more than the 4-point scale increases the likelihood of everyone actually referencing those helpful descriptors you spent so much time creating.

The following are more grading scales to consider. Which ones promote differentiated practices? Which ones are the most useful, efficient, and easy to interpret by students, their families, and our colleagues?

- A, B, C, and "not-yet-achieved"
- A, B, and "You're not done"
- Proficient, capable, adequate, limited, poor
- Sophisticated, mature, good, adequate, naïve understanding (suggested in McTighe and Wiggins 2001, p. 72)
- Consistently, usually, sometimes, seldom
- Exceptional, strong, capable, developing, beginning, emergent

- Exceeds the standard, meets the standard, making progress, getting started, no attempt
- Exemplary, competent, satisfactory, inadequate, unable to begin effectively, no attempt
- Advanced, proficient, basic, below basic (from Donegal School District, Mount Joy, PA, as described in O'Connor 2002, p. 81)

If rubric assessments are more accurate and the feedback is more useful, it makes sense, then, to incorporate more of them during the year.

Summary and Further Thinking

Grading practices represent what we believe about teaching and learning. It's important that they align with our vision for differentiated instruction. Any practice that hinders a student's full development or the expression of that development should be questioned, and some commonly accepted grading practices are in that hindering category. Schools should never be a place where students who learn differently from their classmates—in pace, style, method, or tools—are made to suffer for that difference.

In differentiated classes we grade on a trend, emphasizing patterns of performance over time. We don't hold a student's past performances against him or her. Embracing such an appropriate grading policy for differentiated instruction can be a scary process if a school's grading culture is purely about documenting deficiencies and sorting students. Successfully differentiated schools create a culture that keeps the focus of grades on how they assist students with learning and teachers with teaching.

As teachers who differentiate, we ceaselessly reexamine what grades mean and how they affect students' lives, and we do not grade the way we do because it was done to us. We opt instead for grading that supports sound pedagogy, making the best of an imperfect system, helping it evolve along the way. We recognize that grades are often subjective inferences that come with emotional baggage that might distort what we're trying to communicate. We're careful to minimize subjectivity and maximize usefulness by removing nonacademic factors from academic marks. Though the former is highly influential of the latter, our current grading approaches do not allow us to delineate between work habits and mastery definitively, so we separate the two in order to be accurate with both. We also realize that smaller grading scales often provide better feedback and are more useful to students and teachers. We try to use them whenever possible in an effort to be valid and reliable teacher to teacher.

The issue for differentiating teachers is not, "How do I equitably assign grades?" Instead, it's: "What is fair for each child?" and "What report card feedback best represents what a child truly learns and promotes the most learning?" Rather than perpetuate ineffective, norm-referenced grades that reflect the tools of assessment (such as tests, the number correct on the tests, and how students did on the tests in relation to others), successful, differentiating teachers focus on criterion-based mastery in relation to essential understandings and their learning objectives.

CHAPTER 13

Gradebook Formats for the Differentiated Classroom

E
verything we do should promote student learning, even when our students' learning is differentiated. Our record-keeping should reflect the learning and differentiation. As we enter data on students, we reflect on their growth and how the lessons we provided helped or hindered that growth. Our gradebooks are records of our actions, in this sense. Since our teaching/learning beliefs are revealed via our actions, we better make sure our beliefs and actions are consistent with one another. If we embrace differentiation, then we need to use gradebook practices that support differentiation.

There is no one gradebook format that works best for all teachers. The best advice, then, is to examine several different types and choose the format that serves our needs best, and that may change over time and may vary according to the courses and grade levels we teach. Flexibility, not rigidity, enables trees to withstand the changing winds; it's good advice for our gradebooks as well.

The good news is that many gradebook formats work well for differentiated classes. Gradebooks keep records, reporting what was achieved, not specific strategies, differentiated or not. Some are more responsive than others, however, so it's wise to consider the format(s) we want to use carefully. To fully consider a gradebook format, ask yourself these questions:

Does this format respond to the differentiated approaches I'm using with my students? If so, how?

Does this gradebook format render an accurate statement of students' mastery—what they know and are able to do?

How does using this gradebook format make grading and assessing students more manageable for me?

Does this gradebook format support my teaching/learning beliefs?

Is this gradebook easily understood by others who may need to see and interpret its pages without me being present?

By using this gradebook format, will I be able to keep up with grading and record-keeping so that I can provide feedback to students, document progress, and inform my instructional decisions in a timely manner?

The following sections describe gradebook formats to consider.

Grouping Assignments by Standard, Objective, or Benchmark

For those classrooms dedicated to standards-based instruction and assessment, the gradebook format shown in Figure 13.1 works well. At any given time, a principal, a parent, a student, and, of course, the teacher can ask how the student is doing regarding a particular benchmark, objective, or standard, and see all the data gathered in one place. When it comes time to determine the grade, we consider the grades for the assignments under each standard, benchmark, or objective (for example, the upper, left-hand grade blank for each student corresponds to the upper, left-hand assignment under the standard) and record them, then we simply look at the pattern of scores in the gray squares horizontally.

Ken O'Connor supports this kind of reporting. He reminds teachers to ". . . not set up grading plans according to methods of assessment" (2002, pp. 50–51), but to instead set them up for assessing learning goals. In keeping with this helpful tone, O'Connor recommends establishing an assessment code, such as recording "f" or "s" next to assessments in the gradebook to indicate whether the assessment was formative or summative. Summative grades are used for final grade determination for the grading period while formative grades are used to guide instructional decisions and chart progress. A separate column or row to indicate "f" or "s" seems wise.

Our LA teachers changed categories from the traditional homework, quizzes/tests, and so on to Voice, Organization, Mechanics, and all the rest of the 6+1 Traits®. Some of our math teachers changed their categories to match the objectives for that quarter and Computation. Their reasoning was that when they looked in their gradebooks, they could see what they needed to do for instructional planning and they could give their students some feedback that would help them know their strengths and weaknesses. Kids knew that their grades were strong in linear tables and graphs but not in algorithms. So they knew that's where they needed to work. Their folks knew it, too. Before they just knew that they had low quiz grades and they were missing two homework assignments. . . . Teachers also knew which kids to pull for extra help on which kinds of instructional pieces.

—Marsha Ratzel, secondary teacher

Figure 13.1 Gradebook for Grading According to Standards

Standards:	Analysis		Synthesis		Prediction			
	Test on Alkalinity	Page 23 Questions	Vocabulary Quiz	Summary of Metals Video	Test on Alkalinity	Inert Gases Behavior Activity		
	Essay on Energy and Matter	Dual Nature of Light Lab Explan.	Test on Periodic Table of Elements	Comic Strip of Covalent vs. Ionic Bonds	Heisenberg Uncertainty Principle Lab	Dual Nature of Light Lab Explan.	Average	Grade
Ballard, Bob								
Carson, Rachel								
Ride, Sally								
Sagan, Carl								

Figure 13.2 contains an example of one way to go based on an idea from O'Connor's book, *How to Grade for Learning.*

This is a huge step for teachers. O'Connor quotes a 1996 work by Marzano and Kendall who say:

> *First and foremost, the teacher must stop thinking in terms of assignments, tests, and activities to which points are assigned, and start thinking in terms of levels of performance in the declarative and procedural knowledge specific to her subject area. . . . [T]he use of columns in a gradebook to represent standards, instead of assignments, tests, and activities, is a major shift in thinking for teachers (O'Connor 2002, pp. 147 and 150)*

Imagine the different conversations and the resulting insights we'll have when we stop categorizing a student's achievement in terms of the assessment formats used, and instead use the standards by which he or she was assessed. We move from "Tanika scored well on the first three tests, but blew it on the last one, so her grade is a C," to "Tanika understands the powerful impact of

Figure 13.2 Summary of Evidence Format

Achievement Evidence

Student: Date:

Assessments/ Strands													Summary
Math calculations and problem solving													
Graphing													
Algebraic concepts													
Use of the graphing calculator													
Uses appropriate resources to resolve confusion													
Exponents and radicals													
Comments													

Report Card Grade*: _____

*This is the most consistent level of achievement with consideration for more recent achievement.

the Byzantine Empire in the early Middle Ages as well as the impact of Charlemagne's rule and the ongoing battles among the Turks, Christians, and Muslims, but she is struggling with how events in the last two hundred years of the Middle Ages led to so many changes in government, science, and man's view of himself during the Renaissance." The first comment tells us nothing, but the second one provides plenty of information to which we can respond.

To get an idea of what such a gradebook structure might yield on a report card, look at the example in Figure 14.1, which is based on Robert Marzano's suggested report card format: For it, he used the McREL Institute model described in the next chapter.

One of the potential concerns with this format is that our assessments often incorporate more than one standard, benchmark, or objective. Does this mean we have to record the assignment under more than one standard and, because of that, give more than one grade on each assignment?

Yes. When we see that assignment or assessment are recorded in more than one column, we know that the grade in each column reflects the grade on the assessment for the column's stated standard, not just one overall grade inclusive of everything, simply counted twice (or more, if more than two standards are involved).

Recording more than one grade for the same assignment is more work, sure, but the grades are more accurate and useful. Is it worth it? That depends on where we are in our personal and professional lives. To be honest, recording grades that aren't very accurate or are so generalized as to be relatively useless to teachers and students, also seems like a waste of time. Anything we can do to increase the usefulness of grades is a worthwhile endeavor.

Also, as we grade the fifth and sixth papers of the 180 we have to grade, we catch on to patterns. We know what to look for in students' work. This is a mental "groove" that makes us efficient in assessing students' products. When we're in this state of alertness, we can keep track of more than one rubric in our minds as we assess. It's not that much more of an effort to record two or three grades at the top of a test than it is to write one, especially when clarifying comments are already provided on the rubrics themselves.

Grouping Assignments by Weight or Category

In the gradebook format shown in Figure 13.3, assignments are grouped by weight, and that weight is determined by importance and complexity of the required responses. Writings in the most heavily weighted category are more demanding and more accurately represent students' true learning. In the example in the figure, the teacher determines grades at the end of the grading period by multiplying the writings' grade by three, the tests' grade by two, and the homework grade by one, totaling six grade influences. Then he or she divides by six to get the average.

Is this a good format to use for a differentiated class? It can be. We can get a fairly accurate rendering of student mastery, as long as our assignments were developmentally responsive themselves. Would it be okay to adjust the weights of particular categories for individual students in order to more accurately represent a student's achievements in a particular quarter? Yes. Again, life is full of extenuating circumstances, and "stuff" happens.

If the current category weights (influences) limit a particular student's record from being accurately represented, then change the approach so that his or her achievement gets a fair showing. This might happen, for instance, if a student has a learning disability in writing and can't reveal what he or she knows through writing but understands the concepts and tests very well

Figure 13.3 Grouping Assignments by Weight or Category

	Writings (3X)			Tests (2X)		Homework (1X)			
	Essay on Energy and Matter	Dual Nature of Light Lab Explan.	Summary of Metals Video	Test on Periodic Table of Elements	Test on Alkalinity	Vocab. Practice	Page 23 Questions	Average	Grade
Ballard, Bob									
Carson, Rachel									
Ride, Sally									
Sagan, Carl									

using alternative formats. In such a case, we might reverse the weight—tripling the test grade while only doubling the writing grade. This can only be done, of course, if each category is holding students responsible for comparable objectives.

The principle is true: One size doesn't fit all, even in gradebooks. Of course, if we find ourselves changing the category weights for a particular student often or changing the weights for more than just a few students, we may have a bigger problem and should probably rethink our entire gradebook format.

Listing Assignments by Date

The gradebook format in Figure 13.4 has the advantage of looking at student growth longitudinally. If we want to see students' growth over time, we have it with the patterns created in this approach. The problem, of course, is that each subsequent assessment doesn't necessarily reflect the next level of development in a particular topic. We're a messy bunch, and we combine different factors in multiple assessments. The comparisons drawn between one current assessment and one down the road aren't often reliable or valid.

Fortunately, most of today's electronic gradebook programs provide a chronological listing function, so if we ever want to set up the gradebook this way, we can. By the way, teachers who use this format often color-code differ-

Figure 13.4 Listing Assignments by Date

	Essay on Energy and Matter 9/25	Vocab. Practice 9/27	Test on Periodic Table of Elements 10/5	Page 23 Questions 10/6	Test on Alkalinity 10/14	Dual Nature of Light Lab Explan. 10/20	Summary of Metals Video 10/22	Average	Grade
Ballard, Bob									
Carson, Rachel									
Ride, Sally									
Sagan, Carl									

ent assignments according to category—orange for tests, yellow for quizzes, green for homework, for example.

An important final thought about this format: Most of us find grading on a trend to be fairly accurate. That means we look at students' growth over time, often weighting the most recent scores higher than scores earlier in the grading period or year. This extends to grade-point average, too; Guskey writes:

> *Over how many years should [a student's grade point average] be calculated? Students change dramatically over their high school years; very frequently, underachieving freshmen become high-achieving seniors. Why should their first-year performance be held against them at the end of high school? (Guskey and Bailey 2001, p. 208)*

This is a good point. In addition, an accurate and fair grade requires attention to the greatest preponderance of evidence, not just any evidence. This focuses teachers more on the median and mode of test scores. The median refers to the middle of a set of test scores, half of which are above the median and half of which are below the median. It's a better measure than the mean of something if you have highly differing test scores. The mode refers to the most frequently occurring test score of a student's scores. It provides the general trend of students' proficiency. Though it is a new way of thinking for many of us, the mean or average score is less informative than the median and mode. For those still struggling with this idea, Marzano (2000) makes the case for grading on a trend in *Transforming Classroom Grading.*

It takes courage to commit to grading on a trend or on consistency of performance over time, because we may have a child who has earned a D or C during the first grading period, then received A's in the remaining three quarters. What grade should the student receive?

Without hesitation, the student would earn an A in my class. The A represents the child's current performance in a clear and consistent manner. It's an accurate portrayal of the student as of report card time at the end of the year. If I wove the first-quarter grade into the final tally, I would be holding the student's previous development against him or her; the grade would not be an accurate rendering of current performance. Children grow dramatically in one school year, they are not the same people in June as they were in September. We have to recognize that. In order to be useful to the student, his or her family, and next year's teachers, the student's grades must be accurate as of the latest data available.

Topics-Based Gradebooks

The approach shown in Figure 13.5 is particularly appealing. It's a topics-based gradebook approach put forth by Robert Marzano (2001). The figure shows one example I generated from my own classroom based on Marzano's idea.

Notice that all assignments are recorded for every single student in the form of a shortened letter key that can be referenced at the top. Given today's computer programs and electronic gradebooks, this is easy to create. Also notice that the Final Topic Score is not always an average of the column scores. And yes, using this format means teachers have to assess the assignments in more than one area as warranted, literally recording more than one grade at the top of each student's paper.

On many tests and quizzes, several different subjects are being assessed. One grade at the top of the test does not provide sufficient feedback, documentation, or information for decision making on any of them. The great thing about the Figure 13.5 format is that the grades are very specific, and therefore, useful to everyone involved; and perhaps just as important in a standards-based approach, we can focus on students' mastery with individual standards, benchmarks, and objectives.

At first this approach seems time-consuming, but it gets easier the more we do it and, in the end, is very helpful. Students get specific feedback which results in better learning early in the unit. This can help alleviate the remediation needed down the road, which translates to less time spent reteaching and grading in the long run. Secondary teacher Marsha Ratzel promotes a grade-in-categories approach:

Figure 13.5 Topics-Based Gradebook Approach

Key:

A. Quiz, 9/1
B. Commercial, 9/7
C. Puzzle, 9/9
D. Graphic org., 9/11
E. Quiz, 9/12

F. Web activity, 9/15
G. Rewrite, 9/17
H. Summary, 9/17
I. Parts of speech hunt, 9/21
J. Critique, 9/21

K. Quiz, 9/24
L. Paragraph anal., 9/25
M. Summary, 9/28
N. Oral pres., 9/29
O. Project, 10/11

Students and Assignments		Nouns and Pronouns	Modifiers: Adjectives, Adverbs	Verbs	Prepositions	Conjunctions	Analyzing Parts of Speech
	A	3.5					3.0
	B	4.0	2.5				
	C			3.0			
	D			2.5			
	E	3.5	3.0	3.0			3.0
Ballard, Bob	F				2.5		3.0
	G	3.0	2.5	3.5	3.0	2.0	
	H						3.5
	I				2.5	2.5	
	J						3.0
	K						3.5
	L			3.5			
	M						3.0
	N			3.0			
	O	4.0	3.0	3.0	2.5	2.0	
Final Topic Score		3.75	2.75	3.0	2.75	2.0	3.25
	A	4.0					4.0
	B	4.0	3.5				
	C			4.0			
	D			3.5			
	E	3.5	4.0	4.0			4.0
Carson, Rachel	F				3.5		4.0
	G	4.0	4.0	4.0	4.0	4.0	
	H						3.5
	I				4.0	4.0	
	J						3.5
	K						4.0
	L			4.0			
	M						3.5
	N			4.0			
	O	4.0	3.0	3.5	4.0	3.5	
Final Topic Score		4.0	3.75	4.0	4.0	4.0	3.75

Throughout your quarter you can look down and run your numbers. Look to see where your grades are stacking up. . . . If your students are low-performing on percents . . . that should jump out at you. Then you can attend to reinforcing instruction there. Likewise you can look at individual students in a new light. You can compare them to the rest of the class for strengths and weaknesses. . . . During conferences the data that you will hold is going to be more informative than any you've had before because it will speak to the content directly.

. . . One math teacher who tried this said she will never go back because she is so much stronger at knowing how to plan her instructional delivery. In one IEP meeting she attended, she described her student's abilities in great detail. The parents of that student were so amazed and told her that no one in all his years had understood what he was good at and where he needed help as well as she did.

One of the bottom-line tenets of differentiated instruction is woven through all the *formats* suggested in this chapter: Grades should be clear, undiluted indicators of what students have learned. If the format of an assessment gets in the way of accurate rendering of mastery, we change the format so it's more accurate. The problem, then, is what to write in our gradebooks if we've changed the format for some students.

In situations like this, remember the focus of differentiated instruction: fair and developmentally appropriate curriculum. Go back to your essential and enduring knowledge or your essential understandings and benchmarks, and put them at the top of your gradebook columns instead of the media through which students demonstrated their mastery (such as written summary, oral report, true/false test, Web site, radio play, written response to questions). If a student demonstrates mastery in an alternative manner, it doesn't matter; we have the universal attribute for which he or she was held accountable written at the top. We keep a separate matrix in the back of the gradebook to keep track of individual assignments for students who do things differently from time to time, but for the legal document from which we determine final grades—the gradebook—we have all we need on its primary pages.

For instance, if the whole class is studying the difference between amphibians and reptiles, we can record "Understands difference between amphibians and reptiles, November 8th" at the top of the gradebook column (using shorthand in those tiny gradebook spaces, of course). If students do different tasks in order to learn the material or demonstrate mastery, that's fine. We're still focused on the benchmark, and it is from that benchmark grade that we will determine the final grade.

In another example, suppose a student cannot draw well and the test calls for drawing a novel character's thinking, a particular sports maneuver, or a student demonstrating a proper safety procedure for a tech tools lab. Before assigning the drawing task, we go back and ask ourselves what we really want to assess. In this example, chances are we'll want the student to demonstrate a clear understanding of the novel character's reasoning, the sport maneuver, or the proper tech lab procedure. The student might not be able to demonstrate his or her full level of mastery of the information in the format we've declared all students must use.

Instead of standing on principle and requiring students to do a drawing and labeling the corresponding gradebook column with "Drawing of . . . ," we allow the student to demonstrate solid understanding in whatever way will best reveal his or her level of competence regarding the topic, not the medium, then we make sure to record the degree of achievement under our gradebook column title for this assessment—"Can analyze a character's motivation," "Can demonstrate [insert sport maneuver]," or "Demonstrates safe lab procedures"—accordingly. Unless the specific route (method) taken to demonstrate mastery is the subject the student is actively learning, the route doesn't matter. It's what the student learns, not the hoops through which he or she jumps that matter. We don't want to get in the way of that success.

Teachers looking for the one true gradebook format that best supports differentiated practice will be frustrated. There isn't one. Many of them work, including hybrids. The trick is to constantly assess whether the one we currently are using is the best to meet our needs. The gradebook format must provide clear, accurate reporting of achievement; be responsive to students' learning differences; focus on the essential learnings and their benchmarks; and be easy to manage. Don't be afraid to experiment until you find the format that works best for you.

CHAPTER 14

Responsive Report
Card Formats

According to Grant Wiggins, a report card consultant quoted in the
Christian Science Monitor *article, "Parents Push for Report Cards that*
Don't Require a Users' Manual," the real conflict is not over format. The
problem is that parents and teachers have different goals and different
expectations about the reporting process. "Educators," he says, "want to
get away from comparison and parents want to hold onto it." Teachers
want to measure the success of each child, says Wiggins. They want to
identify each student's strengths and weaknesses and report on the
progress that student is making toward achieving individual goals.
Parents, on the other hand, want to know how their children are per-
forming compared to other children. Knowing what their children are
doing isn't enough, parents say. In order to understand what that infor-
mation means, they need to put it into a recognizable context. They want
to know if their children are working on grade level; if the quality of
their work is work better than, worse than, or the same as the work of
other children in the same classroom and at the same grade level.

—Linda Starr, writing for the on-line publication, *Education World*, 1998

Differentiated instruction appeals to the best of us, both in pedagogy and
civility. What differentiation looks like when reporting to parents and others,
however, is where many of us hesitate to fully embrace its potential. If we do
different things with different students that result in grades with multiple

meanings, what do we write on the report card (or "progress report," grouped here with all references to report card)? In order to continue differentiation's powerful impact on student achievement and our schools' mission, report card formats must be responsive to our students' experience, and they must reflect the differentiated practices provided.

Every year multiple schools around our country and abroad reexamine their report card formats. Among their reasons for doing so, teachers and administrators are looking for a greater range of narrative comments that help them express unique situations with students while also seeking consistency teacher to teacher and among grade levels. In addition, they want report card formats that reflect their district's changing curriculum, new grade definitions, and new grade-level configurations, such as schools moving from separate elementary and middle schools to K–8 schools. Some of us are experiencing frustrations as well as joy with new electronic reporting systems that may or may not account for all we want to do with our grades and reporting. Reexamining report card formats helps us focus on our beliefs and goals. Just imagine the rich conversation we have when we discuss whether to include a separate column for grading effort and work habits.

As we look at the functionality and responsiveness of our report cards for differentiated classrooms, it's important to remember our objective with such reporting: an accurate and developmentally appropriate rendering of mastery that is clearly communicated to students, their parents, and other educators. From these reports, we have insightful knowledge of a student's growth and accomplishment. Our reporting symbols (marks) should provide feedback, document progress, and inform instructional decisions. They better be the best they can be, useful to all who need to use them. There are several report card formats that include these characteristics.

Adjusted (Modified) Curriculum

In this approach, we grade students against their own progression. In each grading period, we examine and report where students were at the beginning of their time with us and how far they move along the learning continuum to where they are today. The difference between the two points is the statement of their growth and the starting point for determining their grades.

Along the way, we may have adjusted or modified the curriculum in some way to better meet the needs of our students. This differentiation may include using an advanced curriculum for gifted students that entailed more breadth, depth, primary sources, challenge, or complexity than the curriculum of a regular student. It may also refer to how we changed the pacing of delivery or restructured content for students who were struggling academically. We may have adjusted vertically, laterally, or some mixture of the two, but the point we need to get across in our report cards is that the curriculum these students experienced is not the same as the curriculum experienced by other students of this grade level and subject area. The grade or mark on the report card may not reflect the same content and skill sets as regular students.

When we adjust the curriculum and it results in a significant difference in a student's final content and skill mastery, we have to indicate the adjustment on the report card. This can be done easily by the course title, such as when we use the terms "Honors," "II," or "Remedial" near the regular course title.

The problem, of course, comes when we modify curriculum but list only the regular education course title. Writing "Adjusted Curriculum" on a report card next to a grade is not allowed in most school districts. This is for good reason: Students may suffer stigmatization or unfair treatment if such a comment is on their permanent transcripts. It's a red flag to future employers and colleges that shouts, "Potential issues with this student." They may read too much into the comment, assuming the student has learning concerns and hasn't learned all that is expected for someone with such grades. They may not want to take him or her on. It is not hyperbole to say that this can ruin not just careers, but whole lives.

In order to prevent any misreading of a report card yet also be accurate and helpful to students, families, and educators, many school districts allow teachers to place an asterisk next to the grade (or a checkmark or an "X" in a box for this purpose) indicating that the viewer of the report card should access a narrative comment recorded about that grade located in the student's cumulative folder. This narrative comment can document anything, from advanced coursework to remedial curriculum to an impressive award the child won to the fact that the child's family relocates a lot, to name a few possibilities. We're careful to note on the card, however, that the asterisk or checkmark is not positive or negative for the child and his or her learning or potential. Some school districts allow teachers to select "Adjusted Curriculum" from the computerized comment choices to be printed on the report card in the comment section, though this can result in the same negatives mentioned before.

Remember that we teach in the best way students learn. It does no service to the student, the teacher, the family, the school, or the community to not differentiate, or to "fudge" the truth with an inaccurate and unusable mark on a report card. Imagine a student who arrives in your class at the start of the year two grade levels below the other students. In the course of time with you, however, the student grows a year and a half in mastery—that's a lot of growth in one year. The student blossoms with your approach, earning high grades on almost all assignments. Clearly, given all his or her growth, the student has earned the top grade; the growth was that significant.

Uh-oh, you worry. When compared to other students, the student is still half a year behind. If you assessed him or her purely on mastery of this year's material, the student would demonstrate understanding of only 50 percent of it, and 50 percent is a failing percentage on most school's grading scales. On the other hand, you've been giving the student high grades to represent his or her tremendous achievements. What do you record on the report card?

Record the higher grade. It more accurately reflects the student's accomplishments and learning. It is therefore more useful to everyone involved.

> To tell a kid who, for example, starts two grade levels behind and finishes the year one grade level behind, "Congratulations, you've done two years worth of work in one year, that's outstanding, here's your F."— What does this accomplish?
>
> —Bill Ivey, secondary educator

Wait a minute, you think next. How can this be? Next year's teacher will think this student has mastered what other students with high grades have mastered.

No, they won't. You've placed the asterisk or checkmark next to the grade to indicate the modified curriculum.

Imagine the results if you didn't do this. The child grows by leaps and bounds and has received feedback all year that he or she is accomplishing a tremendous amount, yet you record a D or an F on the report card. What message does that send? Two big messages are sent loud and clear to the student: 1) There's no correlation among hard work, personal growth, and achievement; and 2) even when I play by the rules, I lose.

It destroys hope, and if we have a child without hope, we have a much bigger problem than our report card format. To give a high grade to a student experiencing an adjusted curriculum that does not reflect the same extent of mastery as children experiencing the regular curriculum does not dilute the rigor of a course or promote grade inflation. It's not making anything easier for the student, as if he or she were getting away with something. Giving the high grade and indicating that it stems from an adjusted curriculum does far more good—we keep the student in the game and the grade is useful to us. The alternatives—giving the student a low grade despite high grade progress, or giving the student a higher grade because he worked hard without indicating an adjusted curriculum—are unacceptable for a teacher bent on teaching.

If the title of the course does not clearly convey the nature of the learning level and hence help parents and others interpret the grade accordingly, we have to do something to provide that clarification.

The Dual Approach: Grading Both Personal Progress and Achievement Against Standards

Another idea some schools consider is to record a symbol or mark indicating a student's personal progress as well as a symbol or mark indicating where the student stands against the standards set for everyone in this subject at this grade level. For example, a student might earn an A3. The first symbol, A, represents the typical letter grade (A, B, C, D, F) and refers to how many of the grade-level standards were demonstrated with full proficiency. The second symbol, 3, is a numerical score representing where the student is in her progression. A 3 might mean tremendous growth, a 2 might mean expected growth, and a 1 might mean little or no growth. An A3 demonstrates a nice correlation between standards and the student's growth—the student mastered a lot of standards and progressed more than expected.

Consider, though, the student who earns an A1. Was it a good year for him or her? No. The child demonstrated a lot of mastery, but grew little or not at all. He or she may have already known the material, in fact. We should have been doing something different with that child, such as providing an advanced program in our class or moving him or her to an advanced class. We can celebrate the A, but if we're honest, it was a waste of a year. A2 or A3 is preferred.

What about the student who earns D3? He's not at the same level as his classmates, but wow, what a fantastic year it was for him! The dual grade provides feedback, affirmation, and guidance for instructional decision making.

Most of the time there will be a correlation between personal progress and standards achieved. Most progress grades will be a 2. For those situations in which there is a significant discrepancy, however, it's a red flag that something is amiss and that corrective action needs to be taken.

Multiple Categories Within One Subject

As we mentioned earlier, the more we aggregate into one symbol, the less reliable it is as an indicator of what students know and can do. If we want to create helpful grades, then it makes sense to focus on more specific areas of study within each grading period or school year. Doing so also makes grading fair for students; they're not penalized in all subtopics of a subject for poor performance in one of them.

One way to create a multiple categories approach is to identify our essential and enduring standards, objectives, or benchmarks for grading, then provide a grade for each one. For example, in a middle school science course, students might be graded in the following areas during the first grading period:

- Consistently demonstrates proper lab procedure
- Successfully employs the scientific method
- Properly uses nomenclature and/or taxonomic references
- Accurately creates and interprets graphs
- Accurately identifies the difference between science and conjecture
- Consistently draws reasonable conclusions from given data

If we didn't provide separate grades for each one, and instead wrote C+ on the report card under one general category called "Science," we wouldn't be able to use the grade to provide much feedback, documentation, or guidance for instruction. If we focus on each benchmark, however, we get a better sense of where the student is achieving and not achieving, and with that knowledge, we better meet his or her needs. This approach removes the one overall grade that we normally use because such an aggregation of varied and important feedback obfuscates mastery.

Some educators may look at such an approach and worry about the time factor. It takes 15 to 20 percent longer to record such grades for students, but as Marzano reminds us: "We make up that time if we grade primarily with rubrics, which do not require time to do calculations of scores" (2000, p. 64). Even better: Many electronic gradebook programs offer the capacity to record and report grades according to benchmarks and standards. Sure, we have to do the data entry, but isn't it great to be able to respond with clarity to inquiries about a student's performances for specific standards? It helps us decide where to spend our time and energy. It's a data-driven teacher's dream.

Marzano offers one of the most interesting examples of what a report card format that favors the multiple categories approach would look like (2001, p. 107). It's actually borrowed from the McREL Institute, but it works very well. I've modified the sample he used in order to provide more details on what he calls "nonachievement factors." See Figure 14.1.

Continuous Progress Report

Educator and differentiation expert Lynda Rice offers a format for a Continuous Progress Report in which we mark growth over two or more years. Figure 14.2 shows an example I modified for a language arts class.

Progress reports and report cards make transparent what we do. If we differentiate to their full intent, our cards need to be responsive. If, for example, we use only aggregate grades, we diminish what we can do with the information. Differentiated classes are more easily achieved when report cards list achievement levels for individual standards, not all-inclusive subjects. They also serve us well when they have separate categories for feedback marks on effort, behavior, citizenship, and attendance.

Teachers breathe a sigh of relief if they know they can record "adjusted curriculum" on the report card or the cumulative folder if necessary when differentiating instruction on a regular basis. Since most course curriculum is spiral in nature and is a multi-year process to master, it's appropriate to be open to different rates and styles of learning for students. Students are not all ready to receive what we have to offer at the moment. The greater gift is to teach students where they are and to report their achievement clearly and honestly.

Figure 14.1 Sample of a Report Card with No Overall Grades

Name: Joe Freshman
Address: 123 Jimmy Buffet Lane
City: Paradise Island, Bahamas   Grade Period Ending: 11/1/07
Course: English 9   Grade Level: 9

	Standard Descriptor	Standards Rating (1)	(2)	(3)	(4)
Standard 1	Usage/Punct/Spelling	————2.5			
Standard 2	Analysis of Literature	———1.75			
Standard 3	6+1 Traits of Writing	—————————3.25			
Standard 4	Reading Comprehension	—————————3.25			
Standard 5	Listening/Speaking	———————2.0			
Standard 6	Research Skills	——————————————4.0			

Additional Comments from Teacher:
(*These can be computerized comments that are printed here according to data entry by teachers, or this space can be used for handwritten comments. The comments recorded here usually refer to academic clarifications and declarations regarding a student's mastery of material.*)

Health and Maturity Records for the Grading Period:
(*These are the teacher's marks for all nonacademic indicators such as attendance, work habits, initiative, tardies, collaboration, citizenship, behavior, and community service. While these factors have great impact on a student's academic achievement, they are not declarations of mastery—what students know and can do—regarding the curriculum standards; therefore, they occupy a separate space from academics.*)

Course: Algebra I	Standard Descriptor	Standards Rating (1)	(2)	(3)	(4)
Standard 1	Number Systems/Sets	—————————3.0			
Standard 2	Solving for the Variable(s)	—————————3.25			
Standard 3	Graphg Linear Equations	—————————3.50			
Standard 4	Roots and Radicals	—————————3.50			
Standard 5	Powers and Exponents	—————————3.0			
Standard 6	Word Problems	—————————3.0			

Additional Comments from Teacher:

Health and Maturity Records for the Grading Period:

(*This format repeats for all of the student's courses, making the report card more than one page in length.*)

Source: Based on a format promoted by the McREL Institute and used in Marzano's *Transforming Classroom Grading* (2000).

Wiggins's (1997) observation at the beginning of this chapter is correct—parents appreciate the specific information regarding their own child's achievement but they also want to know how he or she compares with others. "Is my child developing normally?" is a common concern, whether spoken or not.

Figure 14.2 Continuous Progress Report

This Progress Continuum can be used to cover a two-year block of time.

Student:

Teacher:

School Year(s):

Key:

 IC—Identifies the Concept

 BA—Beginning Application

 IA—Intermediate Application

 BM—Benchmark Mastery

	IC	BA	IA	BM
Reading				
Makes accurate inferences				
Accurately determines main idea				
Uses contextual clues when initially confused by text				
Determines what is important in text				
Connects what is read to personal life				
Adjusts reading strategies according to type of reading material				
Writing				
Strong voice				
Clear organization and logic				
Supportive details are accurate and related to the topic				
Uses a variety of word choices in strategic ways to advance the purpose of the writing				
All sentences advance the reader (no "fluff" or off-topic, toss-away lines)				
Makes good use of the writing process				

Educators should keep their report cards' emphasis on the standards and personal achievement but, when doing so, communicate their rationale for such a focus to parents, and also place a comment on the report card that indicates whether the student is developing the way he or she should be. This one comment, whether it states expected, limited, or advanced progress, will be the first and most important comment on the card to parents. It will supersede grades as the catalyst for parent response to the report card, good or bad. What "expected progress" looks like is subject to debate in each community, however, so it's worth discussing. We can put parents' minds at ease with "expected" and "advanced," and we can raise red flags for parent involvement with "limited," justifiably.

CHAPTER 15

Thirty-Six Tips to Support Colleagues as They Move Toward Successful Practices for Differentiated Classrooms

There are times when I doubt the sanity of my colleagues. They must have been on another planet when we discussed our grading policy last month; their comments seem so alien to what we agreed to do.

As soon as I think this, I realize they're thinking the same thing, and I'm one of the aliens.

It can be a humbling experience to talk with colleagues about grading and assessment: What if our grading approach isn't the most effective, responsive, fair, or accurate? What if my colleague doesn't like the way I do my grades—is this really her business? What if I disagree with my colleague and we can't come to a compromise? What if the principal makes me do something with my grades that I don't want to do? What if we find out we've been doing it all wrong? And in our more absurd yet plaintive moments, we ponder: Is there any way to gather all the students I've taught all these years together and teach them again but, this time, correctly?

In addition, we sometimes find ourselves in situations in which we have to motivate colleagues to examine new ideas and/or do something they'd rather not do. Teachers' hesitations with new or different approaches stem from any number of factors, including complacency, cynicism, ignorance, fear, distrust, unclear outcomes, perceived increase in workload; or because they are in survival mode and cannot extend any more of themselves for any new cause or concept. The school's mission progresses despite these misgivings, however, and we generally find ways to convince colleagues to give something a try.

181

Despite the potential for discomfort, talking with colleagues about grading and assessment is a non-negotiable. It has to be done. There is no one way to grade and assess, but there are lots of commonsense measures that can be taken, and just as many ideas worth exploring together. The good news is that it doesn't have to be a horrible experience. In fact, it can be liberating and insightful, and it can bring a staff closer together.

Tips for Talking with Colleagues

First, when disagreeing with a colleague over grading and assessment issues, assume you're on the same side. It's easy to see the other person as irrational, or worse, the enemy, when he or she doesn't see your side of things. We can quickly get judgmental and extrapolate our negative perception of the person into other areas. This isn't helpful to anyone. You both are teachers, both have worthy ideas, and both deserve to be heard. A person isn't a lesser teacher because his or her opinion is different from our own.

Second, follow Stephen Covey's advice: Seek first to understand, then to be understood (2004). Take steps to fully understand the other person's side of a grading or assessment issue, even paraphrasing back to the person so you are both sure you each heard correctly before forming your response. Such respect goes a long way to engendering respect for your own ideas when it's your turn to share.

One way to express interest in a colleague's ideas even though we may not be sure we agree is to lean toward the colleague and say, "Tell me more about that." This is body and verbal language indicating interest in the person's ideas. When we do this, one or more things happen: the person rethinks his or her position, perhaps becoming even more compelled by it; the person sees the errors of the thinking and corrects himself or herself; and/or we gain clarity and appreciate the person's rationale. Whatever happens, we come across as welcoming of the conversation, not blocking it.

Third, remember that if you're feeling a little stress with a colleague over a grading or assessment issue, chances are your colleague is, too. By breaking the silence and approaching him or her about the issue, you initiate relief on both sides, not disdain.

Fourth, with your colleagues, frequently reflect on the big questions that get circumnavigated in our daily attempts to put out fires. We don't want to be forever focusing on the urgent while the important escapes our grasp. Responding to the big questions re-centers us, helps us identify where to spend our energy and resources, and also helps us make stronger commitments to one another and our school's programs. The big questions include:

- Why do we have schools in America?
- Why do we try to teach everyone rather than just those easiest to teach?
- Why do we grade students?
- What does a grade mean?
- Does the current grading scale best serve students?
- How do we communicate grades and grading to parents?
- How does assessment inform our practice?
- Is what we're doing fair and developmentally appropriate?
- How can we counter the negative impact of poverty on our students' learning?
- How can we provide feedback to students most effectively and efficiently?
- Do our assessments provide us with the information for which we are searching? If not, why not, and how can we change them so that they do?
- What role does practice play in mastery?
- What is mastery for each curriculum we teach?
- What is homework, and how much should it count in the overall grade?
- How are our current structures limiting us?
- Whose voice is not heard in our deliberations?
- What evidence of mastery will we accept?
- What do we know about differentiated practices and the latest in assessment thinking and how are those aspects manifest in our classrooms? If they are not, why not?
- Are we mired in complacency?
- Are we doing things just to perpetuate what has always been done?
- Are we open to others' points of view—why or why not?
- Does our report card format express what we're doing in the classroom?
- How does my grading approach get in the way or support students' learning?
- How are classrooms different from classrooms thirty years ago?
- What will our grading and assessment practices look like fifteen years from now?
- To what extent do we allow state and provincial exams to influence our classroom practices?

Fifth, if a majority of folks are embracing a new grading and assessment approach but a minority are not, concentrate your energy on the majority who are. Lift them up; let them experience your can-do leadership. Most of the others will come along or they will get uncomfortable enough to transfer to other schools. Instead of knocking your head against the wall and draining your finite, personal energy trying to convince the immovable, hold your head high and provide all the resources and energy you can to those who are willing to give the new grading and assessment ideas a go. Students and the school will be better for it in the long run.

The following three dozen ideas provide ample avenues to pursue discussions and training for responsive grading and assessment practices. Although these staff development ideas are appropriate for other topics, such as differentiated instruction, cognitive theory, preparing students for the state exams, meeting the needs of learning disabled children, reading across the curriculum, and teaching in extended-class periods, they are particularly helpful with topics that push people's emotional buttons, like grading. Each description is meant to be a nugget of an idea that you can use as is or as the first step toward something that better meets the needs of your staff. One of these strategies will have little impact, but three, four, or more done at the same time will have great impact.

Culture of Expectancy

Create an atmosphere in which teachers feel a little peer pressure to at least examine the grading and assessing ideas. This means the faculty is immersed in the concept. If it's in sight, it's in mind, so put it in sight. Post, and frequently update, grading and assessment bulletin boards on the wall behind the photocopier so while teachers make copies, they can read about the topics. Post flyers about grading and assessing on the back of the teacher bathroom stall doors, next to the mirror, or above the urinals. Our business in the washroom makes us a captive audience.

In the weekly (or monthly) principal's letter to staff, devote a corner or column to the topics, asking different teachers, departments, grade levels to submit examples of ideas in practice or how they resolved issues with them. Make reference to grading and assessing in every faculty gathering. During principal walk-throughs, ask teachers to share one example of their exploration or use of a new grading or assessing idea they've used in the last few days.

Culture refers to our way of doing things around here, so make exploring grading and assessing ideas an expected element of everyday life in the school. If almost everyone is talking about and experimenting with them, it's difficult for those who aren't doing so to keep their toes dry.

Faculty Meetings

Open each meeting with a different group sharing their experiences with grading and assessing ideas for five to ten minutes. Rotate different departments and grade levels through the presentation duty.

Department Meetings

Request that every department meeting include discussion of an aspect of new grading and/or assessing ideas as they relate to their individual disciplines, and ask departments to share their observations with the administration.

Expert in the Lounge

Invite an expert in grading and assessment to spend a day in the teacher's lounge posing provocative questions, responding to concerns, and facilitating conversations about the topics.

Faculty Portfolio of Ideas

Place a crate containing a hanging file for each subject at every photocopier in the building. Ask teachers to photocopy one extra copy of whatever they're doing regarding grading and assessment practices and file it in their subject's file in the crate. Anything they put in there is now available for anyone in the building to use. At the end of the year, combine all the files into one portfolio of "best thinking" on grading and assessing that everyone can access.

Dedicated Intranet Folder

Maintain a folder dedicated to grading and assessment issues and practices on your school's intranet where teachers can post ideas and questions. A list-serv might be wise, too.

Instructional Roundtables

These are gatherings of one hour or less. Someone posts a topic and a location for the meeting two weeks in advance. In this case, the topics can be anything associated with grading and assessment. Sample topics might include: Dealing with paperwork—what do grades mean? What do I do with report card grades if I do different things for different students in my lessons? How do we tier tests? What are the best ways to set up our electronic gradebook?

Anyone who wants to get ideas on the posted topic is invited to come, but the ticket in the door is one idea photocopied a dozen times to share with those who attend. At the meeting, everyone shares their one idea, the group discusses new ideas generated by the conversation, and everyone leaves with multiple great ideas. This is done grassroots-style: Anyone can declare a topic and meeting date, not just administration or teacher leaders. All subjects are possible, which means there's likely to be one or more useful to each of us.

Teacher In-service

In addition to your own district's in-house experts, there are many professional development organizations with cadres of speakers, many of whom do presentations on grading and assessment. Contact them about working with your staff. Realize that it's usually best to contract with them for more than one day: one or more days to present and one day at a later time to return and answer questions, coach, and debrief. Highly recommended organizations that provide this service include the following: National Middle School Association (www.nmsa.org); the Association for Supervision and Curriculum Development (ASCD) (www.ascd.org); Staff Development for Educators (www.sde.com); AEI Speakers Bureau (www.aeispeakers.com); and professional subject organizations such as the National Council of Teachers of English (www.ncte.org), the National Science Teachers Association (www.nsta.org), The International Reading Association (www.reading.org), the National Council of Teachers of Mathematics (www.nctm.org), the National Education Association (www.nea.org), the American Federation of Teachers (www.aft.org), and Phi Delta Kappa International (www.pdkintl.org). Don't forget to inquire as to whether the organization conducts webcasts or e-seminars for professional development, too. They might be a better option for you.

When teachers have training, they are more inclined to try new ideas. Without professional development, they feel more threatened and less likely to deviate from what they know. Remember, though, one "drive-by" in-service won't cut it. Plenty of follow-up, encouragement, and nurturing will be needed. For every in-service planned, also identify your action plan for supporting teachers' exploration of the topic and maintaining the focus in the months and years ahead.

Figure 15.1 shows a format for helping teachers take in-service learning further.

Monthly or Quarterly Meetings

Regularly gather to debrief in small groups about how things are going with the new grading and assessment ideas. If possible, use teachers rather than administrators to lead the groups. Make sure to have a list of prompts or questions to facilitate discussion at each gathering.

Central Clearinghouse on Students

Establish a central data bank of all information the school has regarding individual students, and invite teachers to enter data as they become aware of it. For example, if you're an encore (elective) teacher, you can look on-line at

Figure 15.1 "3 x 3 x 3" to Use Following an In-service Training Session

Make a plan for your next steps in developing your assessment and grading approaches for differentiated classes. Page through your notes and the handouts and identify *three* attributes or perspectives likely to appear in your practice on your return to the classroom. Next, identify *three* areas of particular interest that you will explore in more depth during the coming school year. Finally, identify *three* specific steps you will take in order to pursue those areas. Examples include:

- Reread and consider notes from today a week from now
- Read a professional book on grading and assessment
- Start a support or study group about assessment and grading
- Implement a new idea (or two) that you've learned at the in-service, then write a reflective piece on how it worked or didn't work with students. If it didn't work, what would you do differently the next time you try it? If it worked, what evidence do you have that it worked?
- Start maintaining an intranet folder dedicated to grading and assessment discussions and ideas for your building
- Seriously reflect on your gradebook setup and how it might be improved
- Reconstruct your tests and other assessments so that they provide better feedback to students
- Write a one- or two-page summary of your assessment and grading philosophy
- Conduct turn-around training for colleagues
- Lobby for a revision of the school's or district's report card format
- Design many other formative assessment opportunities for units of study
- Reexamine redo policies
- Discuss some of the concepts from today with a colleague who wasn't here
- Write an article for an education journal regarding your school's investigation of grading and assessment practices

this data bank to learn about the multiple intelligence (MI) proclivities of your students, as posted by the math teacher who administered MI surveys to all students in the fall. As long as the information isn't highly sensitive, it should be okay to place in this file. If it's something extremely personal, such as that the child is a victim of sexual abuse, it's better to put a flag or mark in the student's database instead of the actual information. The symbol indicates that a school counselor or an administrator has pertinent information on this student that all teachers who work with him or her should see.

The more information we have, the better able we are to serve the student, and that includes assessing and grading.

Model, Model, Model

Begin with teachers who already embrace the new grading and assessing ideas, and support them as they explore the classroom applications. Invite others to observe them. Any aspect of the assessing and grading philosophy that can be applied to all the teachers and administrators in the building should be tried as well. If it's a sound practice for students, it's probably sound when it comes to assessing teachers and administrators, too. We're all teachers and we're all learners and, in both cases, assessing and grading need to be responsive.

Incorporate Grading and Assessing Practices into Professional Goals

This can be attached to teacher evaluation or not, but ask every teacher to establish one or more goals related to grading and assessment. In addition, they should provide an accompanying work plan and evaluative criteria for achieving their goal(s). Work plans might include: read a book, read a few articles, discuss the topic with a mentor or colleague, try three or more ideas during the year and reflect on how they impact student learning, attend a conference and do turn-around training with the faculty, conduct action research, and/or participate in a study group dedicated to the topic. Again, if it's in sight, it's in mind, and professional goals and evaluations are usually kept in sight.

Provide Funding

Find funds for those teachers wishing to pursue additional training in grading and assessment. School business partners are a great source, as are education grants. Corwin Press (www.corwinpress.com) has published several good books about getting education grants, as does ASCD; *Education Week* and *Teacher Magazine* often have multiple grant offers listed.

Tip: As educator and author Todd Whitaker recommends: when sending teachers to conferences and training seminars, send two positive teachers for every negative teacher. This way the reporting and turn-around training following the conference will be balanced for the faculty.

Get Multiple Copies

Purchase multiple copies of books and publications devoted to grading and assessment for study groups, or buy one copy for every teacher. Don't waste money buying just one copy and telling the faculty to circulate it amongst themselves. One copy does not effect change, and your school's limited dollars should effect positive change.

Book Study Groups

Establish and encourage study groups dedicated to books about grading and assessment. Be sure to have one member who distills some of the major points encountered during the study group meetings for sharing with the larger faculty.

Critical Friends Groups and Action Research Groups

Form case study groups, such as those found in Critical Friends Groups and action research groups, that analyze grading and assessment issues in the classroom and devise investigations to explore those issues and potential responses. These groups can be amazingly supportive and keep things moving in a scholarly manner, often yielding substantive and useful data for teacher buy-in and decision making.

Become a Lab for a University or College

Ask to be a lab school for a local university or college. This gets professors and teacher candidates into the building, which often helps veteran teachers take a more objective look at what they're doing and forces them to address issues about which they may have become complacent over the years. Those of us who have had student teachers in our rooms know that our pedagogy is put to the test and, hopefully, reaffirmed as a result of their probing questions. Grading and assessment are great fodder for these interactions.

In many cases, connecting to a university also opens the university's faculty and resources to teachers. Teachers feel affirmed as professionals, and they can get information on the latest thinking and research on grading and assessment. Ask professors who visit the school to focus on grading and assessment practices, in particular. The university connection creates a professional atmosphere similar to that of a teaching hospital. Conversations are a bit more elevated, and teachers are more focused on professional issues. The professors can be a conduit of recent research, too, while the faculty provides frontline reality applications for them.

Make Use of Teacher Mailboxes

Disseminate pertinent articles and ideas about grading and assessment practices in teacher mailboxes. Make sure to provide opportunities and expectations for interaction on the articles' information at future faculty or department gatherings.

Update Parents and the Community

Inform the parents and community about the school's new emphasis and invite them to look for evidence of it in action. Explain in clear terms—not in "education speak"—what you're doing, and provide multiple channels and opportunities for them to provide input. Don't divert attention to other programs or sugarcoat any aspect of the school's new grading and assessment approaches. Straightforward honesty will work. Parents who are educated about the new approaches and who feel like they've had a chance to make their opinions known won't have as many issues as they are implemented. This won't eliminate challenges, but it will decrease them.

Promotional Materials to Inform

Add the new grading and assessment emphasis to the school's publications, such as newsletters, Web site, work plan, accreditation materials, and other school promotional materials. This is as much a public relations campaign as it is a change in grading policy.

Use Humor

Keep a sense of humor and a sense of journey. It's an engaging, three- to five-year process, not an overnight mandate. Welcome the occasional humor and recognize the messy path that reform can take. Three steps forward, two steps back is still progress, and it's easier with a smile. ☺

Affirmation

Regularly affirm and reward small steps of success, as well as what teachers are already doing well. To do this, try: public recognition at faculty gatherings, private notes of thanks and encouragement, taking over a teacher's class in order to give him or her an extra planning period, referring a teacher looking for help to a successful teacher, posting teacher successes somewhere visible, inviting news organizations to interview teachers who have been successful, and asking successful teachers to take on leadership roles regarding the school's grading and assessment practices.

Comparisons

Regularly show how the new grading and assessment strategies enable success and achievement not attainable via former approaches. This helps with naysayers who may be asking, "Why are we doing this?"

Examples and Non-examples

Just like in great instruction, provide examples and non-examples of the new strategy, concept, or principle (Marzano et al. 2001). Clarity is motivating to both students and teachers. If perception of the new idea is vague, nebulous perception among the teachers, they are less likely to explore it. Providing clear examples of sound grading and assessment practices, and contrasting them with examples of grading and assessment that are not sound clarifies the ideas for everyone. "Just show me what it looks like" is a common refrain from teachers struggling with new ideas.

Cognitive Theory

Update everyone on the latest thinking in cognitive science/theory. There is great overlap and mutual reinforcement with grading and assessment practices. Teachers who are well-informed about cognitive theory principles usually embrace responsive grading and assessment for differentiated classrooms readily. In addition, learning about cognitive theory empowers and excites teachers. David Sousa, Marian Diamond, Barbara Strauch, Pat Wolfe, Bruce Campbell, Robert Sylwester, Robert Marzano, and Eric Jensen, are among the many names with resources that might help.

Peer Observations and Mentoring

Maintain a system of peer observation and mentoring. This is a system of collegial feedback in which teachers observe and analyze each other's lessons in light of the new emphasis on grading and assessment. Assign someone the task of coordinating who is partnering with whom and the dates and times for observations and post-observation analysis. Observations can be in person by giving up an occasional planning period or by providing a substitute for a non-planning period slot. It can also be done by videotaping the class and analyzing the lesson with a colleague later. Enlist retirees and parents to do the taping, if that's easier.

Core Values

Focus colleagues on the school's core values. This may take a year or more, but identify those four or five bottom-line values with which everyone agrees. If the faculty has a stake in a commonly held mission, it's easier for them to see the worthiness of new approaches in grading and assessment. They buy into them; they don't see the new initiatives as sacrifices or threats. For example, if teachers really believe that we teach so that students learn, not just to present curriculum, then they will employ whatever practices lead to students learning, not just getting through the units. If they believe all students should be taught in a fair and developmentally appropriate manner, then they will question grading practices that don't seem fair after close examination.

Small Beginnings

Start very small. As with most things, practice new behaviors in short chunks. How about implementing one new grading and assessment idea every month? Then, how about one every week until we use multiple ideas weekly?

School Visits

Visit other schools that are farther along in their grading and assessment reforms than your school, and report back what you find. Invite colleagues on professional listservs to share their "dos and don'ts" about grading and assessment reforms.

Reflective Practitioners

Create an atmosphere of reflective practice and analysis. Ask faculty members to maintain reflection (learning) logs, and to regularly connect dots between decisions they make regarding grading and assessment and the subsequent impact on students and their learning. If something bombs, ask teachers to reflect on what they would do differently next time they teach the unit, and if something succeeds, ask them to analyze why. If you're a teacher leader or administrator, make sure to do your version of this so that folks feel like you're working with them.

Common Planning Times

Facilitate common planning times among subjects/teams so they can really explore grading and assessment practices. This is not always easy to provide, but having time is still one of the most influential and transforming strategies available. Without common planning time, very little gets accomplished; the impact of new ideas dims. It's worth adjusting the master schedule to provide for this time.

Remember, though, that teachers who are not used to having common planning time will need training in how to best use such time when it becomes available. There are many, hard-won common planning times in schools that are squandered on activities best left to personal planning times or before or after school hours. Provide the necessary training to maximize its use.

Publishing

Publish what your school is doing regarding grading and assessment in education journals and magazines. It's very motivating to know that our work will get a broader audience than just us. It lends urgency and legitimacy to the new approaches, and we all have a stake in making the school look good. In addition, it feels great to think our school is making a contribution to the profession, let alone to see our names in print.

Risk-Taking

Affirm risk-taking. Make teachers feel safe in trying new things. It starts at the top with the administration taking risks publicly, and it's promoted weekly. Ask teachers how they've experimented with ideas this week and what they learned as a result—good, bad, or in-between. Give teachers license to experiment for the good of the cause.

Staff Health

Focus on staff physical and emotional well-being. If we're barely surviving ourselves, we have little inclination to explore something new or extend ourselves to students. If we're healthy, we're not threatened by the energy needed to take on something new. Specifically, then, make sure teachers are handling stress positively and feeling good about their work. They also need to be exercising regularly, hydrating, eating, and sleeping well. No problem is too great when we are physically and emotionally in a good place.

CBAM

Consider using CBAM, the Concerns-Based Adoption Model. Check the Internet for specific books and articles devoted to this model; it's worth it. Two suggested sources are:

- *Taking Charge of Change,* Shirley M. Hord, William L. Rutherford, Leslie Huling-Austin, and Gene E. Hall, Association for Supervision and Curriculum Development, 1987
- Southwest Educational Development Laboratory catalog—see www.sedl.org/pubs/catalog/items/cbam15.html

In the model, teachers move through different stages of concern—for themselves, for the task, for the new idea's impact—as well as through stages of use. It's great to use when moving teachers through grading and assessment reforms. If we respond to each level of concern and how teachers are using the idea, teachers are more willing to partake in the new initiative. These are the levels and their corresponding uses.

CBAM Overview

Teacher Concerns	*Teacher Use of the New Idea*
6—Refocusing	6—Renewal
5—Collaboration	5—Integration
4—Consequences	4a/4b—Refinement/Routine
3—Management	3—Mechanical
2—Personal	2—Preparation
1—Informational	1—Orientation
0—Awareness	0—Non-use

Publish Time Lines

Create and reference a time line of implementation. Just like those new building construction time lines and fund drives, we need to graphically portray progress. It's motivating to see where we are compared to where we were. Post the time line in a conspicuous space and identify milestones in the journey. Make sure to celebrate those milestones every time they occur.

One More Idea

Here's a bonus idea that works as well: Ask faculty members to write their own grading policy. Writing a policy helps us do three things 1) affirm our efforts that have proven successful over the years, 2) confront any of our grading philosophies that seem stale and counterproductive, and 3) rededicate our efforts with students and for their learning. When we write about grading and assessment, we discover new ideas about those topics.

It's important to explore those insights with colleagues; once we've articulated what we believe in writing, the next step is to share it. Because we've clarified our thinking through writing, conversations with colleagues are much more productive. We have both language and a framework on which to hook our ideas, but we're also willing to look at our ideas from more than one angle. With all the candor and insight you can muster, write down your own grading philosophy right now.

Martin Luther King Jr. reminded us that progress is not inevitable. In order to move forward, we have to pursue the future actively. This requires diligent attention to motivating colleagues at the micro- and macro-levels: from hall duty to the data analysis we do to close achievement gaps; from outdated, one-size-fits-all grading to responsive grading with grades that are accurate and fair. It still takes a spark to get a fire going, and as colleagues, we can be both flint and kindling for one another.

CHAPTER 16

Putting It All Together: How Do Differentiating Teachers Assess and Grade Differently?

Teachers who grade successfully in differentiated classrooms embrace the concepts of good differentiated practice. While they are technically skilled at such differentiation strategies as scaffolding, tiering, flexible grouping, compacting, and other ways to differentiate, the real harbinger of their success with students is their mind-set.

Differentiated instruction teachers do what's fair and developmentally appropriate for the students they teach, and those students change every year. They respond to the students in front of them rather than generic middle or high school students. Because instruction is inseparable from assessment, differentiating teachers' grading policies are also responsive to the individuals they teach. They agree that one-size-fits-all instruction and assessment approaches inevitably don't.

Differentiating teachers will do different things for different students some or a lot of the time. They will choose fairness over equality, and what is fair won't always be equal. As a result, they see it as fair when they provide scaffolding and support for some students but not for others who do not need it, or when they "ratchet" up or down the challenge level of student tasks in order to meet instructional needs. Grades earned on subsequent assessments are fairly earned by all groups. With this focus, differentiating teachers spend considerable time and energy designing pre-assessments, and formative and summative assessments, to provide feedback, document progress, and inform instructional decisions, being particularly attentive to formative assessments as the most crucial to student success.

Even though most differentiating teachers have a mandated curriculum they must teach, they make every effort to teach that material so that students learn, not just to have presented the material and watch the students sink or swim with it. This means they teach and assess in ways that make the material understood and meaningful—two prerequisites for long-term memory storage and subsequent student success.

Differentiation means doing whatever it takes to maximize students' learning at every turn, including giving them the tools to handle anything that is undifferentiated. Good teachers teach students not just one technique for completing a task but five different techniques, for example; then they teach students how to decide which technique to use in any given situation. Differentiation does not make learning any easier for students than explaining orally that "usted" is the formal, singular "you" reference in Spanish makes things easier for students to learn Spanish. It is straightforward, without deviation from our challenging goals. It is not about changing the difficulty level of a task; it's about changing the nature of the task.

Some students learn at a different pace, in a different manner, with different tools, and while immersed in different cultures. Differentiating teachers use these attributes to help students master what our communities deem important for citizens to know. It goes against every fiber of the differentiating teacher's being to make students suffer for not learning at the same pace, in the same manner, with the same tools, or because they are not from the same culture as the majority of their classmates. This includes the suffering encountered by advanced or honors students whose needs aren't being met, not just those who struggle academically. We do whatever it takes to provide all students, regardless of their differences and stations in life, with the tools and inclination to achieve.

Successful differentiated assessment and grading practices express these sentiments. Good teachers allow students more than one chance to master material, and they give them full credit for the highest levels they achieve, rarely holding past digressions against them. They recognize the developmental nature of learning, and they do not hold students to adult-level competencies, because students are not adults. Differentiating teachers are never coy with assessments; for example, when a teacher says students should study hard because particular content may or may not be on Friday's test. Instead, they create vivid and compelling expectations for achievement in every lesson they teach, as well as how students will be held accountable.

Differentiating teachers use the student's pattern of achievement over time to declare mastery, not allowing one or two immature or unfortunate moments to taint an accurate record. Differentiating teachers do not grade students' practice as they come to know material, which means they do not grade daily homework assignments, though they provide ample feedback on those assignments. These teachers grade only summative demonstrations of proficiency so that the grade is an accurate rendering of mastery.

Teachers who differentiate separate work habits, effort, citizenship, and attendance from academics because 1) it is difficult to objectively evaluate some of these factors; and 2) they know grades are more useful when not distorted by these factors, important as these may be. These teachers are also very cautious with extra credit and bonus points, using them only to entice students, but never to substitute for or significantly alter a grade. They take action as a result of their assessments, so they make the assessments useful to everyone and authentic to the learning experience.

Successful differentiating teachers provide ample opportunity for students to assess themselves. They realize that some students are just now attaining the concept while others have fully grasped it and require experiences that build automaticity and extended applications of the concept. They are clear on what constitutes mastery of the topics they teach as well as what evidence clearly and consistently demonstrates that mastery. If they don't know these aspects of their subjects, they seek the advice of others.

Differentiating teachers tend to use rubrics more than percentage grading, recognizing the need to tie achievement to specific learning, not the number of test items answered correctly. This means they also tend to record any zeros achieved on a 100-point scale as a sixty or the upper range of the F grade in their gradebooks so that the grade has an appropriate influence on the overall indicator of mastery.

All record-keeping media in differentiated classes, including gradebooks and report cards, reflect responsive teaching and the students' experience. The focus for this media is criterion-referenced standards. Differentiating teachers realize that norm-referenced assessment and grading has limited utility and can be damaging to their cause. This means there is no room in the differentiated class for grading on a curve and rarely is it appropriate to assign group grades. If a school's record-keeping media does not allow responsive approaches to be expressed, the differentiating teacher finds another way to communicate the student's achievement appropriately, whether by an addendum to the report card, a separate report card, narrative comments, a conference, an analysis of portfolio work, or something else.

Differentiating teachers design classroom tests that do not attempt to thwart students with confusing prompts or troubling formats. They make every prompt worth asking and clear enough to enable an intelligent response. They design their tests for quick and useful feedback to the student, understanding that they are teaching for successful learning, not just to document students' growth or lack thereof.

In all of this, differentiating teachers do not teach in isolation. They are ceaselessly collaborative, welcoming the scrutiny of colleagues and the chance to learn more about the ways students learn best. They are not threatened by the observations or advice of others, and they take frequent risks in the classroom—teaching in ways that students best learn, not the way they teach best. They shift their thinking from their own state of affairs to empathy for their students.

While visionaries, differentiating teachers are also the ultimate pragmatists—doing whatever works to elevate students and advance the school's mission with each one of them. Well-equipped and clear in their purpose, differentiating teachers teach well. Even better, their students thrive.

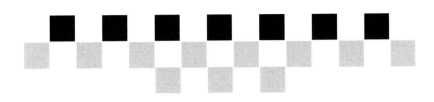

Glossary

Note: While each one of these terms can have different meanings in different contexts, the definitions here refer to the assessment and grading uses of them.

Affective That which appeals to the emotional/social side

Assess To gather data in order to make informed decisions (from "assidēre," meaning "to sit beside")

Checklist A list of behaviors, attributes, or tasks with which teachers tally students' evidence for mastery

Chunking Redistributing or restructuring content and/or experiences in order to clarify, shorten, or connect learning for students

Compacting Shortening lessons or units of study into mini-lessons or small units for students who have already demonstrated mastery of the material

Complexity The extent to which intricate tasks or ideas challenge students' minds; can also refer to the number of variables or facets of something with which one must interact in order to understand and apply it

Content The legal, state- or province-mandated curriculum students must learn; usually made up of specific information, concepts, and skills

Criterion-referenced Using standards, objectives, or benchmarks as the reference points for determining students' achievement

EEK Essential and Enduring Knowledge

Evaluate To judge the worthiness of something, or how a performance, product, or idea compares to standards or criteria set for it

Feedback Telling students what they did, no evaluative component, and helping them compare what they did with what they were supposed to do

Formative assessment Frequent and ongoing assessment, completed en route to mastery; ongoing assessment could be considered as "checkpoints" on students' progress and the foundation for feedback given—the most useful assessment teachers can provide for students and for their own teaching decisions

KUD *Know, Understand,* and *Do,* usually associated with essential understandings in a differentiated lesson

Learning environment Any external factor that affects a student's readiness to learn

Learning styles The ways in which we prefer to learn; when assessed in these ways, the results are accurate indicators of mastery

Multiple intelligence (MI) Proclivities we all have—"It's not how smart we are; it's how we are smart" (Gardner)

Norm-referenced Using other students' performances as the reference point for determining students' achievement

Portfolio A collection of work, some teacher-selected and some student-selected, used to assess a student's growth over time; often includes student's own reflections

Pre-assessment Any kind of assessment completed *prior* to teaching a lesson; informs instructional decisions

Process The ways in which students come to know the curriculum

Product How students demonstrate their mastery of the curriculum

Rubric A smaller-scale continuum of scores in which each score correlates to a clear descriptor of performance

Scaffolding The kind and extent of the teacher's direct support of students; the teacher's goal is to move from heavy scaffolding to zero scaffolding—we might provide many templates and direct instruction experiences early on, but then remove those structures incrementally as students build autonomy regarding the skill or concept

Summative assessment Completed after the learning experiences; usually requires students to demonstrate mastery of all the essential understandings (EEK or KUD), though they can be explored over several different tasks; gradable

Tier To adjust a lesson, assignment, or assessment to a developmentally appropriate level of readiness for students; most often done by increasing or decreasing the complexity, not the workload or difficulty of a task

Bibliography

Armstrong, Thomas. 2000. *Multiple Intelligences in the Classroom*. Alexandria, VA: Association for Supervision and Curriculum Development.

Arter, Judith. 1996. *Assessing Student Performance*. Professional Inquiry Kit (multimedia). Alexandria, VA: Association for Supervision and Curriculum Development. (ASCD has a number of on-line courses and other resources on assessment. You can visit them at www.ascd.org.)

Arter, Judith A., and Jay McTighe. 2000. *Scoring Rubrics in the Classroom: Using Performance Criteria for Assessing and Improving Student Performance*. Thousand Oaks, CA: Corwin Press.

Beamon, Glenda Ward. 2001. *Teaching with the Adolescent Learning in Mind*. Upper Saddle River, NJ: Skylight Professional Development.

Beers, Kylene. 2003. *When Kids Can't Read: What Teachers Can Do*. Portsmouth, NH: Heinemann.

Beers, Kylene, and Barbara G. Samuels. 1998. *Into Focus: Understanding and Creating Middle School Readers*. Norwood, MA: Christopher-Gordon Publishers.

Benjamin, Amy. 2002. *Differentiated Instruction Using Technology: A Guide for Middle and High School Teachers*. Larchmont, NY: Eye on Education.

Bloom, Benjamin S. 1984 *Taxonomy of Educational Objectives*. Needham Heights, MA: Allyn and Bacon.

Borich, Gary D., and Martin L. Tombari. 2003. *Educational Assessment for the Elementary and Middle School Classroom*. 2nd ed. Upper Saddle River, NJ: Prentice Hall.

Brookhart, Susan M. 2004. *Grading*. Upper Saddle River, NJ: Pearson-Merrill-Prentice Hall.

Buckner, Aimee. 2005. *Notebook Know-How*. Portland, ME: Stenhouse. Publishers.

Burke, Kay. 2001. *What to Do With the Kid Who . . . : Developing Cooperation, Self-Discipline, and Responsibility in the Classroom*. Upper Saddle River, NJ: Skylight Professional Development.

Campbell, Linda, Bruce Campbell, and Dee Dickinson. 2004. *Teaching and Learning Through Multiple Intelligences*. Needham Heights, MA: Allyn and Bacon.

Clarke, S. 2001. *Unlocking Formative Assessment*. London: Hodder & Stoughton Educational.

Connors, Neila A. 2000. *If You Don't Feed the Teachers They Eat the Students*. Nashville, TN: Incentive Publications.

Cooper, Harris M. 2001. *The Battle Over Homework: Common Ground for Administrators, Teachers, and Parents*. Thousand Oaks, CA: Corwin Press.

Covey, Stephen. 2004. *The 7 Habits of Highly Effective People*. New York: Free Press.

Forte, Imogene, and Sandra Schurr. 1996. *Integrating Instruction in Science: Strategies, Activities, Projects, Tools, and Techniques*. Nashville, TN: Incentive Publications.

Forsten, Char, Jim Grant, and Betty Hollas. 2002. *Differentiated Instruction: Different Strategies for Different Learners*. Peterborough, NH: Crystal Springs Books.

———. 2003. *Differentiating Textbooks: Strategies to Improve Student Comprehension and Motivation*. Peterborough, NH: Crystal Springs Books.

Frender, Gloria. 1990. *Learning to Learn: Strengthening Study Skills and Brain Power*. Nashville, TN: Incentive Publications.

Gallagher, Kelly. 2004. *Deeper Reading: Comprehending Challenging Texts, 4–12*. Portland, ME: Stenhouse Publishers.

Gardner, Howard. 1991. *The Unschooled Mind: How Children Think and How Schools Should Teach*. New York: Basic Books.

Ginott, Haim G. 1993. *Teacher and Child: A Book for Parents and Teachers*. New York: Collier.

Glynn, Carol. 2001. *Learning on their Feet: A Sourcebook for Kinesthetic Learning Across the Curriculum*. Shoreham, VT: Discover Writing Press. (This is for K–8 classrooms.)

Goleman, Daniel. 1995. *Emotional Intelligence: Why It Can Matter More Than I.Q.* New York: Bantam. (The Brain Store, 800-325-4769, www.thebrainstore.com).

———. 1998. *Working with Emotional Intelligence*. New York: Bantam. (The Brain Store, 800-325-4769, www.thebrainstore.com).

Gruss, Mike. 2005. "Some Teachers Practice Zero Intolerance." *The Virginian-Pilot*, June 29.

Guskey, Thomas. 1997. *Communicating Student Learning: 1996 ASCD Yearbook*. Alexandria, VA: Association for Supervision and Curriculum Development.

Guskey, Thomas R., and Jane M. Bailey. 2001. *Developing Grading and Reporting Systems for Student Learning*. Thousand Oaks, CA: Corwin Press.

Heacox, Diane, Ed. D. 2001. *Differentiating Instruction in the Regular Classroom, Grades 3–12*. Minneapolis: Free Spirit Publishing.

Hord, Shirley M., William L. Rutherford, Leslie Huling-Austin, and Gene H. Hall. 1987. *Taking Charge of Change*. Alexandria, VA: Association for Supervision and Curriculum Development.

Hunter, Robin. 2004. *Madeline Hunter's Mastery Teaching: Increasing Instructional Effectiveness in Elementary and Secondary Schools*. Thousand Oaks, CA: Corwin Press.

Hyerle, David. 2000. *A Field Guide to Visual Tools*. Alexandria, VA: Association for Supervision and Curriculum Development.

Jensen, Eric. 2000. *Different Brains, Different Learners*. San Diego: The Brain Store (800-325-4769, www.thebrainstore.com; also available at Crystal Springs Books—www.crystalspringsbooks.com).

Kohn, Alfie. 2000. *What to Look for in a Classroom*. San Francisco: Jossey-Bass.

Kralovec, Etta, and John Buell. 2001. *The End of Homework: How Homework Disrupts Families, Overburdens Children, and Limits Learning*. Boston: Beacon Press.

Lavoie, Richard. 1999. *How Difficult Can This Be?* The F.A.T. City Workshop. WETA Video, P. O. Box 2626, Washington, D.C., 20013-2631, 703-998-3293. (Also available at www.donline.org.)

Leibowitz, Marian. 1999. *Promoting Learning through Student Data*. Professional Inquiry Kit (multimedia). Alexandria, VA: Association for Supervision and Curriculum Development.

Levine, Mel. 1992. *All Kinds of Minds*. Cambridge, MA: Educators Publishing Service.

———. 2003. *The Myth of Laziness*. New York: Simon & Schuster.

Lewin, Larry, and Betty Jean Shoemaker. 1998. *Great Performances: Creating Classroom-Based Assessment Tasks*. New York: John Wiley & Sons.

Marzano, Robert J. 1992. *A Different Kind of Classroom: Teaching with Dimensions of Learning*. Alexandria, VA: Association for Supervision and Curriculum Development.

———. 2000. *Transforming Classroom Grading*. Alexandria, VA: Association for Supervision and Curriculum Development. (Dr. Marzano can be contacted at bmarzano@mcrel.org, McREL, 2550 South Parker Road, Suite 500, Aurora, CO, 80014, or at 303-337-0990).

Marzano, Robert J., Jay McTighe, and Debra J. Pickering. 1993. *Assessing Student Outcomes: Performance Assessment Using the Dimensions of Learning Model*. Alexandria, VA: Association for Supervision and Curriculum Development.

Marzano, Robert J., Debra J. Pickering, and Jane E. Pollock. 2001. *Classroom Instruction That Works: Research-Based Strategies for Increasing Student Achievement*. Alexandria, VA: Association for Supervision and Curriculum Development.

Mathews, Jay. 2005. "Where Some Give Credit, Others Say It's Not Due: Across the Nation, Teachers' Views Vary on Whether Struggling Students Deserve Points Simply for Trying." *The Washington Post,* June 14: A10.

McTighe, Jay, and Grant Wiggins. 1999. *Understanding by Design Handbook*. Alexandria, VA: Association for Supervision and Curriculum Development.

———. 2001. *Understanding by Design*. Alexandria, VA: Merrill-Prentice Hall with the Association for Supervision and Curriculum Development.

Millan, James H. 2000. *Classroom Assessment: Principles and Practice for Effective Instruction*. 2nd ed. Needham Heights, MA: Allyn & Bacon.

Newton, Cathy Griggs. 1996. *Risk It! Empowering Young People to Become Positive Risk Takers in the Classroom & Life*. Nashville, TN: Incentive Publications.

Nolen, Susan Bobbitt, and Catherine S. Taylor. 2005. *Classroom Assessment: Supporting Teaching and Learning in Real Classrooms*. Upper Saddle River, NJ: Pearson-Merrill-Prentice Hall.

Northey, Sheryn Spencer. 2005. *Handbook on Differentiated Instruction for Middle and High Schools*. Larchmont, NY: Eye on Education.

Nunley, Kathie F. 2004. *Layered Curriculum®*. Amherst, NH: Nunley (http://brains.org.).

O'Connor, Ken. 2002. *How to Grade for Learning: Linking Grades to Standards*. Upper Saddle River, NJ: Pearson Education.

Parks, S., and H. Black. 1992. *Organizing Thinking: Book Two*. Pacific Grove, CA: Critical Thinking Press & Software.

Popham, W. James. 2003. *Test Better, Teach Better: The Instructional Role of Assessment*. Alexandria, VA: Association for Supervision and Curriculum Development.

———. 2004. *Classroom Assessment: What Teachers Need to Know*. 4th ed. Upper Saddle River, NJ: Pearson Education.

Purkey, William W., and John M. Novak. 1984. *Inviting School Success: A Self-Concept Approach to Teaching and Learning*. 2nd ed. Belmont, CA: Wadsworth Publishing.

Reeves, Douglas B. 2002. *Making Standards Work: How to Implement Standards-Based Assessments in the Classroom, School, and District*. Denver: Advanced Learning Press.

Renzulli, Joseph S. 2001. *Enriching Curriculum for All Students*. Arlington Heights, IL: Skylight Training and Publishing.

Rogers, Spence, Jim Ludington, and Shari Graham. 1998. *Motivation & Learning: Practical Teaching Tips for Block Schedules, Brain-Based Learning, Multiple Intelligences, Improved Student Motivation, Increased Achievement*. Evergreen, CO: Peak Learning Systems. (To order, call 303-679-9780.)

Rutherford, Paula. 1998. *Instruction for All Students*. Alexandria, VA: Just ASK Publications (800-240-5434).

Sousa, David A. 2001. *How the Special Needs Brain Learns*. Thousand Oaks, CA: Corwin Press.

Sprenger, Marilee. 2005. *How to Teach So Students Remember*. Alexandria, VA: Association for Supervision and Curriculum Development.

Sternberg, Robert J., and Elena L. Grigorenko. 2001. *Teaching for Successful Intelligence: To Increase Student Learning and Achievement*. Arlington Heights, IL: Skylight Training and Publishing.

Stiggins, Richard J. 2000. *Student-Involved Classroom Assessment*. 3rd ed. Upper Saddle River, NJ: Prentice Hall.

Stiggins, Richard J., Judith Arter, Jan Chappuis, and Stephen Chappuis. 2004. *Classroom Assessment for Student Learning: Doing It Right–Using It Well*. Portland, OR: Assessment Training Institute.

Strong, Richard W., Harvey F. Silver, and Matthew J. Perini. 2001. *Teaching What Matters Most: Standards and Strategies for Raising Student Achievement*. Alexandria, VA: Association for Supervision and Curriculum Development.

Strong, Richard W., Harvey F. Silver, Matthew J. Perini, and Gregory M. Tuculescu. 2002. *Reading for Academic Success: Powerful Strategies for Struggling, Average, and Advanced Readers, Grades 7–12*. Thousand Oaks, CA: Corwin Press.

Tatum, Alfred. 2005. *Teaching Reading to Black Adolescent Males: Closing the Achievement Gap*. Portland, ME: Stenhouse Publishers.

Templeton National Report on Acceleration. 2005. *A Nation Deceived: How Schools Hold Back America's Brightest Students.* West Conshohocken, PA: John Templeton Foundation.

Tomlinson, Carol Ann. (Association for Supervision and Curriculum Development [ASCD], publisher. Carol's many books are worth reading. Each one has significant portions devoted to assessment, and her book on leadership for the differentiated classroom has a section on grading. Here they are; all are recommended.)

- 1995. *How to Differentiate Instruction in Mixed-Ability Classrooms.*
- 1999. *The Differentiated Classroom: Responding to the Needs of All Learners.*
- 2001. *At Work in the Differentiated Classroom* (video).
- 2003. *Differentiation in Practice: A Resource Guide for Differentiating Curriculum,* Grades 5–9 (There is one for K–5 and 9–12 as well.).
- 2003. *Fulfilling the Promise of the Differentiated Classroom.*

Tomlinson, Carol Ann, and Jay McTighe. 2006. *Integrating Differentiated Instruction and Understanding by Design: Connecting Content and Kids.* Alexandria, VA: Association for Supervision and Curriculum Development.

Tovani, Cris. 2001. *I Read It, but I Don't Get It.* Portland, ME: Stenhouse Publishers.

Walvoord, Barbara E. 1998. *Effective Grading: A Tool for Learning and Assessment.* San Francisco: Jossey-Bass.

Westley, Joan. 1994. *Puddle Questions: Assessing Mathematical Thinking.* DeSoto, TX: Creative Publications.

Wiggins, Grant. 1997. *Educative Assessment: Designing Assessment to Inform and Improve Performance.* San Francisco: Jossey-Bass. (Wiggins's organization is The Center on Learning, Assessment, and School Structure [CLASS], e-mail classnj@aol.com; he can also be contacted at www.grantwiggins.org, 648 The Great Road, Princeton, NJ 08540, 609-252-1211.)

Wolfe, Patricia. 2001. *Brain Matters: Translating Research into Classroom Practice.* Alexandria, VA: Association for Supervision and Curriculum Development.

Wormeli, Rick. 2001. *Meet Me in the Middle.* Portland, ME: Stenhouse Publishers.

———. 2003. *Day One and Beyond.* Portland, ME: Stenhouse Publishers.

———. 2005. *Summarization in Any Subject.* Alexandria, VA: Association for Supervision and Curriculum Development.

Index